THE PHILOSOPHICAL MISHNAH

Number 163
THE PHILOSOPHICAL MISHNAH
Volume One
The Initial Probe

by
Jacob Neusner

THE PHILOSOPHICAL MISHNAH
Volume One
The Initial Probe

by
Jacob Neusner

Scholars Press
Atlanta, Georgia

THE PHILOSOPHICAL MISHNAH
Volume One
The Initial Probe

Library of Congress Cataloging in Publication Data

Neusner, Jacob, 1932-
   The philosophical Mishnah.

   (Brown Judaic studies ; no. 163-   )
   Includes index.
   Contents: V. 1. The initial probe.
   1. Mishnah--Philosophy. I. Title. II. Series:
Brown Judaic studies ; no. 163, etc.
BM497.8.N4865   1988   296.1'2306   88-33716
ISBN 1-55540-310-7 (alk. paper)

Printed in the United States of America
on acid-free paper

For
my friend and colleague
on the National Council on the Arts

PROFESSOR ROBERT GARFIAS
UNIVERSITY OF CALIFORNIA

ETHNOMUSICOLOGIST AND MASTER OF LANGUAGES,
HE BRINGS TO THE COUNCIL AN APPRECIATION FOR
THE DIVERSITIES OF CULTURES
BUT ALSO FOR THEIR UNITY.

SCHOLAR OF ACCOMPLISHMENT,
ILLUMINATING CO-WORKER,
COLLEAGUE AND FRIEND,
I LEARN FROM EVERY ENCOUNTER,
DERIVE INSTRUCTION FROM EACH INTERVENTION,
ABOVE ALL,
FIND A MODEL OF INTELLECT AND CHARACTER
IN ALL CIRCUMSTANCES GRACED BY HIS PRESENCE.

CONTENTS

Part One
THE PHILOSOPHICAL GRID OF THE MISHNAH

Chapter

Part Two
FROM REGULATION TO RULE:
ARE MISHNAH TRACTATES UQSIN, ORLAH, BESAH, QIDDUSHIN, AND MEILAH PHILOSOPHICAL?

Part Three
A HYPOTHESIS ON
THE MISHNAH'S METHOD AND MESSAGE

Preface

This book begins a systematic account of the Mishnah in the context of philosophy. The purpose is spelled out in the Introduction. The second part of the monograph-series will analyze the other fifty-eight tractates of the Mishnah from the perspectives shaped in this initial probe. The third part of the same series will catalogue the instances in which the Mishnah's authorship addresses a philosophical program, terms defined in the Introduction and in Chapter One, with the methods explained in Chapter Five.

The organization of the book is very simple. The philosophical method of the document is rapidly surveyed in Chapters One through Four, and the particular question I raise here is defined in Chapter Five. The rest of the book then spells out the answer and at the end sets forth what has to be done next. Chapter Thirty-Two summarizes the main results and thereby presents the theory as to the philosophy of the Mishnah that emerges in this preliminary survey. There I answer two simple questions. First, precisely how philosophical is the Mishnah as represented by the five tractates before us? Second, about what does the philosophical Mishnah philosophize? On the basis of the answers to these questions Chapter Thirty-Three explains the next phase in the project.

In order to make it possible to read this book without first reading five or six other books of mine, I rapidly summarize in the opening part of the book, Chapters One through Four, as well as in part of Chapter Five, results already set forth elsewhere. This will give readers the information they require to follow the principal argument laid out here. At the same time the context for the present work is established. There is no alternative, in a sustained project of the dimensions of this one, but to review as succinctly as I can results that form the basis for new work. Then I set forth the experiment that occupies the shank of the book. Readers familiar with items listed below may wish to begin immediately with the Introduction, Chapter One, and then Chapter Five, skipping Chapters Two, Three, and Four.

Clearly, this work flows from a long sequence of earlier studies of (a particular) Judaism and the social order – terms explained in Chapter One – and carries forward ideas and problems that have occupied me in inquiries of a quite different order. Prior publications of mine relevant to this program are as follows:

Judaism. The Evidence of the Mishnah. Chicago: University of Chicago Press, 1981. *Choice,* "Outstanding academic book list" 1982-3. Paperback edition: 1984. Second printing, 1985. Third printing, 1986. Second edition, augmented: Atlanta: Scholars Press for Brown Judaic Studies, 1987.

Judaism in Society: The Evidence of the Yerushalmi. Toward the Natural History of a Religion. Chicago: The University of Chicago Press, 1983. *Choice,* "Outstanding Academic Book List, 1984-1985."

Death and Birth of Judaism. The Impact of Christianity, Secularism, and the Holocaust on Jewish Faith, New York: Basic Books, 1987.

Self-Fulfilling Prophecy: Exile and Return in the History of Judaism. Boston: Beacon Press, 1987.

Judaism and its Social Metaphors. Israel in the History of Jewish Thought. New York: Cambridge University Press, 1988.

The Making of the Mind of Judaism. Atlanta: Scholars Press for Brown Judaic Studies, 1987.

The Economics of Judaism. The Initial Statement. Chicago: The University of Chicago Press, 1989.

The Politics of Judaism. The Initial Structure and System. Forthcoming.

The Formation of the Jewish Intellect. Making Connections and Drawing Conclusions in the Traditional System of Judaism. Atlanta: Scholars Press for Brown Judaic Studies, 1988.

Take Judaism, for Example. Studies toward the Comparison of Religions. Ed. J. Neusner. Chicago: University of Chicago Press, 1983.

First Principles of Systemic Analysis. The Case of Judaism in the History of Religion. Lanham: University Press of America, 1988. *Studies in Judaism* series.

The Systemic Analysis of Judaism. Atlanta: Scholars Press for Brown Judaic Studies, 1988.

The Ecology of Religion: From Writing to Religion in the Study of Judaism. Nashville: Abingdon, 1989.

Understanding Seeking Faith. Essays on the Case of Judaism. Volume Two. *Literature, Religion, and the Social Study of Judaism.* Atlanta: Scholars Press for Brown Judaic Studies, 1987.

Understanding Seeking Faith. Essays on the Case of Judaism. Volume Three. *Society, History, and the Political and Philosophical Uses of Judaism.* Atlanta: Scholars Press for Brown Judaic Studies, 1988.

A Religion of Pots and Pans? Modes of Philosophical and Theological Discourse in Ancient Judaism. Essays and a Program. Atlanta: Scholars Press for Brown Judaic Studies, 1988.

Social Foundations of Judaism. Case-Studies of Religion and Society in Classical and Modern Times. Edited with Calvin Goldscheider. Englewood Cliffs: Prentice Hall, 1989.

Many of these papers emerged in conversations with my colleague, teacher, and friend, Professor Calvin Goldscheider, Professor of Judaic Studies and of Sociology at Brown University, and benefited also from discussions with Professor Francis K. Goldscheider, Professor of Sociology at Brown University. I discussed and planned this project, as I do all of my books of essays and many other things as well, with Professor William Scott Green, University of Rochester. I owe to Professor Green the title of this book. To Professors Ernest S. Frerichs and Wendell S. Dietrich I express my ongoing thanks for companionship of a highly enlightening sort; I learn more than, at times, they think they are teaching (or imagine I am hearing).

I once again call attention to the excellent craftsmanship of Joshua Bell, Verbatim Word Processing, Inc., who carefully and conscientiously prepared the camera-ready copy of this book, as of so many other books of mine. I appreciate the extra effort and intelligence he invests in my books for the two series in which I publish my monographic research, Scholars Press/Brown Judaic Studies and for University Press of America/Studies in Judaism.

JACOB NEUSNER

November 11, 1988

The eve of my trip to University of Bologna
for the conference on religious studies and
the social sciences in international perspective

Program in Judaic Studies
Brown University
Providence, Rhode Island

Introduction

On the surface the Mishnah, ca. A.D. 200, a principal holy book of Judaism, is a compilation of rules. In this and companion studies, aiming ultimately at preparing the way for my planned systematic work, *The Philosophy of Judaism: The First Principles*, I shall show that these rules yield regulations on a program of a distinctively and particularly philosophical character, so that the Mishnah in fact is a philosophical writing. That explains my title for this sequence of monographic studies in several sequential volumes, *The Philosophical Mishnah*. True, the Mishnah's is a philosophy in an odd and peculiar idiom to be sure. But the document will emerge as a work of systematic thought on a sustaining program of issues that, in the Mishnah's authorship's time and place, other philosophers addressed and people in general recognized as philosophical. The rules of classification and generalization, the issues of mixtures, the resolution of doubts, the relationship of the actual to the potential (chicken, egg), the role of attitude or intention in the assessment of an action and its consequences (a subset of the foregoing), and the like – these abstract issues of general intelligibility turn out to form the intellectual program of considerable portions of the Mishnah as well. When philosophers did philosophy, these are some of the things that concerned them.

My intent when I speak of philosophy, therefore, is very specific. I mean more than that there was a rather general philosophy expressed by the law, that is, "philosophy of law." I mean, further, something more particular than that the intellects represented here thought in a manner philosophers respected, e.g., in accord with rules of order and intelligibility. I mean, very concretely, that, in the medium and idiom of rules, the authorship of the Mishnah worked out positions on matters of distinctively philosophical interest. They were not lawyers who had a general philosophy, e.g, of society and the social order. They were philosophers who happened also to produce law. The bulk of their writing, though not all of it, is philosophy in the form of law. That is my claim, and that claim separates the project of which this is

1

the initial monograph from all consideration of the philosophy of Jewish law, which is a different subject altogether and is worked out in terms of different data and different disciplines. So I shall show in this and the next volumes of the preliminary studies that bear the overall title of this book. Then, in the principal work, I shall make stick my basic claim as to the fundamentally and particularly, distinctively *philosophical* character of the Mishnah's program. This I shall do when I place into philosophical context the program of thought I find paramount in the Mishnah, showing that that program indeed is philosophical as philosophers who work in a more conventional idiom define philosophy.

In this initial probe, the present monograph begins in a very simple way. I start with an analysis of the modes of thought and premises of inquiry and issues of a single group of tractates, Uqsin, Orlah, Besah, Qiddushin, and Meilah. The tractates are in different divisions and are of a quite diverse character. I chose these tractates because they are fairly brief and cover five of the six divisions of the Mishnah. In this way I shall form a thesis as to the philosophical character – I mean, the *program* of thought, not merely the *modes* of thought – of the writing, with a fairly detailed picture of the philosophical principles at stake in that document. The program concerns topics, e.g., potentiality and actuality, intention and action, as well as rules of philosophical thought, e.g., the correct manner of classification, that is, assessing mixtures on the one side and hierarchization on the other, or the proper rules governing resolutions of matter of doubt. These rules of thought are specific to philosophy, in that they guide not merely scientific inquiry as does *Listenwissenschaft* but inquiry of a very particular order and into a very distinctive set of questions. Once again, my claim is clearly that we deal with discourse of a peculiarly philosophical order, if in an idiom otherwise alien to philosophy as it was carried on in the age and place under study (and in any other age known to me).

In the next monograph(s) in the sequence of studies within the project of *The Philosophical Mishnah*, I shall test against the evidence of the other fifty-eight tractates that same hypothesis, worked out in this monograph, concerning the sustaining philosophical principles and engagements that animate the Mishnah as a whole. I shall treat the tractates one by one, as I do here. In the third and last part of the monographic work I shall compile a catalogue of what the Mishnah says about the philosophical issues I maintain are treated therein. So what is to follow will be a complete account of the philosophical grid: the documents, read in detail for their philosophical program (if any), then the philosophical issues, stated in detail for the entire Mishnah.

On that basis, as I said, my planned *The Philosophy of Judaism: The First Principles* will be composed.

The Mishnah is not ordinarily read as a work of philosophy. It has been and now is memorized in the circle of all those who participate in the religion, Judaism. It stands at the beginning of a religious tradition and is represented as a corpus of "traditions," that is, true teachings which lay claim to authority or to meaning by virtue of the authorities cited therein. Of still greater weight, the two great documents formed around the Mishnah and so shaped as to serve, in part, as commentaries to the Mishnah, namely, the Babylonian Talmud and the Palestinian Talmud, form the center of the curriculum of Judaism as a living religion. Consequently, the Mishnah is necessary to the understanding of Judaism, but not deemed a writing of a philosophical order. That is a reasonable reading, since, on the surface, the Mishnah does not exhibit the indicative traits associated with philosophy. It speaks of very particular matters and does not explain what they exemplify or how they do so. It moreover does not address philosophical issues in the explicit, abstract terms and categories we should expect for its time and circumstance. Whether or not it is traditional, it scarcely appears to be philosophical.

But the Mishnah does not follow the expected form of documents that claim merely to represent prior traditions, for instance, appeal to prior authority not in detail but in essential form, use of historical reference as authority. The name of an authority rarely serves as a redactional fulcrum. The tense-structure is ahistorical and anti-historical. Sequences of actions generally are stated other than in the descriptive present tense. Rules attain authority not because of who says them but because (it would seem) no specific party, at a specific time, stands behind them. Traits of philosophical, not traditional, thought prevail. The Mishnah is descriptive of how things are. It is indifferent to who has said so, uninterested in the cumulative past behind what it has to say. It is organized topically and for purposes of classification, that is, of discovering the prevailing rule, the Mishnah investigates the traits or properties of things. These are not the traits of a corpus of "traditions." I am inclined to think that law-code, schoolbook, and corpus of traditions all are not quite to the point of the accurate characterization of the Mishnah.

But what then serves to characterize the document? In prior writings I have invoked the language, "a philosophy in the form of a law code." Now I begin the work of justifying that description as a matter of fact. The Mishnah's authorship (a term explained later on) calls one to participate in the process of discovering principles and uncovering patterns of meaning. The very form of the mishnaic rhetoric, its formalization and function of that form – all testify to the role of the learner and hearer, that is, the student, in the process of definitive and indicative description (not communication) of what is, and of what is real. And, beyond the specificities on which we shall concentrate in this monograph, that basic mode of recognition of reader as active intellect marks the document and identifies it. So while people may make the case for the Mishnah as a law-code, a schoolbook, and a corpus of tradition, and I think it is epiphenomenologically all of these things, I shall show its true character. While the Mishnah was edited into final form was to create such a multipurpose document, a tripartite goal attained in a single corpus of formed and formal sayings, it is something other than these three things in one. It transcends the three and accomplishes more than the triple goals which on the surface form the constitutive components of its purpose. By analyzing a tractate and then comparing the results with the traits of two other tractates, I mean to demonstrate that hypothesis, preparatory to testing it against the characteristics of the Mishnah as a whole.

The stakes in this rather substantial program are considerable. Let me briefly announce what I think forms a possible consequence of the program just now commencing, even though I stand at a considerable distance from the end-point. My ultimate goal in the present project of the social study of Judaism, with special reference to economics, politics, and philosophy, is to correct the historic error of Maimonides, who identified Aristotle and his philosophical method as the source of correct knowledge, science, in his day, in his misreading of the requirements of theology and philosophy of Judaism. He supposed to present philosophy outside of the framework of law, and law without sustained and specific engagement with philosophy. This came about because he did not realize the full extent to which the Mishnah, Maimonides' correct choice of the foundation-document of Judaism after Scripture, stood squarely within the Aristotelian philosophical tradition. Specifically, when Maimonides systematized philosophy in his original *Guide to the Perplexed* and law in his imitative *Mishneh Torah*, he misunderstood the fact that the law, for the Judaism of the Dual Torah, constitutes the medium for theological and philosophical reflection and expression. And that is the fact, even though at numerous specific examples, he introduced into the explanation or elucidation of the law philosophical considerations. All of these preliminary impressions await sustained clarification, but they do serve to place this project into perspective.

In his separation of the presentation of law from philosophy, he tore apart what in the Mishnah had been inextricably joined in a lasting union, which was (and is) the law of that Judaism and both its theology and also its philosophy. Seeing the law in *Mishneh Torah* as a problem merely of organization and rationalization, Maimonides did not perceive that that same law contained within itself, and fully expressed, the very same principles of theology and philosophy that in the *Guide to the Perplexed* are invoked to define what we should call Judaism. Maimonides therefore did not grasp that the law in the very document that, in his (correct) judgment contained its classic formulation, that is, the Mishnah, also set forth precisely those principles of philosophy that, in Aristotle's system as Maimonides adapted it, would frame the proposed philosophy and theology of Judaism of *The Guide to the Perplexed*. Then, in the *Guide* Maimonides (mis)represented philosophy and theology by divorcing them from their legal media of articulation, as though these could come to expression entirely outside the framework of the legal sources of Judaism. So the greatest scholar of the Mishnah of all time and the greatest Aristotelian Judaism has ever known misperceived the profound intellectual structure of the Mishnah.

The reason for this error, in my view, is that Maimonides did not understand the deeply Aristotelian character of the Mishnah, which is the initial and definitive statement of the law of Judaism. And that is the error that I am in the process of correcting in these papers and in the companion studies and volumes of which they form an offshoot and a byproduct, as even the concluding remarks of Chapter Thirty-Three will suggest. I am showing, point by point, that the economics, politics, and philosophy, that is, the social order set forth by the Judaism of the Mishnah, finds its intellectual home in Aristotle's philosophy, method and (in the main) results as well. The modes of thought and the basic categorical structures correspond to those of Aristotle. This has already been accomplished in my *Economics of Judaism* and *Politics of Judaism*. Now when we realize that the Mishnah stands squarely within the Aristotelian philosophical tradition in its economics, politics, and philosophical principles (a proposition, as I said, I already have shown for the first two of the three main lines of social thought), then we can understand what happened to mislead Maimonides. And from Maimonides onward, the law has served only episodically and notionally, not systematically and totally, in the formation of the theology and philosophy of Judaism. The scholars of the law in the main knew no theology and could not understand philosophy; the scholars of theology and philosophy, whether or not they knew the law, did not understand in a systematic way that the law would provide the very principles of philosophy that they thought the classic sources of Judaism did not afford. Seeing the law of

Judaism, from the Mishnah forward, as essentially distinct from the philosophical science of Aristotle, Maimonides and everyone since then, if they dealt with law at all, simply arranged the law and turned to the philosophy and theology.

What Maimonides should have done, which I therefore am in the course of doing, was in a systematic and rigorous manner to show the philosophy within the law. That meant not merely that the law has or exhibits a philosophy. Everyone recognizes that simple and commonplace observation. At numerous points in his *Mishneh Torah* Maimonides articulates the principle at hand; and, as to theology, this is encompassed within the *Mishneh Torah Sefer Ahabah*. But the fundamental modes of thought and some of the principal problems of reflection of Aristotle guide the intellectual processes of the Mishnah, and that fact Maimonides did not grasp; if he had, he would have worked out the *Guide to the Perplexed*'s main points within the very framework of legal exposition. In this way the marriage of law and philosophy, which, as a systematic program, eluded Maimonides, could have been consummated, yielding for the history of Judaism a very different result from the one that followed their divorce. For understanding the philosophical modes of thought and also the philosophical problematic of the Mishnah – issues of mixtures, issues of the potential and the actual, for instance – should have meant that the law is part of, and expresses in its distinctive idiom of rules, the rules of a well-composed and clearly defined philosophical tradition.

Not only so, but the earliest intellectual critiques of the Mishnah recognized its fundamental Aristotelianism and rejected it, as I demonstrated in *Uniting the Dual Torah: Sifra and the Problem of the Mishnah*. And, as I now am showing in its principal components, that philosophical tradition in which the Mishnah stands is the very tradition that so engaged Maimonides to begin with, the Aristotelian one. Had he understood that fact, he would have allowed Aristotle to teach him law and its structure and system – that is, the law of the social order that the Judaism of the Dual Torah set forth, and not only philosophy and its principles and rules. So the stakes in this large-scale enterprise are considerable, since, after all, it is not in every century that someone claims to correct a centuries-old misunderstanding, which lies, now, at the heart of the received misreading of Judaism. And what is at issue in this book and in its related *Vorstudien* on the philosophy of the Mishnah is not trivial. But more of this anon, since it will take a number of volumes to prove the point and then a major synthetic work to show its inner structure and outer context.

The long-term stakes in this work therefore are very high. But even the near-at-hand consequences are not inconsequential. For, whatever the outcome of the discussion on the Mishnah and Maimonides, the analysis of the philosophical character of the Mishnah in its own terms will place into perspective what I believe to be the character of the first phase, and the development of the second and third phases, of the Judaism of the Dual Torah. The entire characterization of the first phase of the Judaism of the Dual Torah, that is, the system attested by the Mishnah in particular, rests upon the results. And the comparison of the initial system of Judaism, that is, the politics, philosophy, and economics of the Judaic system of the Mishnah, with the next sequential and connected Judaic system becomes possible, the one attested by the Talmud of the Land of Israel, Genesis Rabbah, and Leviticus Rabbah. And with that comparison, perspect on both systems for the first time becomes plausible.

When in the second phase, we ask the same questions, e.g., concerning economics, politics, and philosophy, we shall be on firm ground in claiming (as I suspect I shall allege in due course), a deep movement away from philosophy altogether, a movement in which the inherited structure is preserved in form but reshaped in all essential aspects. The politics will change altogether; the economics will persist; the entire philosophical character and program will fall away, except within the narrow limits of the exegesis of specific Mishnah-passages, and be replaced with a theological program, in a form found theologically appropriate, as much as the philosophical program of the Mishnah comes to us in that list-making form that was found philosophically appropriate. The characterization of the third phase, the one represented by the Talmud of Babylonia and associated writing, I cannot yet imagine. But we have gotten far ahead of our story. Let us rather turn to the project at hand.

Part One
THE PHILOSOPHICAL GRID OF THE MISHNAH

1

Philosophy and the Social Order

Philosophy comprises both how thought takes place and also what thought defines. When we can identify the method and the message of the intellect in the most abstract form, we can define the philosophy that animates that intellect. Represented as a grid of intersecting lines, philosophy emerges at the intersection of modes of thought and immediate occasions of thought, that is to say, the logic and the topic of the active mind. When the lines of the grid are written on paper, then the paper of philosophy is its rhetoric, the rules of language by which well-crafted thought – the meeting of logic and topic – is set forth. When we know how people think and can explain the medium by which they frame their questions, we can account for their results, that union of disciplined rhetoric, logic, and topic, that comprise a well-crafted philosophical system. Those results that make up a philosophical system, then, are formed in accord with two distinct sets of rules, These govern the modes of thought and the media of thought, how people think, about what they think.

When the modes and media of thought address concrete issues of the social order, then philosophy takes on a public dimension, becoming an indicator of a shared intellect and community of mind. Philosophy within the social order serves to explain and account for a system's world-view, its governing theory of the common culture and sustaining society. Inquiry into the world-view of a social entity then requires sustained analysis of the traits of the shared intellect that philosophy defines. In that sense, philosophy attests to the ethos of a social system. A religion that proposes an account of the social system by definition will fall into the classification of a philosophical religion.[1]

---

[1]This is the counterpart to my argument in *The Politics of Judaism* that a religion that appeals to the sanction of legitimate violence is to be classified as

To be sure, philosophy in the abstract need not define the world-view of a social entity. But, when the theory of the social order addressed to a social entity sets forth a world-view with clearly defined philosophical traits of logical rules and topical discipline, then that social entity builds thought upon a philosophical foundation.

Properly analyzed, the foundation-documents of that (imagined) social entity will guide us deep into the modes of thought – logical and topical alike – that produce the results realized in the world-view of that theory of the social order. For philosophy within the document that sets forth a social system – way of life, world-view, definition of the social entity, covered by the words ethics, ethos, and ethnos – brings to high abstraction those modes of thought and foci of recurrent concern through which a social entity defines and explains the world it realizes. Setting forth the media by which a social entity shapes its world-view, philosophy tells us not so much the specifics of what the social entity (within the systemic foundation-writing) thinks as how that group defines its questions and discovers the answers to them.

When, therefore, we can describe the mind of a social entity through sorting out the rules governing how authorships reach and set forth discrete conclusions on a variety of disparate and even unrelated subjects, we can claim to understand (within the representation of a systemic foundation-document) the philosophy of that social entity, that is to say, the method and medium of its world-view. That philosophy portrays how the mind of a society of like-minded people is formed. In the study of that philosophy, then, we gain access to the generative rules of culture that are stated in intellectual form. We can then set forth regulations of systemic thought – how questions are identified, how answers are attained – that succeeding generations receive in the family and village from infancy and transmit to an unknowable future. Attitudes shift. Values and beliefs change. One generation's immutable truths come to the coming age as commonplace truths, banalities, or nonsense. But processes of reflection about the sense of things, modes of thought concerning how we identify and solve problems, above all, the making of connections between this and that – these endure. Through intellect, that is, philosophy, the foundations of all social life, the framework of all culture, reach definition and intelligible statement. That is why systemic analysis takes up philosophy defined as it is here: modes of thought, media of thought.

---

a political religion, and in *The Economics of Judaism* that a religion that addresses the (systemically) rational disposition of scarce resources will be classified as a religion setting forth a political economy.

Exactly what do we mean by "media of thought"? Stated most simply, the things about which people think constitute the media of their intellect. If, to make matters more concrete, I had to specify a simple rule that tells me that about which people think, it is this: people think about what makes a difference and do not think about what makes no difference. The media of thought, therefore, guide reflection into paths that lead to a desired goal, which permits an answer to the question: what is this? And if I want to know, what is this? then I have also to find out, what is that? and the answer will locate itself in the difference between this and that. It is where a system identifies and explains difference ("what makes a difference? what makes no difference") that I gain access to the system's critical center, its point of generative tension, its focus of systemic interest. And that brings us to the principal point of philosophical description of a system, which is to identify, as a matter of fact, the points of differentiation important in a systemic construction and to take note also of the points of indifference and undifferentiation. Where a system differentiates, there the system focuses its reflective power. The media of thought, then, are those guidelines that direct reflection to differentiate this from that, define the things about which people will think, and identify matters of no account and no concern. So philosophy is made up of modes of thought and media of thought, that is to say, a program of mind that sets forth both how people think, and about what they think. The simplest names for the how and the what are logic and topic.

Thus far I have treated philosophy as a principal component of the social order. But since philosophy emerges from individual intellects, we must wonder just what philosophy has to do with the analysis of a theory of the social order put forth by a system, religious or secular. While philosophy may speak only for an individual, when we deal with documents adopted as authoritative by a social entity, then we analyze thought in its public and shared realization. The philosophy that generates that thought, that is, the logic and topic expressed through the rhetoric, in such a public document forms a systemic and public, not merely a personal and individual, philosophy. The logic then is shared and signals public discourse. The rhetoric makes possible intelligible speech. The topical program makes a difference, which is to say, effects that differentiation that is socially consequential (within the system's theory of the social order). So philosophy stated in a socially recognized writing, such as a law-code for example, forms a social fact, not merely a private reflection. Under the specified circumstances, philosophy affords access to the world-view of a society as that world-view comes to formation and expression.

Now in the study of a systemic writing on the social order, whose processes of thought are subject to analysis, and for whom does a piece of writing, a document, speak? To respond to that question, I have invoked the word "an authorship," meaning, a consensus that a document represents, rather than "an author," meaning, the individual choices of a private person. It is, I maintain, the system of an authorship that a document preserved in a social setting speaks. An authorship may not make up all the materials it has assembled; it may pick and choose among available resources, e.g., paragraphs or even whole chapters (to use, anachronistically, divisions of writing familiar to us). The document testifies to taste and judgment, program and system. Accordingly, I call the framers of a Mishnah-tractate "an authorship." That collectivity – from one to an indeterminate number of persons, flourishing for from ten minutes to five hundred or a thousand years – determined and then followed fixed and public rules of orderly discourse – rules of thought, rules of expression, rules of topical priority – that govern a given authoritative book's logic, rhetoric, and topic. These fixed rules, seen all together, permit us to describe the intent and program of those responsible for this writing: the authorship.

What has been said about a Mishnah-tractate and the Mishnah as a whole applies, of course, to all rabbinic writings. Received in a canonical process of transmission under the auspices of a religious system, a rabbinic writing enjoys authority and status within that canon and system. Hence it is deemed to speak for not a private person but a community and to represent, and contribute to, the consensus of that community. No document has a named author, for such a designation would deprive the document of all standing and authority. Accordingly, a piece of writing is represented, on the surface, as the statement of a consensus. That consensus derives not from an identifiable writer or even school but from the anonymous authorities behind the document as we have it. That is the meaning of the word "authorship," those who made up the rules of a document or later on followed them in adding to that document.

In analyzing the intellectual infrastructure of any piece of writing, we have to ask whether this writing exhibits a cogent character and shows conformity to laws and regularities, therefore derives from a considered set of decisions of (once again my trilogy of analytical issues) a rhetorical, logical, and topical order. If it does, then, as a matter of definition, it derives from an authorship, a collectivity that stands beyond the consensus exhibited in this particular writing. Accordingly, if I can find regularities of rhetoric, logic, and topical program, I claim to discern the consequences of rules people – an authorship – have made, decisions they have reached, concerning the character of this writing of theirs: its structure, organization, proposition, cogent statement. If I find no regularities and indications of an orderly program, then I may fairly claim that this writing is different from one that speaks in behalf of people who have made rules or adopted them for the inclusion of fresh ideas of their own. It belongs in a classification not of a composition but of a scrapbook, not of a collage, which uses fixed materials in a fresh way, let alone of a sustained statement of a single system, but of a mishmash of this and that that fell together we know not how. What we shall see in this initial probe of the Mishnah is that our tractate does conform to rules, and we can say what those rules are. That is the basis for all that follows.

When we address an authorship, we propose to identify those rules that govern thought and the expression of thought in the Mishnah: its modes of thought and its prevailing and recurrent points of differentiation, which I call its method. These two define the intellectual process of the program for the social order that that authorship sets forth. The matter of process grasped, we know how the mind of that social entity frames the propositions that it proposes as its system and the foundation of its order. Accordingly, by definition the logic of intelligible discourse, the premise of self-evident comprehension, above all, the intangible sensibility that makes connections between one thing and something else and yields conclusions transcending them both – these form the infrastructure of a system, that is to say, a theory of the social order. They are what in the imagination of an authorship hold together many minds in one community of shared and mutually intelligible speech that, in the aggregate, we may call society, in our instance, the society of a Judaism or of the "Israel" at hand. The evidence for that shared intellect, that mind in common, therefore comes to us in how people speak to one another, in the connections each makes between two or more sentences and in the connections all make with one another. The formation of a shared intellect, the making of a mind in common – these derive from process and connection.

Now how shall we identify the evidence that makes that study feasible? And what is at stake in the study? The evidence is first of all in language. From the language people used to say to one another what they were thinking, I propose to move backward to the processes of thought encapsulated in that language. If people state a proposition, I want to know the argumentation in behalf of that proposition, the kind of evidence and the manner of marshalling that evidence, and why they took for granted other people would find it all persuasive. Still more to the point, if people see a connection, I want to ask what makes the connection self-evident to them, so that one thing fits with some other, and another thing does not. At stake is an understanding of how philosophy at the most abstract level reached expression in acutely concrete sentences. The authors of the canonical writings of the Judaism of the formative age mastered the requirements of applied reason and practical logic. But that means they also were masters of intellect and logical acumen. Consequently, we have in hand ample evidence, in concrete terms, of both the decisions people reached, the ways in which they framed their propositions, and also, the expectation that others within the group educated in their writings and manners of thought would find the result compelling. We may reconstruct how people think from what they say.

The bridge from proposition, that is, *what* people think, to process, *how* they think, therefore is built of modes of discourse preserved and transmitted in mutually intelligible exchanges of ideas, in fully articulated language made up of words and sentences that follow a public syntax. Discourse thus refers to the way in which people make their statements so that the connections within their thought are intelligible and cogent to others (and that by definition, hence the stress on the public). To describe the modes of discourse which attest to modes of thought at the deep structure of mind, we ask how people place on display not only the conclusions they have reached but also the manner in which they wish to announce and argue in favor of those conclusions – all together, the way in which they make their statement of their position. Accordingly, it is in cogent argument concerning proposition that mind becomes incarnate. That is why I work my way back from the way in which people compose their cogent and persuasive statements to the mind, the intellect, that teaches them not only or mainly what to think, but rather, how to think. My claim, now fully set forth, is that the intellect, an abstraction, finds form in a fully exposed manner of reaching and demonstrating a particular statement of sense. That mind takes place, for instance, in the framing of a proposition, complete in exposition, from beginning statement through middle demonstration and argumentation to end conclusion and the drawing of consequences.

Philosophy represents mind, and, under circumstances such as those prevailing in this context, it is mind that is social in orientation (if not origination). Philosophy thus speaks to the social order, people living together and doing things with others in a shared and persistent organization of their lives. But, in the context of the Mishnah, mind is not conceived to endure in abstract theory, contemplating itself alone, but has its work to do. And not only so, but mind or intellect also flourishes in society, and that means, within a tradition of thought and a context of ongoing process. These two then, logic of cogent discourse, characteristic of mind, and tradition of thinking, definitive of the context of mind, combine in the process that yields systemic construction and composition. And the task of intellect is always and everywhere both to think afresh but also to state the results within the setting of the society that is meant to receive and embody the consequent system of intellect. Through a considerable argument, we shall now see that the two work together, logic and system, to produce order and structure, and that the textual community has then to place into enduring cultural and social context the order and structure of the hour. When we know how a Judaic system not only did its work but also established its place in an ongoing labor of culture, we shall understand the method and message of the philosophy of that Judaism.

That explains why in reading the tractates at hand I want to know three things to which the documentary statement attests, first, the rhetorical conventions an authorship has found affective, second, the logical modes by which they proposed to convey intelligible thought, third, the topical or propositional or thematic range they identified as urgent. That third point of analyzing a piece of writing attends to the argumentation in behalf of that proposition, the kinds of evidence and the manner of marshalling evidence. If people see a connection – whether in rhetoric, logic, or topic – between one thing and something else, for instance, I want to ask what makes the connection self-evident to them, so that one thing fits with some other, and another thing does not. The authors of the Mishnah mastered the requirements of applied reason and practical logic. But that means they also were masters of intellect and logical acumen. And, in the nature of things, they also produced a literature that enjoyed extraordinary power to sustain attention and compel interest not in the time of the writing alone but for two thousand years thereafter, no mean achievement. Consequently, we have in hand ample evidence, in concrete terms, of both the decisions people reached and the ways in which they framed their propositions. That is why I claim the philosophy of a system of a Judaism finds ample documentation in the writings of that Judaism. We reconstruct how people think – their system, their Judaism – from what they say and the way in which they say it. But among the three points of interest – rhetoric, logic, topic – it is topic that gains the closest reading. The reason is that, if as I maintain there are recurrent considerations of issues of philosophy, that is, problems of general intelligibility framed here in an arcane formulation, then I have to show that that is the fact. And I must show it in detail. And, finally, I must distinguish stretches of the tractate, and ultimately, the document as a whole, that cover philosophical territory from ranges of the writing that do not touch upon issues of general intelligibility and philosophical interest at all. So we shall rapidly run by the matters of rhetoric and logic, to which in any event I have devoted ample attention, and concentrate our detailed analytical reading solely upon postulate and premise of philosophical concern.

In arguing that philosophy forms a principal plank in the platform of the social order, I carry forward my work on the study of the initial social order set forth by Judaism. In fact, this work is meant to prepare the way for writing the third in a three-part account of the Judaic system of the social order: politics, philosophy, and economics. *The Politics of Judaism* and *The Economics of Judaism*, treating the Mishnah's stage in the unfolding of the Judaism of the Dual Torah, form the first two parts of the work, and, as I said, in this and companion work, I lay the foundations for the third. Let me therefore place the whole into context. The social study of Judaism addresses the way in which a Judaism sets forth its conception of the social order. Systems of thought concerning the social order work out a cogent picture, self-evidently true for those who make them up, of *how* things are correctly to be sorted out and fitted together, of *why* things are done in one way, rather than in some other, and of *who* they are that do and understand matters in this particular way. These systems of thought then are composed of three elements: ethics, ethos, ethnos, that is, world-view, way of life, and an account of the social entity at hand. Such systems need not fall into the category of religion or invariably be held to form religions, and it is the fact that not all religions set forth accounts of the social order. But when, as has often been the case, people invoke God as the foundation for their world-view, maintaining that their way of life corresponds to what God wants of them, projecting their social entity in a particular relationship to God, then we have a system that is, as a matter of fact. And when, finally, a religious system appeals as an important part of its authoritative literature or canon to the Hebrew Scriptures of ancient Israel or "Old Testament," we have a Judaism.

In the scholarly initiative of which this book forms a part, I therefore propose to describe Judaism as a social system, hence the title of the venture as a whole, the social study of Judaism. In doing so, I carry forward my sustained interest in the systemic study of religion, exemplified by Judaism. That is to say, reading a text in its context and as a statement of a larger matrix of meaning, I propose to ask larger questions of systemic description of a religious system represented by the particular text and its encompassing canon. In the first three parts of the work I take up the initial systemic statement of the paramount document of Judaism of all time, which is the Mishnah, the first document of the Judaism of the Dual Torah beyond Scripture. When we ask that a religious composition such as the Mishnah speak to a society with a message of the *is* and the *ought* and with a meaning for the everyday, we focus on the power of that system to hold the whole together: the society the system addresses, the individuals who compose the society, the ordinary lives they lead, in ascending order of consequence. And that system then forms a whole and well-composed structure. What is the rationality of that structure? Philosophy will answer that question for us.

Beyond this work, dealing with the evidence of the period ending at ca. A.D. 200, lie two further stages in the unfolding of the Judaism of the Dual Torah in its formative age. These are marked by the writings that come to closure at ca. A.D. 400 and ca. A.D. 600, respectively. The second is attested by the Talmud of the Land of Israel and associated writings, the third, by the Talmud of Babylonia and its companions. Each of these stages in the continuation of the Judaism adumbrated by the Mishnah demands synchronic description in its own terms and also diachronic comparison and contrast with the Judaisms fore and aft, that is, a three-dimensional account of the formative age of Judaism. In seeing the unfolding, stage by stage, of the deep logic, the rationality, of a Judaism, I mean to make possible for Judaism the address to a variety of questions emerging in the generative problematic of social science in its theoretical aspect: why science here, not there? why capitalism in the West and not in the East? why democracy as mass participation in the political process where it has taken root? And, contrariwise, why no science, why no capitalism, why no democracy, in other civilizations beside the Western one? The answers to these questions make possible the comparative study of rationalities, such as Max Weber intended to carry out in his study of India, China, Christianity, and Judaism. In the case of his "Judaism," of course, he was unable to analyze what had up to his day been described in an uncritical and conceptually bungling way, as a monolith, lacking history, lacking context, lacking nuance. In these and associated works, I mean to correct the errors that prevented the purposeful analysis of what Weber would call "the rationality," and what I call, "the social order," of Judaism. Weber asked the right questions of the wrong data. Here are the right data, rightly construed: in historical context, in social nuance, in the interplay of context and contents.

What is at stake in the project as a whole? I conceive this project of social study to form a chapter in the study of the rise of Western civilization to world dominance. Just as Weber understood the issue, why has the West defined the world, so I want to explain in what ways Judaism has formed a Western religion, and in what ways it has not. Just as Weber asked questions of comparison and contrast in finding out what is particular and what common, so I want to find points of commonality and difference. At issue in academic debate in the next half-century will be the place of the West in the world. Since, as a matter of fact, everywhere in the world, people aspire to those material advantages that flow, uniquely I think, from the modes of social organization that the West has devised – the West's economics, its science and technology, and also – let us say it straight out – its politics and also its philosophy as modes of thought and inquiry, I think it is time to stop apologizing and start analyzing what has made Western civilization the world-defining power that it has become. When Weber asked why no capitalism in India, China, or Judaism, he opened, in that exemplary manner, a much broader set of questions. When, nowadays, people rightly want to find a place, in the study of civilization that the academy sustains, for Africa, Asia, peoples indigenous to every region and land, we all need to frame a global program of thought and reflection. And if we are not merely to rehearse the facts of this one and that one, we shall require modes of comparison and in particular the comparative study of rationalities.

Hence sustaining questions, applying to all areas because of their ubiquitous relevance, why this, not that? have to come to definition. And since the simple fact of world civilization is that the West has now defined the world's economy, politics, and philosophy, and since all social systems measure themselves by Western civilization in its capacity to afford to large masses of people both the goods of material wealth and the services of political power, the indicative traits of the West demand close study. These are, I think, in politics, mass distribution of power in political structures and systems, in economics, capitalism, and in philosophy, the modes of thought and inquiry we call scientific. That explains how I have now undertaken to revise the entire program of the study of the Jews and Judaism. And, it is self-evident, what I mean to do is provide a model for others to follow in the study of all other social entities and their social systems. So the stakes in this scholarly program of mine are as high as I can make them.

As I have made clear, I plan a sequence of three sets of three studies, on the philosophy, politics, and economics of Judaism in the three stages of its initial development, the system of the Mishnah (ca. A.D. 200), the system represented by the Talmud of the Land of Israel and closely allied writings such as Genesis Rabbah and Leviticus Rabbah (ca. A.D. 400), and the system adumbrated by the Talmud of Babylonia and its closest affines (ca. A.D. 600). These nine books then will allow both synchronic pictures of the successive Judaisms as these came to expression in the designated periods and places, and also diachronic pictures of the interrelationships among those same successive Judaisms. It is a somewhat complex project, but I think worth attempting. The nine planned books are of course underway, so it is not premature to announce the plan and to set forth initial results.

These first results pertain to two of the three principal components of what I conceive to be any theoretical system of the social order. Among the three, philosophy (world-view, ethics), politics (social entity, ethnos), and economics (way of life, ethos), I already have taken up the second and the third. The work on philosophy cannot be undertaken without prior monographs, such as were not required for economics and politics. In respect to the other components of the theory of the social order, I was able to appeal without mediation of prior studies to the Mishnah's evidence, to its well-composed theory of market, the unit of production, wealth and money, value, and the like, and to its equally cogent account of the agencies that legitimately employ violence to gain assent, that is, the politics. But the Mishnah is not written as a philosophy in the way in which it is written to answer questions of politics and economics, and in the work at hand, I am attempting to do for the document what its authorship did not do at all: [1] as a matter of hypothesis, uncover the philosophical program and [2] as a matter of sustained inquiry, demonstrate that, indeed, the document does follow such a program. The reader must now wonder whether my insistence on the analysis of regularities of rhetoric, logic, and topic is sustained in the literary evidence at hand. For even though, as a matter of theory, one concedes my points on the social power of intellectual process, still the evidence subject to analysis must permit inquiry into these specified traits. We therefore turn to an account of the Mishnah's rhetoric and logic, so that I can demonstrate that both modes of discourse in the Mishnah follow orderly rules and regulations, the first and necessary indicator of philosophical thought.

2

Philosophical Discourse of the Social Order [I]: The Mishnah's Rhetoric

The bridge from proposition, that is, *what* people think, to process, *how* they think, is built of modes of discourse. "Discourse" thus refers to the way in which people make their statements so that the connections within the sequences and propositions that comprise their thought are intelligible and cogent to others (and that by definition, hence the recurrent stress on the public dimension of philosophy). To describe the modes of discourse which attest to modes of thought at the deep structure of mind and validate the claim that philosophical thought operates, we ask how people place on display not only the conclusions they have reached but also their sense of language, the manner in which they wish to announce and argue in favor of those conclusions – all together, the way in which they make their statement of their position.

Let us begin with the matter of rhetoric, then proceed to logic and finally to topic. In nearly all tractates the Mishnah (as in other documents within the same canon) highly formalized modes of composition convey ideas. Fixed literary structures (that is, rhetoric) dictate to the authorships of nearly all documents the repertoire of choices available for saying whatever it is that they wish to say. What this means is that individual preferences, personal modes of forming sentences for instance, rarely come into play. Nothing is allowed to remain private and idiosyncratic; speech is public and conventional not only in intent but also in form. Thoughts are set forth in a few well-defined ways, and not in the myriad diverse ways in which, in a less formalized literature, people say their piece. That fact vastly facilitates the comparison of document to document, since the range of rhetorical choices is limited to the forms and literary structures paramount in the documents subject to description and analytical comparison, and that range is remarkably circumscribed. Not only so, but the work of comparison is made still more reliable by the very extrinsic character of forms and structures; identifying them is not a matter of taste and judgment.

Once we have defined a form or rhetorical pattern or structure, we know whether or not it is present by appeal to some few facts that are readily accessible to the naked eye. Consequently, there can be irrefutable proof that one set of forms or literary structures, and not another, predominates in a given document, and that proof can even take the form of the statistics which describe the total number of units of thought subject to description and the proportion of those units of thought that fall into the several defined categories of form or structure, as against the proportion of those that do not. Defining these rhetorical conventions therefore sets forth the first step in describing the documents, one by one, and then comparing them to one another. For the forms or literary structures paramount in one differ from those found useful in another, and hence the work of comparison and contrast commences in the simplest and most extrinsic matter. Only when we establish the distinctive traits of documents by appeal to such external matters, in which matters of taste and judgment do not figure, do we move on to substantive differences of topic and even proposition, in which they do – if we let them.

Let me proceed to some simple definitions, beginning with language for rhetorical analysis. A *form* or *literary structure* comprises a set of rules that dictate those recurrent conventions of expression, organization, or proportion, the grammar and syntax of thought and expression, that occur invariably in the ordinary patterning of language and also are *extrinsic* to the message of the author. The conventions at hand bear none of the particular burden of the author's message, so they are not idiosyncratic but systemic and public. A form or literary structure or language-pattern of syntax and grammar imposes upon the individual writer a limited set of choices about how he will convey whatever message he has in mind. Or the formal convention will limit an editor or redactor to an equally circumscribed set of alternatives about how to arrange received materials. These conventions then form a substrate of the literary culture that preserves and expresses the world-view and way of life of the system at hand.

When we can define the form or literary structures, we also can ask about the program and policy of thought – recurrent modes of analysis and exercises of conflict and resolution – that dictate the content of the commentary. For how I think and what the syntax of my language and thought permits me to say dictates what I shall think and why I shall think it: this, not that. How are we to recognize the presence of such structures? On the basis of forms that merely appear to be patterned or extrinsic to particular meaning and so entirely formal, we cannot allege that we have in hand a fixed form or literary structure. Such a judgment would prove subjective. Nor shall we benefit from bringing to the text at hand recurrent syntactic or grammatical patterns shown in *other* texts, even of the same canon of literature, to define conventions for communicating ideas. Quite to the contrary, we find guidance in a simple principle: *A text has to define its own structures for us.*

Patterning of language is readily discerned. For authors do so simply by repeatedly resorting to a severely circumscribed set of literary conventions and to no others. These patterns, we shall soon see, not only dictate formal syntax and principles of composition but also define the deep structure of logical analysis and the modes of proof for particular propositions of argument. On the basis of inductive evidence alone, therefore, a document will testify that its authors adhere to a fixed canon of literary forms. That canon of forms shows that forms guide the authors to the propositions for, or against, which they choose to argue: the program of the book, not only its plan. If demonstrably present, these forms present an author or editor with a few choices on how ideas are to be organized and expressed in intelligible – again, therefore, public – compositions. So internal evidence and that alone testifies to the form or literary structures of a given text. And when we can identify no limited set of forms or structures but only a mass of fixed forms, randomly employed, we further ask whether the authorship of that document also proposes to argue for or against a limited and identifiable set of propositions.

In form-analysis or the study of rhetoric of the Mishnah, the adjective "recurrent" obviously constitutes a redundancy when joined to the noun "structure" or "pattern." For we cannot know that we have a structure if the text under analysis does not repeatedly resort to the presentation of its message through a disciplined structure entirely external to its message on any given point. A pattern used episodically defines nothing about a writing as a whole. And, it follows self-evidently, we do know that we have a structure when the text in hand repeatedly follows recurrent conventions of expression, organization, or proportion *extrinsic* to the message of the author. The form or literary structures or patterns find definition in entirely formal and objective facts: the placement of the key-verse subject to discussion in the composition at hand, the origin of that verse. No subjective or impressionistic judgment intervenes. That is why anyone may replicate the results of form-analysis carried on inductively in any rabbinic writing.[1]

Second in order of analysis, as we shall see presently, is the logic of a document. I use the simple word, logic, to stand for the principle of intelligibility and cogency of thought and the expression of thought in public discourse. Logic is what joins one sentence to the next and forms the whole into paragraphs of meaning, intelligible propositions, each with its place and sense in a still larger, accessible system. Because of logic one mind connects to another, public discourse becomes possible, debate on issues of general intelligibility takes place, and an *anthology* of statements about a single subject becomes a *composition* of theorems about that subject. What people think – exegesis in accord with a fixed hermeneutic of the system – knows no limit. How they think makes all the difference. Now to the issue at hand: language and how it is structured.

The Mishnah's language is notional and episodic; it invariably focuses upon specific cases and details of those cases. But it is so framed as to repeat certain rigid patterns of syntax. This rather special language is filled with words for neutral things of humble existence. But because of the peculiar and particular way in which it is formed and formalized, this same language not only adheres to an aesthetic theory but expresses a deeply embedded ontology and methodology of the sacred, specifically of the sacred within the secular, and of the capacity for regulation, therefore for sanctification, within the ordinary.[2] Since that is the principal focus of interest in the inductive exercise to follow, we shall first treat the document's rhetoric and logic. These traits predominate throughout. Only when we reach our sample-tractate shall we address the more difficult and special problem of identifying a program of principles that I allege underlies the topical repertoire of a given tractate.

The Mishnah's authorship everywhere (in sixty-three of the sixty-four tractates, tractate Avot being the exception) organizes

---

[1]Replicate, but also improve upon those results. All of my form-analytical work has been carried on with attention only to the most gross and crude traits of language-patterning. Refinement will show many more patterns and a much more subtle and intricate sense for implicit structure – poetic structure, I should claim – than I have found it necessary to display for the purpose of my sustained and encompassing demonstration of the traits of the literature as a whole. Now that this work is done, a second generation of form-analysis can render it obsolete.

[2]All things in order, all things then hallowed by God who orders all things, so had said the priests' creation-tale.

discourse in a topical way and also expresses its ideas in highly formalized language. Let me summarize the criteria of linguistic formalization and editorial organization of the Mishnah, criteria that apply throughout. There are two criteria that account for the organization of the entire document and all but one of its tractates, subject-matter and form. The one is topical, the other formal.

The first of the two criteria derives from the nature of the principal divisions themselves: subject-matter or theme. What it means to organize a document by topics is self-evident: we talk about this subject here, then that subject there. Within a given subject, we identify the subtopic that comes prior to some other when we know what I must know first to understand the subject, and what I may know only later on in the same sequence of exposition. So the topical organization is familiar to us, since most of the information we receive comes to us within that simple manner of setting things out.

Topical organization necessarily results from a choice, for, in fact, there were (and are) other ways of organizing a piece of writing beside the abstract one of a subject and its inner requirements of order, e.g., what, in that subject, comes first, and what must I know then. One can organize by number-sequences, e.g., there are five this's and five that's; by names of authorities, e.g., Rabbi X rules on the following five discrete subjects; by language-patterns, e.g., There is no difference between this and that except for the other thing, and the like. All of these modes of organizing thought do occur in the Mishnah. But there is only one paramount principle of cogent order, and that is defined by the requirements of the exposition of a topic and its indicative traits. It is along thematic lines that the redactors organized vast corpora of materials into principal divisions, tractates. These fundamental themes themselves were subdivided into smaller conceptual units. The principal divisions treat their themes in units indicated by the sequential unfolding of their inner logical structure. Accordingly, one established criterion for the deliberation of an aggregate of materials from some other, fore or aft, will be a shift in the theme, or predominant and characteristic concern, of a sequence of materials. For most tractates, we can account for the layout of themes or problems, meaning, explain why the framers have treated a given problem within their topic before, or after, they addressed another problem within that same topic.

The second fundamental criterion is the literary character, the syntactical and grammatical pattern, which differentiates and characterizes a sequence of primitive (that is, undifferentiable, indivisible) units of thought. Normally, when the subject changes, the mode of expression, the formal or formulary character, the patterning of language, will change as well. That simple fact of the redaction of the document requires us to turn to the way in which sentences and paragraphs and chapters are put together. Let us begin in the middle, with a paragraph, since all chapters are made up of such paragraphs, and all paragraphs form expositions of a principle or conception, however limited in scope. Understanding how this formal-literary mode of cogent discourse works draws us deep into the orderly thought-patterns of this writing.

By a "paragraph" (which is a metaphor drawn from our own circumstance) I mean a completed exposition of thought, the setting forth of a proposition whole and complete, now without regard to the larger function, e.g., in a sustained discourse of argument or proposition, served by that thought. Two or more lapidary statements, e.g., allegations as to fact, will make up such a sustained cognitive unit. And collections of such units form chapters, or what I call "intermediate units." Intermediate divisions of these same principal divisions (we might call them chapters of tractates or books) are to be discerned on the basis of internal evidence, through the confluence of theme and form. That is to say, a given intermediate division of a principal one (a chapter of a tractate) will be marked by a particular, recurrent, formal pattern in accord with which sentences are constructed, and also by a particular and distinct theme, to which these sentences are addressed. When a new theme commences, a fresh formal pattern will be used.

And this now brings us back to the point with which we commenced, which is the matter of the formalization of syntax or forms. Within the intermediate divisions, we are able to recognize the components, or smallest whole units of thought (hereinafter, cognitive units, defined presently), because there will be a recurrent pattern of sentence structure repeated time and again within the unit and a shifting at the commencement of the next theme. Each point at which the recurrent pattern commences marks the beginning of a new cognitive unit. In general, an intermediate division will contain a carefully enumerated sequence of exempla of cognitive units, in the established formal pattern, commonly in groups of three or five or multiples of three or five (pairs for the first division). A single rhetorical pattern will govern the whole set of topical instances of a logical proposition. When the logical-topical program changes, the rhetorical pattern will change too. So the mnemonics of the Mishnah and the foundations of its discourse alike throughout rest on the confluence of (1) deep logic, (2) articulated topic, and (3) manifest rhetoric.

Before proceeding, let me give a concrete case of how the Mishnah is so formulated as to facilitate memorization.

A.   Honeycombs: from what point are they susceptible to
        uncleanness in the status of liquid?

B.   The House of Shammai say, "When one smokes out [the bees
        from the combs, so that one can potentially get at the honey]."

C.   The House of Hillel say, "When one will actually have broken up
        [the honeycombs to remove the honey]."

M[ishnah-tractate] Uqs[in] 3:11

The authors begin with an announcement of the topic at hand,
honeycombs, and then ask our question, A. We have a single sentence by
way of an answer:

> *Honeycombs: from what point are they susceptible to uncleanness in
> the status of liquid? When ["it is from the point at which"] one smokes
> out [the bees from the combs, so that one can get at the honey].*

or:

> *Honeycombs: from what point are they susceptible to uncleanness in
> the status of liquid? "When one will actually have broken up [the
> honeycombs to remove the honey]."*

We see, therefore, a question followed by a selection of answers,
and each answer can stand on its own to respond to the question. Not
only so, but the simple analysis involving identifying successive
sentences shows us how the sentences are broken up and brought together
into a single coherent statement. This is done by creating a dispute out
of several autonomous statements. We assign a statement to an
authority, the Houses of Shammai and Hillel. Then we make all the
statements bearing attributions into a sequence of responses to a simple
problem, thus a dispute. The formulation of the passage is very tight, a
kind of poetry. For the Hebrew shows closer balance than does the
English, since, at M. Uqs. 3:11, the statements of the two Houses are
made up of precisely the same number of syllables. So the match is
more precise than we should have expected.

We need hardly notice that it is very easy to memorize such highly
patterned language. In point of fact, most of the Mishnah is written not
in narrative prose, flowing declarative sentences for instance, but in
these brief thought units with a question (normally implicit) and an
answer, set forth in a disciplined way. There will be a set of thought-
units following a single syntactic and grammatical pattern. Put
together, they will set forth three or five cases, and if you reflect on
the examples, you can readily recover the principle that explains all
three or five rulings. Accordingly, we deal with a piece of writing quite
different from simple narrative, in that the author wants us to learn
the point by putting together things that are given to us to draw a

conclusion that is not spelled out for us – a very warm compliment to us as readers.

To return to the main point: the criteria of formalization and organization of the Mishnah, criteria that apply throughout, are two. The first of the two criteria derives from the nature of the principal divisions themselves: theme. That is, it is along thematic lines that the redactors organized vast corpora of materials into principal divisions, tractates. These fundamental themes themselves were subdivided into smaller conceptual units. The principal divisions treat their themes in units indicated by the sequential unfolding of their inner logical structure. So one established criterion for the deliberation of an aggregate of materials from some other, fore or aft, will be a shift in the theme, or predominant and characteristic concern, of a sequence of materials. The second fundamental criterion, as we now see, is the literary character, the syntactical and grammatical pattern, which differentiates and characterizes a sequence of primitive (that is, undifferentiable, indivisible) units of thought. Normally, when the subject changes, the mode of expression, the formal or formulary character, the patterning of language, will change as well. From the basic traits of large-scale organization, which appeal to the characteristics of subject-matter, we turn to the way in which sentences and paragraphs are put together. By a "paragraph" (which is a metaphor drawn from our own circumstance) I mean a completed exposition of thought, the setting forth of a proposition whole and complete, now without regard to the larger function, e.g., in a sustained discourse of argument or proposition, served by that thought. Two or more lapidary statements, e.g., allegations as to fact, will make up such a sustained cognitive unit. The cognitive units in the Mishnah in particular resort to a remarkably limited repertoire of formulary patterns, and the document as a whole exhibits remarkable formal uniformity.

The matter of rhetoric now comes to the fore. As a matter of simple fact, the authorship of the Mishnah manages to say whatever it wants in one of the following ways:

1.   the simple declarative sentence, in which the subject, verb, and predicate are syntactically tightly joined to one another, e.g., he who does so and so is such and such;

2.   the duplicated subject, in which the subject of the sentence is stated twice, e.g., He who does so and so, lo, he is such and such;

3.   mild apocopation, in which the subject of the sentence is cut off from the verb, which refers to its own subject, and not the one with which the sentence commences, e.g., He who does so and so..., it [the thing he has done] is such and such;

4.   extreme apocopation, in which a series of clauses is presented, none of them tightly joined to what precedes or follows, and all of them cut off from the predicate of the sentence, e.g., He who does so and so..., it [the thing he has done] is such and such..., it is a matter of doubt whether...or whether...lo, it [referring to nothing in the antecedent, apocopated clauses of the subject of the sentence] is so and so...

5.   In addition to these formulary patterns, in which the distinctive formulary traits are effected through variations in the relationship between the subject and the predicate of the sentence, or in which the subject itself is given a distinctive development, there is yet a fifth. In this last one we have a contrastive complex predicate, in which case we may have two sentences, independent of one another, yet clearly formulated so as to stand in acute balance with one another in the predicate, thus, *He who does...is unclean, and he who does not...is clean.*

It naturally will be objected, is it possible that "a simple declarative sentence" may be asked to serve as a formulary pattern, alongside the rather distinctive and unusual constructions which follow? True, by itself, a tightly constructed sentence consisting of subject, verb, and complement, in which the verb refers to the subject, and the complement to the verb, hardly exhibits traits of particular formal interest. Yet a sequence of such sentences, built along the same gross grammatical lines, may well exhibit a clear-cut and distinctive pattern. And here the mnemonics of the document enter into consideration. The Mishnah is not a generalizing document; it makes its points by repeating several cases that yield the same, ordinarily unarticulated, general principle. Accordingly, the Mishnah, as I said, utilizes sets of three or five repetitions of cases to make a single point. Now when we see that three or five "simple declarative sentences" take up one principle or problem, and then, when the principle or problem shifts, a quite distinctive formal pattern will be utilized, we realize that the "simple declarative sentence" has served the formulator of the unit of thought as aptly as did apocopation, a dispute, or another more obviously distinctive form or formal pattern. The contrastive predicate is one example; the Mishnah contains many more.

The important point of differentiation, particularly for the simple declarative sentence, therefore appears in the intermediate or the whole cognitive unit, thus in the interplay between theme and form. It is there that we see a single pattern recurring in a long sequence of sentences, e.g., *the X which has lost its Y is unclean because of its Z. The Z which has lost its Y is unclean because of its X.* Another example will be a long sequence of highly developed sentences, laden with relative clauses and other explanatory matter, in which a single syntactical pattern will govern the articulation of three or six or nine exempla. That sequence will be followed by one repeated terse sentence pattern, e.g., *X is so and so, Y is such and such, Z is thus and so.* The former group will treat one principle or theme, the latter some other. There can be no doubt, therefore, that the declarative sentence in recurrent patterns is, in its way, just as carefully formalized as a sequence of severely apocopated sentences or of contrastive predicates or duplicated subjects.   None of the Mishnah's secondary and amplificatory companions, e.g., the Tosefta, the Talmud of the Land of Israel or Yerushalmi, the Talmud of Babylonia or Bavli, exhibits the same tight and rigidly adhered to rhetorical cogency.   These cursory remarks suffice to characterize the writing before us and so to prepare the way for our study of the philosophical medium and message of the document: its logic and its sustained debate about the premises of being, which I call its medium (of thought) and its (philosophical) message.

3

Philosophical Discourse
of the Social Order [II]:
The Mishnah's Repertoire of
Logics

If the strict conventions of forms and literary structures make their mark on the very surface of documents, the inquiry into the logics of cogent discourse, a term explained immediately, carries us to the depths of the structures of thought of those same documents.[1] For rhetoric dictates the material arrangement of words, while logics govern the possibilities of thought. These define how thought, arranged or set forth in one way, makes sense, in another way, nonsense. And yet whether we explore the extrinsic traits of formal expression or the most profound layers of intelligible discourse and coherent thought that hold sentences together and form of them all propositions or presentations that can be understood, we produce a single result. It is that each document's authorship does make choices and therefore works out a rationality of its own. Choosing modes of cogent discourse and coherent thought involves a repertoire that is exceedingly limited. Options in rhetoric by contrast prove quite diverse. But the work of comparison and contrast in both sorts of choices proves entirely feasible, since with regard to both rhetoric and logic we are required to compare fixed and external traits. There is no appeal to subjective taste and judgment.

Now let me explain what is at issue when I speak of "logic." We begin from the beginning: what do I mean by "cogent discourse"? As I have already explained, people wish not only to frame, but also to

---

[1]Not only structures of thought, but structures of social order.

communicate, their ideas, and when they propose propositions for others' attention, they do so only by appeal to shared conventions of thought. To be understood by others, the one who frames ideas has as a matter of premise to compose thought in ways that others understand. That understanding requires in particular a shared conception of the connections between one thing and another, for instance, between one fact and another. When we know and can describe the character of those connections, which can be quite diverse, we point to what I designate the logics of intelligible discourse for a given group. Such logics serve where and how they serve, whether an entire culture or only two people who form a social entity of some sort – in our case, for an authorship. For that authorship presents statements, whether or not aimed at constituting propositions, to reach others and make sense to them – and that by definition. Such intelligible expression must evoke a shared logic, so that others make the same connections that, to the authorship, prove self-evident. It is that repertoire of logics that makes the thought of one person or our authorship intelligible to some other person(s).

In concrete terms, what this means is simple. One sentence not only stands beside, but generates another; a consequent statement follows from a prior one. We share a sense of connection, pertinence, relevance – the aptness of joining thought A to thought B to produce proposition X. These (only by way of example) form intelligible discourses, turning facts into statements of meaning and consequence. To conduct intelligible discourse, therefore, people make two or more statements which, in the world in which they say their piece, are deemed self-evidently to hang together and form a proposition understood by someone else in that same world. It is the matter of self-evident cogency and intelligibility, in the document at hand, that now gains our attention.

Discourse shared by others begins when one sentence joins to a second one in framing a statement (whether or not presenting a proposition) in such a way that others understand *the connection* between the two sentences. In studies of other documents of the canon of the Judaism of the Dual Torah I have identified four different logics by which two or more sentences are deemed to cohere and to constitute a statement of consequence and intelligibility. One is familiar to us as philosophical logic, the second is equally familiar as the logic of cogent discourse attained through narrative. These two, self-evidently, are logics of a propositional order, evoking a logic of a philosophical character. The third is not propositional, and, as a matter of fact, it also is not ordinarily familiar to us at all. It is a mode of joining two or more statements – sentences – not on the foundation of meaning or sense or proposition but on the foundation of a different order altogether. The fourth mode of coherent discourse, distinct from the prior three, establishing connections at the most abstract and profound level of thought, which is through highly methodical analysis of many things in a single way. That forms the single most commonplace building block of thought in our document. It is, as a matter of fact, stunning in its logical power. But like the third logic it also is not propositional, though it yields its encompassing truths of order, proportion, structure, and self-evidence.

We turn to the two familiar modes of turning two sentences into a coherent statement, one weight and meaning, which both connects the two sentences, forming them into a whole, and also presents a statement that in meaning and intelligible proposition transcends the sum of the parts. Then I shall point to the third and fourth logics before us.

1. The first logic, most familiar to us in the West, establishes propositions that rest upon philosophical bases, e.g., through the proposal of a thesis and the composition of a list of facts that prove the thesis. This – to us entirely familiar, Western – mode of scientific expression through the classification of data that, in a simple way, we may call the science of making lists (*Listenwissenschaft*), is best exemplified by the Mishnah, but it dominates, also, in such profoundly philosophical-syllogistic documents as Leviticus Rabbah as well. Within the idiom of the canonical writings of the Dual Torah, those documents bring us closest to the modes of thought with which we are generally familiar. A broad range of philosophical modes of stating and then proving or establishing propositions also characterizes Sifra and Sifré to Deuteronomy, but, in proportions and use, the proportions are quite different in the two writings. No philosopher in antiquity will have found unintelligible these types of units of thought.

This philosophical logic of cogent discourse works in a familiar way. Its issue is one of connection, not of fact but of the relationship between one fact and another. The two or more facts, that is, sentences, are connected through or in a conclusion. The conclusion or proposition is different from the established facts. When we set up as a sequence two or more facts and claim out of that sequence to propose a proposition different from, transcending, the facts at hand, we join the two sentences or facts in the philosophical logic of cogent discourse that is most common in our own setting. We may call this the logic of propositional discourse. We demonstrate propositions in a variety of ways, appealing to both a repertoire of probative facts and also a set of accepted modes of argument. In this way we engage in a kind of discourse that gains its logic from what, in general, we may call philosophy: the rigorous analysis and testing of propositions against the canons of an accepted reason. Philosophy accomplishes the miracle of making the whole more – or less – than the sum of the parts, that is, in the simple language I have used up to now, showing the connections between fact 1 and fact 2, in such wise as to yield proposition A. We begin with the irrefutable fact; our issue is not how facts gain their facticity, rather, how, from givens, people construct propositions or make statements that are deemed sense and nonsense or gibberish. So the problem is to explain the connections between and among facts, so accounting for the conclusions people draw, on the one side, or the acceptable associations people tolerate, on the other, in the exchange of language and thought.

Propositional logic also may be syllogistic, e.g., a variant on a famous syllogistic argument:

1.   All Greeks are philosophers.
2.   Demosthenes is a Greek.
3.   Therefore Demosthenes is a philosopher.

At issue is not mere facticity, rather, broadly speaking, the *connections* between facts. The problem subject to analysis here then is how one thing follows from something else, or how one thing generates something else, thus, as I said, connection. In that context, then, the sentences, 1, 2, and 3, standing entirely by themselves convey not a proposition but merely statements of a fact, which may or may not be true, and which may or may not bear sense and meaning beyond itself. Sentence 1 and sentence 2 by themselves state facts but announce no proposition. But the logic of syllogistic discourse joins the two into No. 3, which indeed does constitute a proposition and also (by the way) shows the linkage between sentence 1 and sentence 2. But there are more ways for setting forth propositions, making points, and thus for undertaking intelligible discourse, besides the philosophical, and syllogistic one with which we are familiar in the West. We know a variety of other modes of philosophical-propositional discourse, that is to say, presenting, testing, and demonstrating a proposition through appeal to fact and argument.

No less familiar to us is yet another way of carrying on cogent discourse through propositional logic. It is to offer a proposition, lay out the axioms, present the proofs, test the proposition against contrary argument, and the like. The demonstration of propositions we know, in general, as *Listenwissenschaft*, that is, a way to classify and so establish a set of probative facts, compels us to reach a given conclusion based on evidence and argument. These probative facts adduced in evidence for a proposition may derive from the classification of data, all of which point in one direction and not in another. A catalogue of facts, for example, may be so composed that, through the regularities and indicative traits of the entries, the catalogue yields a proposition. A list of parallel items all together point to a simple conclusion; the conclusion may or may not be given at the end of the catalogue, but the catalogue – by definition – is pointed. All of the catalogued facts are taken to bear self-evident connections to one another, established by those pertinent shared traits implicit in the composition of the list, therefore also bearing meaning and pointing through the weight of evidence to an inescapable conclusion. The discrete facts then join together because of some trait common to them all. This is a mode of classification of facts to lead to an identification of what the facts have in common and an explanation of their meaning. These and other modes of philosophical argument are entirely familiar to us all. In calling all of them "philosophical," I mean only to distinguish them from the other three logics we shall presently examine.

2. This brings us to the second, equally familiar logic of cogent, therefore intelligible discourse, which is narrative or, as I shall explain, teleological in character. A proposition emerges not only through philosophical argument and analysis, e.g., spelling out in so many words a general and encompassing proposition, and further constructing in proof of that explicit generalization a syllogism and demonstration. We may state and demonstrate a proposition in a second way, which resorts to narrative (itself subject to a taxonomy of its own) both to establish and to explain connections between naked facts. Let me spell out this second logic, which derives from narrative and evokes a teleology to connect one sentence, fact, or thought, to another. A proposition (whether or not it is stated explicitly) may be set forth and demonstrated by showing through the telling of a tale (of a variety of kinds, e.g., historical, fictional, parabolic, and the like) that a sequence of events, real or imagined, shows the ineluctable truth of a given proposition. The logic of connection demonstrated through narrative, rather than philosophy, is simply stated. It is connection attained and explained by invoking some mode of narrative in which a sequence of events, first this, then that, is understood to yield a proposition, first this, then that *because of this.* That sequence both states and establishes a proposition in a way different from the philosophical and argumentative mode of propositional discourse. Whether or not the generalization is stated in so many words rarely matters, because the power of well-crafted narrative is to make unnecessary explicit drawing of the moral.

That is why I argue that this second logic, besides the logic of philosophy and syllogistic argument, is one of that narrative, that sees cogency in the purpose, the necessary order of events seen as causative.

That is then a logic or intelligibility of connection that is attained through teleology: the claim of purpose, therefore cause, in the garb of a story of what happened because it had to happen. Narrative conveys a proposition through the setting forth of happenings in a framework of inevitability, in a sequence that makes a point, e.g., establishes not merely the facts of what happens, but the teleology that explains those facts. Then we speak not only of events – our naked facts – but of their relationship. We claim to account for that relationship teleologically, in the purposive sequence and necessary order of happenings. In due course we shall see how various kinds of narratives serve to convey highly intelligible and persuasive propositions.

3. We come, third, to the one genuinely odd, mode of discourse in the canon of the Judaism of the Dual Torah, one present in the Mishnah in only tractate Avot. I call it the logic of fixed association, by which distinct facts or sentences or thoughts are held together without actually joining into sequential and coherent propositions of any kind. What we have is a sequence of absolutely unrelated sentences, made up in each instance of a clause of a verse, followed by a phrase of amplification. Nothing links one sentence (completed thought) to the ones fore or aft. Yet the compositors have presented us with what they represent side by side with sentences that do form large compositions, that is, that are linked one to the next by connections that we can readily discern. That seems to me to indicate that our authorship conceives one mode of connecting sentences to form a counterpart to another.

How then does the logic of cogent discourse supplied by fixed association accomplish its goal? In the sample we have examined, we find side by side a sequence of sentences that bear no relationship or connection at all between one another. These discrete sentences appear in "commentary-form," for instance:

"Clause 1": "this means A."
"Clause 2": "this refers to Q."

Nothing joins A and Q. Indeed, had I used symbols out of different classifications altogether, e.g., A, a letter of an alphabet, and a symbol such as #, which stands for something else than a sound of an alphabet, the picture would have proved still clearer. Nothing joins A to Q or A to # except that clause 2 follows clause 1. The upshot is that no proposition links A to Q or A to # and so far as there is a connection between A and Q or A and # it is not propositional. Then is there a connection at all? I think the authorship of the document that set forth matters as they did assumes that there is such a connection. For there clearly is – at the very least – an order, that is, "clause 1" is prior to "clause 2," in the text that out of clauses 1 and 2 does form an intelligible statement, that is, two connected, not merely adjacent, sentences.

This third way in which two or more sentences are deemed, in the canonical literature of Judaism, to constitute a more than random, episodic sequence of unrelated allegations, A, X, Q, C, and so on, on its own, out of context, yields gibberish. That is, this mode of connection establishes itself with no proposition, no sense, no joining between two sentences, no implicit connection accessible without considerable labor of access. But this third way can see cogent discourse even where there is no proposition at all, and even where the relationship between sentence A and sentence X does not derive from the interplay among the propositions at hand. It is hard for us even to imagine non-propositional, yet intelligible discourse, outside the realm of feeling or inchoate attitude, and yet, as we shall see, before us is a principle of intelligible discourse that is entirely routine, clearly assumed to be comprehensible, and utterly accessible. This third logic rests on a premise of education – that is, of prior discourse attained through processes of learning a logic not accessible, as are the logics of philosophy and narrative, but through another means.

The third logic rests upon the premise that an established sequence of words, joins whatever is attached to those words into a set of cogent statements, even though it does not form of those statements propositions of any kind, implicit or explicit. The established sequence of words may be made up of names always associated with one another. It may be made up of a received text, with deep meanings of its own, e.g., a verse or a clause of Scripture. It may be made up of the sequence of holy days or synagogue lections, which are assumed to be known by everyone and so to connect on their own. The fixed association of these words, whether names, whether formula such as verses of Scripture, whether lists of facts, serves to link otherwise unrelated statements to one another and to form of them all not a proposition but, nonetheless, *an entirely intelligible sequence of connected or related sentences.* Even though these negative definitions intersect and in a measure cover the same ground, each requires its own specification – but I shall ask only a mite more of the reader's indulgence.

4. The fourth logic of intelligible discourse is discourse in which one analytical method applies to many sentences, with the result that many discrete and diverse sentences are shown to constitute a single intellectual structure. This I call the logic of methodical analysis. A variety of explanations and amplifications, topically and propositionally unrelated, will be joined in a methodical way so as to produce a broadly applicable conclusion that many things really

conform to a single pattern or structure. Such methodologically coherent analysis imposes upon a variety of data a structure that is external to all of the data, yet that imposes connection between and among facts or sentences. The connection consists in the recurrent order and repeated balance and replicated meaning of them all, seen in the aggregate. This is commonly done by asking the same question to many things and producing a single result many times. Unity of thought and discourse therefore derives not only from what is said, or even from a set of fixed associations.

Methodical analysis may be conducted by addressing a set of fixed questions, imposing a sequence of stable procedures, to a vast variety of data. That will yield not a proposition, nor even a sequence of facts formerly unconnected but now connected, but a different mode of cogency, one that derives from showing that many things follow a single rule or may be interpreted in a single way. It is the intelligible proposition that is general and not particular, that imposes upon the whole a sense of understanding and comprehension, even though the parts of the whole do not join together. What happens, in this mode of discourse, is that we turn the particular into the general, the case into a rule, and if I had to point to one purpose of our authorship overall, it is to turn the cases of the book of Deuteronomy into rules that conform, overall, to the way in which the Mishnah presents its rules: logically, topically, a set of philosophically defensible generalizations.

Prima facie evidence that the Mishnah may be read as a philosophical writing derives from the character of the logic of the document. One logic prevails (though the other three are present here and there). The Mishnah's paramount logic of cogent discourse establishes propositions that rest upon philosophical bases, e.g., through the proposal of a thesis and the composition of a list of facts that (e.g., through shared traits of a taxonomic order) prove the thesis. The Mishnah presents rules and treats stories (inclusive of history) as incidental and of merely taxonomic interest. Its logic is propositional, and its intellect does its work through a vast labor of classification, comparison, and contrast generating governing rules and generalizations.

That people made choices as to the appropriate logic for their discourse emerges in the contrast between the Mishnah's and the Pentateuch's choices in this matter. The composite produced by the pentateuchal authorship provides an account of how things were in order to explain how things are and set forth how they should be, with the tabernacle in the wilderness the model for (and modeled after) the Temple in the Jerusalem abuilding. The Mishnah speaks in a continuing present tense, saying only how things are, indifferent to the *were* and the *will-be*. The Pentateuch focuses upon self-conscious "Israel," saying who they were and what they must become to overcome how they now are. The Mishnah understands by "Israel" as much the individual as the nation and identifies as its principal actors, the heroes of its narrative, not the family become a nation, but the priest and the householder, the woman and the slave, the adult and the child, and other castes and categories of person within an inward-looking, established, fully landed community. Given the Mishnah's authorship's interest in classifications and categories, therefore in systematic hierarchization of an orderly world, one can hardly find odd that (re)definition of the subject-matter and problematic of the systemic social entity.

While, therefore, the Pentateuch appeals to the logic of teleology to draw together and make sense of facts, so making connections by appeal to the end and drawing conclusions concerning the purpose of things, the Mishnah's authorship knows only the philosophical logic of syllogism, the rule-making logic of lists. The pentateuchal logic reached concrete expression in narrative, which served to point to the direction and goal of matters, hence, in the nature of things, of history. Accordingly, those authors, when putting together diverse materials, so shaped everything as to form of it all as continuous a narrative as they could construct, and through that "history" that they made up, they delivered their message and also portrayed that message as cogent and compelling. If the pentateuchal writers were theologians of history, the Mishnah's aimed at composing a natural philosophy for supernatural, holy Israel. Like good Aristotelians, they would uncover the components of the rules by comparison and contrast, showing the rule for one thing by finding out how it compared with like things and contrasted with the unlike.[2] Then, in their view, the unknown would become known, conforming to the rule of the like thing, also to the opposite of the rule governing the unlike thing.

That purpose is accomplished, in particular, though list-making, which places on display the data of the like and the unlike and implicitly (ordinarily, not explicitly) then conveys the role. That is why, in exposing the interior logic of its authorship's intellect, the Mishnah had to be a book of lists, with the implicit order, the nomothetic traits, dictating the ordinarily unstated general and encompassing rule. And all this why? It is in order to make a single statement, endless times over, and to repeat in a mass of tangled detail

---

[2]Compare G. E. R. Lloyd, *Polarity and Analogy. Two Types of Argumentation in Early Greek Thought* (Cambridge: Cambridge University Press, 1966). But the core-logic of *Listenwissenschaft* extends back to Sumerian times.

precisely the same fundamental judgment. The Mishnah in its way is as blatantly repetitious in its fundamental statement as is the Pentateuch. But the power of the pentateuchal authorship, denied to that of the Mishnah, lies in their capacity always to be heard, to create sound by resonance of the surfaces of things. The Pentateuch is a fundamentally popular and accessible piece of writing. By contrast, the Mishnah's writers spoke into the depths, anticipating a more acute hearing than they ever would receive. So the repetitions of Scripture reenforce the message, while the endlessly repeated paradigm of the Mishnah sits too deep in the structure of the system to gain hearing from the ear that lacks acuity or to attain visibility to the untutored eye. So much for the logic. What of the systemic message? Given the subtlety of intellect of the Mishnah's authorship, we cannot find surprising that the message speaks not only in what is said, but in what is omitted. Precisely how does the Mishnah's logic do its work? Only with the answer to that question shall we see with great clarity the philosophical character of that writing. Then we may turn to the question of the document's program and ask where and how what is discussed states in a concrete way an issue of philosophical depth.

4

The Mishnah's Philosophical Method

The Mishnah's philosophical method, we know full well, is that of *Listenwissenschaft*, which is to say, the search for the rule governing many things by classification of things by shared traits. The framers of the Mishnah in defining those taxonomic indicators that dictate what belongs on one list, what on some other, appeal solely to the intrinsic traits of things.[1]   When we understand the logical basis of *Listenwissenschaft*, we shall understand the deeply philosophical character of the Mishnah's authorship's mode of thought.   For *Listenwissenschaft* defines a way of proving propositions through classification, so establishing a set of shared traits that form a rule which compels us to reach a given conclusion. Probative facts derive from the classification of data, all of which point in one direction and not in another. And that defines philosophical method from Aristotle forward.

Listenwissenschaft does its work by defining the way of proving propositions through classification, so establishing a set of shared traits that form a rule which compels us to reach a given conclusion. Probative facts derive from the classification of data, all of which point in one direction and not in another. A catalogue of facts, for example, may be so composed that, through the regularities and indicative traits of the entries, the catalogue yields a proposition. A list of parallel items all together point to a simple conclusion; the

---

[1]That that is what is at stake is shown by Sifra. The authorship of Sifra by contrast insists that by themselves, the traits of things do not settle anything. Only Scripture designates classifications that serve. I have spelled out this matter in *Uniting the Dual Torah: Sifra and the Problem of the Mishnah* (Atlanta: Scholars Press for Brown Judaic Studies, 1989).

conclusion may or may not be given at the end of the catalogue, but the catalogue – by definition – is pointed. All of the catalogued facts are taken to bear self-evident connections to one another, established by those pertinent shared traits implicit in the composition of the list, therefore also bearing meaning and pointing through the weight of evidence to an inescapable conclusion. The discrete facts then join together because of some trait common to them all. This is a mode of classification of facts to lead to an identification of what the facts have in common and – it goes without saying, an explanation of their meaning.

A catalogue of facts, for example, may be so composed that, through the regularities and indicative traits of the entries, the catalogue yields a proposition. A list of parallel items all together point to a simple conclusion; the conclusion may or may not be given at the end of the catalogue, but the catalogue – by definition – is pointed. All of the catalogued facts are taken to bear self-evident connections to one another, established by those pertinent shared traits implicit in the composition of the list, therefore also bearing meaning and pointing through the weight of evidence to an inescapable conclusion. The discrete facts then join together because of some trait common to them all. This is a mode of classification of facts to lead to an identification of what the facts have in common and an explanation of their meaning. These and other modes of philosophical argument are entirely familiar to us all.

The diverse topical program of the Mishnah, time and again making the same points on the centrality of order, works itself out in a single logic of cogent discourse, one which seeks the rule that governs diverse cases. Two pericopes of the Mishnah show us the logic that joins fact to fact, sentence to sentence, in a cogent proposition, that is, in our terms, a paragraph that makes a statement. To see how this intellect does its work we turn first to Mishnah-tractate Berakhot, Chapter Eight, to see list-making in its simplest form, and then to Mishnah-tractate Sanhedrin, Chapter Two, to see the more subtle way in which list-making yields a powerfully argued philosophical theorem. In the first of our two abstracts we have a list, carefully formulated, in which the announcement at the outset tells us what is catalogued, and in which careful mnemonic devices so arrange matters that we may readily remember the conflicting opinions. So in formal terms, we have a list that means to facilitate memorization. But in substantive terms, the purpose of the list and its message(s) are not set forth, and only ample exegesis will succeed in spelling out what is at stake. Here is an instance of a Mishnah-passage which demands an exegesis not supplied by the Mishnah's authorship.

Mishnah-tractate Berakhot Chapter Eight

8:1

A These are the things which are between the House of Shammai and the House of Hillel in [regard to] the meal:

[1] B. The House of Shammai say, "One blesses over the day, and afterward one blesses over the wine."

And the House of Hillel say, "One blesses over the wine, and afterward one blesses over the day."

8.2

[2] A The House of Shammai say, "They wash the hands and afterward mix the cup."

And the House of Hillel say, "They mix the cup and afterward wash the hands."

8:3

[3] A The House of Shammai say, "He dries his hands on the cloth and lays it on the table."

And the House of Hillel say, "On the pillow."

8:4

[4] A The House of Shammai say, "They clean the house, and afterward they wash the hands."

And the House of Hillel say, "They wash the hands, and afterward they clean the house."

8:5

[5] A The House of Shammai say, "Light, and food, and spices, and *Havdalah*."

And the House of Hillel say, "'Light, and spices, and food, and *Havdalah*."

[6] B. The House of Shammai say, "'Who created the light of the fire.'"

And the House of Hillel say, "'Who creates the lights of the fire.'"

The mnemonic serving the list does its work by the simple reversal of items. If authority A has the order 1, 2, then authority be will give 2, 1. Only entry [3] breaks that pattern. What is at stake in the making of the list is hardly transparent, and why day/wine vs. wine/day, with a parallel, e.g., clean/wash vs. wash/clean, yields a general principle the authorship does not indicate. All we know at this point, therefore, is that we deal with list-makers. But how lists work to communicate principles awaits exemplification.

The next abstract allows us much more explicitly to identify the *and* and the *equal* of mishnaic discourse, showing us through the making of connections and the drawing of conclusions the propositional and essentially philosophical mind that animates the Mishnah. In the following passage, drawn from Mishnah-tractate Sanhedrin Chapter Two, the authorship wishes to say that Israel has two heads, one of state, the other of cult, the king and the high priest, respectively, and that these two offices are nearly wholly congruent with one another, with a few differences based on the particular traits of each. Broadly speaking, therefore, our exercise is one of setting forth the genus and the species. The genus is head of holy Israel. The species are king and high priest. Here are the traits in common and those not shared, and the exercise is fully exposed for what it is, an inquiry into the rules that govern, the points of regularity and order, in this minor matter, of political structure. My outline, imposed in bold-face type, makes the point important in this setting.

Mishnah-tractate Sanhedrin Chapter Two

I. The rules of the high priest: subject to the law, marital rites, conduct in bereavement

2:1

A.   A high priest judges, and [others] judge him;

B.   gives testimony, and [others] give testimony about him;

C.   performs the rite of removing the shoe [Deut. 25:7-9], and [others] perform the rite of removing the shoe with his wife.

D.   [Others] enter levirate marriage with his wife, but he does not enter into levirate marriage,

E.   because he is prohibited to marry a widow.

F.   [If] he suffers a death [in his family], he does not follow the bier.

G.   "But when [the bearers of the bier] are not visible, he is visible; when they are visible, he is not.

H.   "And he goes with them to the city gate," the words of R. Meir.

I.   R. Judah says, "He never leaves the sanctuary,

J.   "since it says, *'Nor shall he go out of the sanctuary'* (Lev. 21:12)."

K.   And when he gives comfort to others,

L.   the accepted practice is for all the people to pass one after another, and the appointed [prefect of the priests] stands between him and the people.

M.   And when he receives consolation from others,

N.   all the people say to him, "Let us be your atonement."

O.   And he says to them, "May you be blessed by Heaven."

P.   And when they provide him with the funeral meal,

Q.   all the people sit on the ground, while he sits on a stool.

II. The rules of the king: not subject to the law, marital rites, conduct in bereavement

2:2

A. The king does not judge, and [others] do not judge him;

B. does not give testimony, and [others] do not give testimony about him;

C. does not perform the rite of removing the shoe, and others do not perform the rite of removing the shoe with his wife;

D. does not enter into levirate marriage, nor [do his brother] enter levirate marriage with his wife.

E. R. Judah says, "If he wanted to perform the rite of removing the shoe or to enter into levirate marriage, his memory is a blessing."

F. They said to him, "They pay no attention to him [if he expressed the wish to do so]."

G. [Others] do not marry his widow.

H. R. Judah says, "A king may marry the widow of a king.

I. "For so we find in the case of David, that he married the widow of Saul,

J. "For it is said, *'And I gave you your master's house and your master's wives into your embrace'* (2 Sam. 12:8)."

2:3

A. [If] [the king] suffers a death in his family, he does not leave the gate of his palace.

B. R. Judah says, "If he wants to go out after the bier, he goes out,

C. "for thus we find in the case of David, that he went out after the bier of Abner,

D. "since it is said, *'And King David followed the bier'* (2 Sam. 3:31)."

E. They said to him, "This action was only to appease the people."

F. And when they provide him with the funeral meal, all the people sit on the ground, while he sits on a couch.

III. Special rules pertinent to the king because of his calling

2:4

A. [The king] calls out [the army to wage] a war fought by choice on the instructions of a court of seventy-one.

B. He [may exercise the right to] open a road for himself, and [others] may not stop him.

C. The royal road has no required measure.

D. All the people plunder and lay before him [what they have grabbed], and he takes the first portion.

E. *"He should not multiply wives to himself"* (Deut. 17:17) – only eighteen.

F. R Judah says, "He may have as many as he wants, so long as they *do not entice him* [to abandon the Lord (Deut. 7:4)]."

G.   R. Simeon says, "Even if there is only one who entices him [to abandon the Lord] – lo, this one should not marry her."

H.   If so, why is it said, "He should not multiply wives to himself"?

I.   Even though they should be like Abigail (1 Sam. 25:3).

J.   *"He should not multiply horses to himself"* (Deut. 17:16) – only enough for his chariot.

K.   *"Neither shall he greatly multiply to himself silver and gold"* (Deut. 17:16) – only enough to pay his army.

L.   *"And he writes out a scroll of the Torah for himself"* (Deut. 17:17).

M.   When he goes to war, he takes it out with him; when he comes back, he brings it back with him; when he is in session in court, it is with him; when he is reclining, it is before him,

N.   as it is said, *"And it shall be with him, and he shall read in it all the days of his life"* (Deut. 17:19).

2:5

A.   [Others may] not ride on his horse, sit on his throne, handle his sceptre.

B.   And [others may] not watch him while he is getting a haircut, or while he is nude, or in the bath-house,

C.   since it is said, *"You shall surely set him as king over you"* (Deut. 17:15) – that reverence for him will be upon you.

The subordination of Scripture to the classification-scheme is self-evident. Scripture supplies facts. The traits of things – kings, high priests – dictate classification-categories on their own, without Scripture's dictate.

The philosophical cast of mind is amply revealed in this essay, which in concrete terms effects a taxonomy, a study of the genus, national leader, and its two species, [1] king, [2] high priest: how are they alike, how are they not alike, and what accounts for the differences. The premise is that national leaders are alike and follow the same rule, except where they differ and follow the opposite rule from one another. But that premise also is subject to the proof effected by the survey of the data consisting of concrete rules, those systemically inert facts that here come to life for the purposes of establishing a proposition. By itself, the fact that, e.g., others may not ride on his horse, bears the burden of no systemic proposition. In the context of an argument constructed for nomothetic, taxonomic purposes, the same fact is active and weighty. The whole depends upon three premises: [1] the importance of comparison and contrast, with the supposition that [2] like follows the like, and the unlike follows the opposite, rule; and [3] when we classify, we also hierarchize, which yields the argument from hierarchical classification: if this, which is the lesser, follows rule X, then that, which is the greater, surely should follow rule X.

And that is the whole sum and substance of the logic of *Listenwissenschaft* as the Mishnah applies that logic in a practical way.

No natural historian can find the discourse and mode of thought at hand unfamiliar; it forms the foundation of all disposition of data in quest of meaning. For if I had to specify a single mode of thought that established connections between one fact and another, it is in the search for points in common and therefore also points of contrast. We seek connection between fact and fact, sentence and sentence in the subtle and balanced rhetoric of the Mishnah, by comparing and contrasting two things that are like and not alike. At the logical level, too, the Mishnah falls into the category of familiar philosophical thought. Once we seek regularities, we propose rules. What is like another thing falls under its rule, and what is not like the other falls under the opposite rule. Accordingly, as to the species of the genus, so far as they are alike, they share the same rule. So far as they are not alike, each follows a rule contrary to that governing the other.

So the work of analysis is what produces connection, and therefore the drawing of conclusions derives from comparison and contrast: the *and*, the *equal*. The proposition then that forms the conclusion concerns the essential likeness of the two offices, except where they are different, but the subterranean premise is that we can explain both likeness and difference by appeal to a principle of fundamental order and unity. To make these observations concrete, we turn to the case at hand. The important contrast comes at the outset. The high priest and king fall into a single genus, but speciation, based on traits particular to the king, then distinguishes the one from the other. All of this exercise is conducted essentially independently of Scripture; the classifications derive from the system, are viewed as autonomous constructs; traits of things define classifications and dictate what is like and what is unlike.

That the authorship of the Mishnah has made a choice within an available repertoire of logics does not require demonstration. But that others who inherited the document took a different position on the correct mode of classification – by appeal to the traits of things – does. For in our own context, that is the sole basis commonly serving for any sort of systematic and analytical thought. But to show how, in its own setting, the Mishnah's authorship has opted for a philosophical mode of thought, I have now to demonstrate that another mode of thought, serving the same purposes and within the same structure of internal logic, was available and indeed was selected. For that purpose I turn to Sifra's authorship's critique of the mode of classification chosen by the authorship of the Mishnah. Specifically, as we shall see, that authorship recognized the principles of classification, which we identify as philosophical, and rejected them in favor of another principle. This other principle shows a deep affinity for the logic of fixed association, because it appeals to a received and not an intrinsic mode of classification. Specifically, it is *Scripture's* classifications, and not those inherent in things by their very nature, that serves to dictate how we make our lists and so derive our general principles.

The basic critique addressed by Sifra's authorship to the Mishnah's philosophical logic is this: time and again, we can easily demonstrate, things have so many and such diverse and contradictory indicative traits that, comparing one thing to something else, we can always distinguish one species from another. Even though we find something in common, we also can discern some other trait characteristic of one thing but not the other. Consequently, we also can show that the hierarchical logic on which we rely, the argument *a fortiori* or *qol vehomer*, will not serve. For if on the basis of one set of traits which yield a given classification, we place into hierarchical order two or more items, on the basis of a different set of traits, we have either a different classification altogether, or, much more commonly, simply a different hierarchy. So the attack on the way in which the Mishnah's authorship has done its work appeals to not merely the limitations of classification solely on the basis of traits of things. The more telling argument addresses what is, to *Listenwissenschaft*, the source of power and compelling proof: hierarchization. That is why, throughout, we must designate the Mishnah's mode of *Listenwissenschaft* a logic of hierarchical classification. Things are not merely like or unlike, therefore following one rule or its opposite. Things also are weightier or less weighty, and that particular point of likeness of difference generates the logical force of *Listenwissenschaft*.

Let us consider a sustained example of how Sifra's authorship rejects the principles of the logic of hierarchical classification precisely as these are worked out by the framers of the Mishnah. I emphasize that the critique applies to the way in which a shared logic is worked out by the other authorship. For it is not the principle that like things follow the same rule, unlike things, the opposite rule, that is at stake. Nor is the principle of hierarchical classification embodied in the argument *a fortiori* at issue. What our authorship disputes is that we can classify things on our own by appeal to the traits or indicative characteristics, that is, utterly without reference to Scripture.

The argument is simple. On our own, we cannot classify species into genera. Everything is different from everything else in some way. But Scripture tells us what things are like what other things for what purposes, hence Scripture imposes on things the definitive classifications, that and not traits we discern in the things themselves. When we see the nature of the critique, we shall have a clear picture of what is at stake when we examine, in some detail, precisely how the Mishnah's logic does its work. That is why at the outset I present a complete composition in which Sifra's authorship tests the modes of classification characteristic of the Mishnah, resting as they do on the traits of things viewed out of the context of Scripture's categories of things.

V. Parashat Vayyiqra Dibura Denedabah Parashah 3

V:I.1

A. "[If his offering is] a burnt-offering [from the herd, he shall offer a male without blemish; he shall offer it at the door of the tent of meeting, that he may be accepted before the Lord; he shall lay his hand upon the head of the burnt-offering, and it shall be accepted for him to make atonement for him]" (Lev. 1:2):

B. Why does Scripture refer to a burnt-offering in particular?

C. For one might have taken the view that all of the specified grounds for the invalidation of an offering should apply only to the burnt-offering that is brought as a freewill-offering.

D. But how should we know that the same grounds for invalidation apply also to a burnt-offering that is brought in fulfillment of an obligation [for instance, the burnt-offering that is brought for a leper who is going through a rite of purification, or the bird brought by a woman who has given birth as part of her purification rite, Lev. 14, 12, respectively]?

E. It is a matter of logic.

F. Bringing a burnt-offering as a freewill-offering and bringing a burnt-offering in fulfillment of an obligation [are parallel to one another and fall into the same classification].

G. Just as a burnt-offering that is brought as a freewill-offering is subject to all of the specified grounds for invalidation, so to a burnt-offering brought in fulfillment of an obligation, all the same grounds for invalidation should apply.

H. No, [that reasoning is not compelling. For the two species of the genus, burnt-offering, are not wholly identical and can be distinguished, on which basis we may also maintain that the grounds for invalidation that pertain to the one do not necessarily apply to the other. Specifically:] if you have taken that position with respect to the burnt-offering brought as a freewill-offering, for which there is no equivalent, will you take the same position with regard to the burnt-offering brought in fulfillment of an obligation, for which there is an equivalent? [For if one is obligated to bring a burnt-offering by reason of obligation and cannot afford a beast, one may bring birds, as at Lev. 14:22, but if one is bringing a freewill-offering, a less expensive form of the offering may not serve.]

I.   Accordingly, since there is the possibility in the case of the burnt-offering brought in fulfillment of an obligation, in which case there is an acceptable equivalent [to the more expensive beast, through the less expensive birds], all of the specified grounds for invalidation [which apply to the in any case more expensive burnt-offering brought as a freewill-offering] should not apply at all.

J.   That is why in the present passage, Scripture refers simply to "burnt-offering," [and without further specification, the meaning is then simple:] all the same are the burnt-offering brought in fulfillment of an obligation and a burnt-offering brought as a freewill-offering in that all of the same grounds for invalidation of the beast that pertain to the one pertain also to the other.

2. A.   And how do we know that the same rules of invalidation of a blemished beast apply also in the case of a beast that is designated in substitution of a beast sanctified for an offering [in line with Lev. 27:10, so that, if one states that a given, unconsecrated beast is to take the place of a beast that has already been consecrated, the already-consecrated beast remains in its holy status, and the beast to which reference is made also becomes consecrated]?

B.   The matter of bringing a burnt-offering and the matter of bringing a substituted beast fall into the same classification [since both are offerings that in the present instance will be consumed upon the altar, and, consequently, they fall under the same rule as to invalidating blemishes].

C.   Just as the entire protocol of blemishes apply to the one, so in the case of the beast that is designated as a substitute, the same invalidating blemishes pertain.

D.   No, if you have invoked that rule in the case of the burnt-offering, in which case no status of sanctification applies should the beast that is designated as a burnt-offering be blemished in some permanent way, will you make the same statement in the case of a beast that is designated as a substitute? For in the case of a substituted beast, the status of sanctification applies even though the beast bears a permanent blemish! [So the two do not fall into the same classification after all, since to begin with one cannot sanctify a permanently blemished beast, which beast can never enter the status of sanctification, but through an act of substitution, a permanent blemished beast can be placed into the status of sanctification.]

E.   Since the status of sanctification applies [to a substituted beast] even though the beast bears a permanent blemish, all of the specified grounds for invalidation as a matter of logic should not apply to it.

F. That is why in the present passage, Scripture refers simply to "burnt-offering," [and without further specification, the meaning is then simple:] all the same are the burnt-offering brought in fulfillment of an obligation and a burnt-offering brought as a substitute for an animal designated as holy, in that all of the same grounds for invalidation of the beast that pertain to the one pertain also to the other.

3. A. And how do we know [that the protocol of blemishes that apply to the burnt-offering brought as a freewill-offering apply also to] animals that are subject to the rule of a sacrifice as a peace-offering?

B. It is a matter of logic. The matter of bringing a burnt-offering and the matter of bringing animals that are subject to the rule of a sacrifice as a peace-offering fall into the same classification [since both are offerings and, consequently under the same rule as to invalidating blemishes].

C. Just as the entire protocol of blemishes apply to the one, so in the case of animals that are subject to the rule of a sacrifice as a peace-offering, the same invalidating blemishes pertain.

D. And it is furthermore a matter of an argument *a fortiori*, as follows:

E. If a burnt-offering which is valid when in the form of a bird, [which is inexpensive], the protocol of invalidating blemishes apply, to peace-offerings, which are not valid when brought in the form of a bird, surely the same protocol of invalidating blemishes should also apply!

F. No, if you have applied that rule to a burnt-offering, in which case females are not valid for the offering as male beasts are, will you say the same of peace-offerings? For female beasts as much as male beasts may be brought for sacrifice in the status of the peace-offering. [The two species may be distinguished from one another].

G. Since it is the case that female beasts as much as male beasts may be brought for sacrifice in the status of the peace-offering, the protocol of invalidating blemishes should not apply to a beast designated for use as peace-offerings.

H. That is why in the present passage, Scripture refers simply to "burnt-offering," [and without further specification, the meaning is then simple:] all the same are the burnt-offering brought in fulfillment of an obligation and an animal designated under the rule of peace-offerings, in that all of the same grounds for invalidation of the beast that pertain to the one pertain also to the other.

The systematic exercise proves for beasts that serve in three classifications of offerings, burnt-offerings, substitutes, and peace-offerings, that the same rules of invalidation apply throughout. The comparison of the two kinds of burnt-offerings, voluntary and obligatory, shows that they are sufficiently different from one another so that as a matter of logic, what pertains to the one need not apply to the other. Then come the differences between an animal that is consecrated and one that is designated as a substitute for one that is consecrated. Finally we distinguish between the applicable rules of the sacrifice; a burnt-offering yields no meat for the person in behalf of whom the offering is made, while one sacrificed under the rule of peace-offerings does. What is satisfying, therefore, is that we run the changes on three fundamentally different differences and show that in each case, the differences between like things are greater than the similarities. I cannot imagine a more perfect exercise in the applied and practical logic of comparison and contrast.

The upshot is very simple. The authorship of Sifra concurs in the fundamental principle that sanctification consists in calling things by their rightful name, or, in philosophical language, discovering the classification of things and determining the rule that governs diverse things. Where that authorship differs from the view of the Mishnah's concerns – I emphasize – *the origins of taxa*: how do we know what diverse things form a single classification of things. Taxa originate in Scripture. Accordingly, at stake in the critique of the Mishnah is not the principles of logic necessary for understanding the construction and inner structure of creation. All parties among sages concurred that the inner structure set forth by a logic of classification alone could sustain the system of ordering all things in proper place and under the proper rule. The like belongs with the like and conforms to the rule governing the like, the unlike goes over to the opposite and conforms to the opposite rule. When we make lists of the like, we also know the rule governing all the items on those lists, respectively. We know that and one other thing, namely, the opposite rule, governing all items sufficiently like to belong on those lists, but sufficiently unlike to be placed on other lists. That rigorously philosophical logic of analysis, comparison and contrast, served because it was the only logic that could serve a system that proposed to make the statement concerning order and right array. Let us first show how the logic of proving propositions worked, then review Sifra's authorship's systematic critique of the way in which the Mishnah's framers applied that logic, specifically, proposed to identify classifications.

No natural historian can find the discourse and mode of thought at hand unfamiliar; it forms the foundation of all disposition of data in quest of meaning. For if I had to specify a single mode of thought that established connections between one fact and another, it is in the search for points in common and therefore also points of contrast. We seek connection between fact and fact, sentence and sentence in the subtle and balanced rhetoric of the Mishnah, by comparing and contrasting two things that are like and not alike. At the logical level, too, the Mishnah falls into the category of familiar philosophical thought. Once we seek regularities, we propose rules. What is like another thing falls under its rule, and what is not like the other falls under the opposite rule. Accordingly, as to the species of the genus, so far as they are alike, they share the same rule. So far as they are not alike, each follows a rule contrary to that governing the other.

So the work of analysis is what produces connection, and therefore the drawing of conclusions derives from comparison and contrast: the *and*, the *equal*. The proposition then that forms the conclusion concerns the essential likeness of the two offices, except where they are different, but the subterranean premise is that we can explain both likeness and difference by appeal to a principle of fundamental order and unity. To make these observations concrete, we turn to the case at hand. The important contrast comes at the outset. The high priest and king fall into a single genus, but speciation, based on traits particular to the king, then distinguishes the one from the other. All of this exercise is conducted essentially independently of Scripture; the classifications derive from the system, are viewed as autonomous constructs; traits of things define classifications and dictate what is like and what is unlike.

As is now clear, the source of classifications proves decisive. No one denies the principle of hierarchical classification. That is an established fact, a self-evident trait of mind. The argument of Sifra's authorship is that, by themselves, things do not possess traits that permit us finally to classify species into a common genus. There always are traits distinctive to a classification. Accordingly, it is the argument of Sifra's authorship that without the revelation of the Torah, we are not able to effect any classification at all, are left, that is to say, only with species, no genus, only with cases, no rules. That appeal to Scripture forms the counterpart, in analytical logic, to the principle of cogent discourse that rests upon the dictated order of verses of Scripture, that is, the logic of fixed association. The authorship of the Mishnah appeals to philosophical logic of classification and philosophical logic of cogent discourse, and in doing so, we now realize, it made choices others recognized and rejected.

Time and again Sifra's authorship demonstrates that the formation of classifications based on monothetic taxonomy, that is to say, traits that are not only common to both items but that are shared throughout both items subject to comparison and contrast, simply will not serve. For at every point at which someone alleges uniform, that is to say, monothetic likeness, Sifra's authorship will demonstrate difference. Then how to proceed? Appeal to some shared traits as a basis for classification: this is not like that, and that is not like this, but the indicative trait that both exhibit is such and so, that is to say, polythetic taxonomy. The self-evident problem in accepting differences among things and insisting, nonetheless, on their monomorphic character for purposes of comparison and contrast, cannot be set aside: who says? That is, if I can adduce in evidence for a shared classification of things only a few traits among many characteristic of each thing, then what stops me from treating all things alike? Polythetic taxonomy opens the way to an unlimited exercise in finding what diverse things have in common and imposing, for that reason, one rule on everything. Then the very working of *Listenwissenschaft* as a tool of analysis, differentiation, comparison, contrast, and the descriptive determination of rules yields the opposite of what is desired. Chaos, not order, a mass of exceptions, no rules, a world of examples, each subject to its own regulation, instead of a world of order and proportion, composition and stability, will result. And that *anomie*, we shall now see, is precisely what the authorship of the Mishnah wishes to avoid.

5

From Regulation to Rule: The Topical Program of the Mishnah and its Philosophical Principles

The Mishnah's authorship took as its mode of expression not the statement of generalization, but the implicit communication of generalization only through grouped examples of a common rule, which rule would rarely be articulated. What these fundamental traits tell us about our authorship is two important facts.

First, they proposed to make an autonomous, free-standing statement, which did not appeal to some other writing – Scripture, for instance – for order and proportion. Rather, they treated the topics of their choice within an autonomous logic dictated by the requirements of those topics. Specifically, they exhibit the sense that a given topic has its own inner tension and generates its own program of thought and exposition.

Second, their free-standing statement was set forth in a highly systematic and rhetorically careful way. Since the exposition bore the burden of clarifying itself, unable to appeal to some other document for structure and cogency, the formulation of that exposition would have to exhibit those signals of sense, beginnings, middles, endings, that instructed the reader (or hearer) on how to follow the whole.

The system of philosophy expressed through concrete and detailed law presented by the Mishnah, thus unites rhetoric and logic appropriate to the task. The system furthermore presents a cogent world-view and comprehensive way of living. The world-view speaks of transcendent things, a way of life responds to the supernatural meaning of what is done with a heightened and deepened perception of the sanctification of Israel in deed and in deliberation. That paramount concern accounts for the centrality of classification. It accounts for the appeal of the logic of hierarchical classification in the demonstration of comparisons and contrasts, in the formation of the thought of the document. For what sanctification in the Mishnah's system means is to establish the stability, order, regularity, predictability, and reliability of the world of nature and supernature in particular at moments and in contexts of danger in the existence of Israel, the holy people. And it is through assigning to all things their rightful name, setting of all things in their proper position, that we discover the laws of stability, order, regularity, and predictability. Danger means instability, disorder, irregularity, uncertainty, and betrayal. Each topic of the system as a whole takes up a critical and indispensable moment or context of social being. Through what is said in regard to each of the Mishnah's principal topics, what the system as a whole wishes to declare is fully expressed. Yet if the parts severally and jointly give the message of the whole, the whole cannot exist without all of the parts, so well joined and carefully crafted are they all.

What this means for the requirements of logical demonstration is quite obvious. To show something to be true, one has to demonstrate that, in logic, it conforms to the regularity and order that form the guarantee of truth. Analytical thought is meant to discover order. It is meant to uncover the rule that covers diverse, by nature disorderly, things, the shared trait, the general and prevailing principle of regularity. And to discover the prevailing rule, one has to know how to classify things that seem to be each sui generis, how to find the rule that governs diverse things. And that explains the centrality in the system of the Mishnah of the classification of things. Proof that for the framers of the Mishnah classification and the correct rules for taxonomy define the critical systemic concern derives from the critique of the Mishnah by the authorship of Sifra, as we just noted. For at issue between the framers of the Mishnah and the authorship of Sifra is the correct sources of classification. The framers of the Mishnah effect their taxonomy through identifying and treating as taxonomically indicative the (natural, inherent) traits of things (just as does Aristotle). The authorship of Sifra insists that the source of classification is Scripture. So much for the exalted principles of logic and rhetoric that make the Mishnah a cogent piece of thought.

But what about the topical program of the document? To this point nothing has been said about the actualities of mishnaic discourse, only about abstractions of a philosphical and aesthetic order. On the basis of what I have emphasized, readers might anticipate a document that deals with vast generalizations, topics analyzed in terms of their most profound governing principles. Then the Mishnah as it is will present a considerable surprise. For the Mishnah does not speak of holy things but of ordinary things, which everyone must have known. Mishnaic discourse is not symbolic in its substance, and the authorship does not invoke sacred symbols. All points are made through talk of pots and pans, of menstruation and dead creeping things, of ordinary water which, because of the circumstance of its collection and location, possesses extraordinary power; of the commonplace corpse and ubiquitous diseased person; of genitalia and excrement, toilet seats and the flux of penises, of stems of pomegranates and stalks of leeks; of rain and earth and wood, metal, glass and hide.

The Mishnah therefore provides an extreme example of how practical logic and applied reason come to expression and are worked out solely through the nitty-gritty of ordinary and everyday life and speech. The Mishnah not only speaks in acutely concrete terms about what I shall try in the remainder of this book to show are profound engagements and principles of philosophy, what are often called simply values. Even its mode of speech – the way it speaks, not only what it says – is testimony to its distinctive value, which is the conception that within the everyday are contained the highest and most abstract truths of not merely wisdom but knowledge, in our language, natural philosophy or science. Just as in contemporary empirical, experimental science the case stands for the principle, so in the Mishnah, the cases bear the entire burdened of analytical and principled thought. The single most indicative trait of speech and thought of the Mishnah's authorship is the specificity in which all thought goes forward. At stake in all that follows is my claim that the specifics serve to stand for general terms, that the Mishnah speaks through cases about principles.

Let us then turn back to the actual facts of the Mishnah's topical program. Organized, as we realize, in terms of subjects, the Mishnah sets forth laws on six topics, divisions (Hebrew: seder/sedarim). The six divisions of the Mishnah are (1) agricultural rules; (2) laws governing appointed seasons, e.g., Sabbaths and festivals; (3) laws on the transfer of women and property along with women from one man (father) to another (husband); (4) the system of civil and criminal law (corresponding to what we today should regard as "the legal system"); (5) laws for the conduct of the cult and the Temple; and (6) laws on the preservation of cultic purity both in the Temple and under certain domestic circumstances, with special reference to the table and bed. Let me now describe and briefly interpret the six components of the Mishnah's whole system. What we shall immediately see is that the interest of the Mishnah's authorship in any given topic is dictated by the authorship's overall problematic; they present not merely useful information, but those facts or rules that are deemed essential in the formation of a larger principle. When we identify the problematic of the parts, we shall also see the cogency of the whole, and that, in turn, justifies the initiative of this inquiry into the philosophy that is supposed, in my view, to be expressed in that whole.

The critical issue in the economic life, which means, in farming, is in two parts, revealed in the first division. First, Israel, as tenant on God's holy Land, maintains the property in the ways God requires, keeping the rules which mark the Land and its crops as holy. Next, the hour at which the sanctification of the Land comes to form a critical mass, namely, in the ripened crops, is the moment ponderous with danger and heightened holiness. Israel's will so affects the crops as to mark a part of them as holy, the rest of them as available for common use. The human will is determinative in the process of sanctification.

Second, in the second division, what happens in the Land at certain times, at Appointed Times, marks off spaces of the Land as holy in yet another way. The center of the Land and the focus of its sanctification is the Temple. There the produce of the Land is received and given back to God, the one who created and sanctified the Land. At these unusual moments of sanctification, the inhabitants of the Land in their social being in villages enter a state of spatial sanctification. That is to say, the village boundaries mark off holy space, within which one must remain during the holy time. This is expressed in two ways. First, the Temple itself observes and expresses the special, recurring holy time. Second, the villages of the Land are brought into alignment with the Temple, forming a complement and completion to the Temple's sacred being. The advent of the appointed times precipitates a spatial reordering of the Land, so that the boundaries of the sacred are matched and mirrored in village and in Temple. At the heightened holiness marked by these moments of Appointed Times, therefore, the occasion for an affective sanctification is worked out. Like the harvest, the advent of an appointed time, a pilgrim festival, also a sacred season, is made to express that regular, orderly, and predictable sort of sanctification for Israel which the system as a whole seeks.

If for a moment we now leap over the next two divisions, the third and fourth, we come in the fifth and sixth divisions, on Holy Things and Purities, to the counterpart of the divisions of Agriculture and Appointed Times. Holy Things and Purities deal with the everyday and the ordinary, as against the special moments of harvest, on the one side, and special time or season, on the other. The fifth division is about the Temple on ordinary days. The Temple, the locus of sanctification, is conducted in a wholly routine and trustworthy, punctilious manner. The one thing which may unsettle matters is the intention and will of the human actor. This is subjected to carefully prescribed limitations and remedies. The division of Holy Things generates its companion, the sixth division, the one on cultic cleanness, Purities. The relationship between the two is like that between Agriculture and Appointed Times, the former locative, the latter utopian, the former dealing with the fields, the latter with the interplay between fields and altar.

Here too, in the sixth division, once we speak of the one place of the Temple, we address, too, the cleanness which pertains to every place. A system of cleanness, taking into account what imparts uncleanness and how this is done, what is subject to uncleanness, and how that state is overcome – that system is fully expressed, once more, in response to the participation of the human will. Without the wish and act of a human being, the system does not function. It is inert. Sources of uncleanness, which come naturally and not by volition, and modes of purification, which work naturally, and not by human intervention, remain inert until human will has imparted susceptibility to uncleanness, that is, introduced into the system, that food and drink, bed, pot, chair, and pan, which to begin with form the focus of the system. The movement from sanctification to uncleanness takes place when human will and work precipitate it.

This now brings us back to the middle divisions, the third and fourth, on Women and Damages. They take their place in the structure of the whole by showing the congruence, within the larger framework of regularity and order, of human concerns of family and farm, politics and workaday transactions among ordinary people. For without attending to these matters, the Mishnah's system does not encompass what, at its foundations, it is meant to comprehend and order. So what is at issue is fully cogent with the rest. In the case of Women, the third division, attention focuses upon the point of disorder marked by the transfer of that disordering anomaly, woman, from the regular status provided by one man, to the equally trustworthy status provided by another. That is the point at which the Mishnah's interests are aroused: once more, predictably, the moment of disorder. In the case of Damages, the fourth division, there are two important concerns. First, there is the paramount interest in preventing, so far as possible, the disorderly rise of one person and fall of another, and in sustaining the status quo of the economy, the house and household, of Israel, the holy society in eternal stasis. Second, there is the necessary concomitant in the provision of a system of political institutions to carry out the laws which preserve the balance and steady state of persons.

What has been said hardly portrays the Mishnah as a promising arena for philosophical inquiry. Compared to any of the writings of Aristotle, the Mishnah simply falls into a different classification altogether. The one, abstract and speculative, the other concrete and practical, on the surface the two bodies of writing scarcely meet. Nor is the topical program going to provide evidence even of shared interests. Philosophers in antiquity wrote treatises about politics and the good life, truth and justice, how we know things and what we can know. None of these subjects engages the articulated attention of the authorship of the Mishnah. And, vice versa, the things that that authorship does dwell upon hardly struck any philosophers of the age as promising candidates for philosophizing.

The sages of the late first and second centuries produced a document to contain the most important things they could specify, they chose as their subjects six matters, of which, I am inclined to think, for the same purpose any philosopher of ancient times should have rejected as arcane or merely theological at least four, and probably all six. That is, four of the divisions of the Mishnah are devoted to purity law, tithing, laws for the conduct of sacrifice in the Temple cult, and the way in which the sacrifices are carried on at festivals – four areas of reality which, I suspect, would not have found a high place on a list of our own most fundamental concerns. The other two divisions, which deal with the transfer of women from one man to another and with matters of civil law – including the organization of the government, civil claims, torts, and damages, real estate and the like – complete the list. But when philosophers talked of politics, and nearly all of them did, they were not likely to take up so mundane a program of thought. When we attempt to interpret the sort of world the rabbis of the Mishnah proposed to create, therefore, at the very outset we realize that that world in no way conforms, in its most profound and definitive categories of organization, to any philosophy we can identify. It follows that the critical work of making sense and use of the Mishnah is to learn how to hear the philosophical discourse that, I maintained, is contained within what the Mishnah wishes to say in its own setting and to the people addressed by those who made it up.

We have therefore to do the work of translation from one world to another of values that, when grasped, turn out to address perennial and utopian issues of social existence, applicable at all times and everywhere. So the most interesting encounter begins when we remember that the Mishnah is separated from us by the whole of Western history, philosophy, and science. The critical problem is to recognize the distance between us and the Mishnah. Our task is the work of allowing strange people to speak in a strange language about things quite alien to us, and yet of learning how to hear what they are saying. That is, we have to learn how to understand them in their language and in their terms. Once we recognize that they are fundamentally different from us, we have also to lay claim to them, or, rather, acknowledge their claim upon us. And what that means is to find in the cases the philosophical principles that we can comprehend and also find engaging and important.

How to proceed? We have to find out whether cases generate rules, whether examples express in concrete ways general principles of intelligibility, such as philosophy will have investigated. I know no better course than to take a sample tractate and ask of each of its propositions, singly or in groups, a simple question: is what is on the surface all that is at issue? Or do the debates about details in fact treat issues that transcend the case at hand? If the former, then all we have is a rule book. If the latter, then we deal with something more. And if we surmise that at stake is an issue that rises above the specific case to a level of generality, then how shall we know where and when we are right? One simple test of the claim that at stake is not the case but the issue is to locate in other cases the same issue. If we can find in three or five or fifteen cases recurrent debates about what appears to be the same fundamental principle, then we stand on firm ground in alleging that it is the principle, not solely the case, that is at stake.

But what about the characterization of the Mishnah, which I have offered up to this point, as not merely cases but rules? To show that that is the fact, I have to estimate what proportion of any given tractate, and of all sixty-three usable tractates (excluding tractate Avot), covers recurrent principles. And I have further to assess what proportion of a given tractate is made up of ad hoc and particular cases, refering to nothing beyond themselves and settled only by the conflicting particular rules exemplified within their own data.

And, finally, if, in studies that presently lie over the distant horizon, I can demonstrate that the principles at stake are general and not specific, then I have further to show that these principles also are philosophical, with philosophy defined by what (some) other philosophers of antiquity investigated in their philosophies. That is to say, I must show that important principles investigated by the authorship of the Mishnah in their idiom address concerns common to philosophy, in one or another of its major representatives and representations, in ancient times. These then are the tasks that lie ahead.

As is my way, I begin with a single tractate and conduct the simple experiment of examining each of its paragraphs and setting forth what I conceive to be the issue under discussion. If, as I anticipate, this yields a program of issues that transcend the cases, then I have to test that result – that method, that program – against two other tractates. The test will show me whether or not my claim that cases illustrate general principles is valid for other tractates, and, further, will tell me whether the general principles that seem to me to be at stake in one tractate prove pertinent to others; and also whether these other tractates produce a further repertoire of issues of broad concern. The outcome, should all the experiments yield positive results, will be a program of research that I can bring to the entire Mishnah.

What precisely do I mean by the claim that I can discern an issue beyond the specificities of a case? And what sort of issue will transcend the details of the case? Let me give a single example of the simple program of questions I have in mind. For that purpose, I turn directly to the tractate for initial study, and to the concluding paragraph of that tractate.

A.   Honeycombs: from what point are they susceptible to uncleanness in the status of liquid?

B.   The House of Shammai say, "When one smokes out [the bees from the combs, so that one can potentially get at the honey]."

C.   The House of Hillel say, "When one will actually have broken up [the honeycombs to remove the honey]."

M[ishnah-tractate] Uqs[in] 3:11

As we noted above, there is a single sentence by way of an answer:

> *Honeycombs: from what point are they susceptible to uncleanness in the status of liquid? When ["it is from the point at which"] one smokes out [the bees from the combs, so that one can get at the honey].*

or:

> *Honeycombs: from what point are they susceptible to uncleanness in the status of liquid? "When one will actually have broken up [the honeycombs to remove the honey]."*

What is at stake in this rather odd dispute is the status, as to uncleanness or cleanness, of liquid, which is susceptible to the uncleanness deriving from sources of uncleanness specified by Leviticus Chapters Eleven through Fifteen. The premise of the question, "from what point does liquid become susceptible," is that liquid may or may not be susceptible to uncleanness at all.

Let us work our way back from the answer to the question, beginning with the shared principle. From the answers to the question we derive the principle shared by both parties. One party maintains that the liquid of honeycombs is susceptible to uncleanness when one has smoked out the bees, the other, when one has broken the honeycombs. Clearly, therefore, when I have access to the honey, so that I may make use of it, the honey is susceptible; hence liquid that is not accessible to human use (in this context) is deemed insusceptible; Lev. 11:34, 37 are read to make that point. So much for the concrete issue.

But what is the principle at hand? I have interpolated some words to make clear in context the issue that transcends the case, which in my judgment is whether what is potential is real. That is to say, do I take account of what potentially may happen? Or do I treat as fact only what has happened? The House of Shammai say that once you have smoked out the bees, you have access to the honey. What is potential is treated as equivalent to what is actual. Since you can get at the honey, the honey can be useful to you and so is susceptible. The House of Hillel say that only when you actually have broken the honeycombs by a concrete deed is the honey susceptible. What is potential is not taken into account, only what is actual. So at stake in this odd passage is a very familiar debate. It specifically concerns the old philosophical problem of the acorn and the oak, the egg and the chicken, the potential and the actual. Clearly we are in the hands of a very odd author, who mounts discourse at three dimensions all at once: [1] through *how* things are said, [2] through *what* is said, and [3] through *what lies beneath the surface* of things as well. If, then, I can demonstrate that the same issue occurs in an unrelated case, I shall be able to show that the document as a whole addresses not merely cases but principles that transcend the case.

To show that the issue of the relationship of potentiality to actuality is a recurrent one, I turn to Mishnah-tractate Makhshirin. The relationship of the actual to the potential is worked out in discussion of how we assess a farmer's intention in relationship to his action. Do I take account of what someone might be thinking and might do, or only of what he actually does or has done? This point is worked out in connection with the law that what is deliberately wet down is susceptible and what is wet down not with the farmer's assent or by his intention is insusceptible. In that regard we work out diverse theories of the interplay between intention and action. The intention represents what is potential, and what we want to know is whether we take account of what has been done or only of what might be done in accord with the farmer's intent. Mishnah-tractate Makhshirin is formed of five successive layers of generative principles, in sequence, and it is at point five that our transcendent principle emerges:

1.   Dry produce is insusceptible, a notion which begins in the plain meaning of Lev. 11:34, 37.

2. Wet produce is susceptible only when *intentionally* wet down, a view expressed in gross terms by Abba Yosé as cited by Joshua.

3. Then follow the refinements of the meaning and effects of *intention*, beginning in 'Aqiba's and Tarfon's dispute, in which the secondary matter of what is tangential to one's primary motive is investigated.

4. This yields the contrary views, assuredly belonging to second-century masters, that what is essential imparts susceptibility and what is peripheral to one's primary purpose does not; and that both what is essential and what is peripheral impart susceptibility to uncleanness. (A corollary to this matter is the refinement that what is wet down under constraint is not deemed wet down by deliberation.)

5. The disputes on the interpretation of intention – Is it solely defined by what one actually does or modified also by what one has wanted to do as well as by what one has done? – belonging to Yosé and Judah and his son Yosé.

We see from this catalogue of successive positions, assigned to authorities who lived in successive generations, that the paramount theme of the tractate is the determination of the capacity of the eligible liquids to impart susceptibility to uncleanness. The questions addressed are these: What is the relationship between intention and action? Does intention to do something govern the decision in a case, even though one's action has produced a different effect? For example, if I intend to wet down only part of an object, or make use of only part of a body of water, but then wet down the whole or dispose of the whole, is the whole deemed susceptible? Does my consequent action revise the original effects of my intention?

The deep thought on the relationship between what one does and what one wants to see happen explores the several possible positions. Judah and his son, Yosé, take up the position that ultimate deed or result is definitive of intention. What happens is retrospectively deemed to decide what I wanted to happen (M. Makhsirin 3:5-7). Other Ushans, Yosé in particular (M. Makhsirin 1:5), maintain the view that, while consequence plays a role in the determination of intention, it is not exclusive and definitive. What I wanted to make happen affects the assessment of what actually has happened. Now the positions on the interplay of action and intention are these:

1. Judah has the realistic notion that a person changes his mind, and therefore we adjudge a case solely by what he does and not by what he says he will do, intends, or has intended, to do. Judah then rejects potentiality in favor of actuality. If we turn Judah's statement around, we come up with the conception predominant throughout his rulings: *A case is judged in terms solely of what the person does.* We do not take account of potentialities, even though these are very real. If he puts on water, that water in particular that he has deliberately applied imparts susceptibility to uncleanness. If he removes water, only that water he actually removes imparts susceptibility to uncleanness, but water that he intends to remove but that is not actually removed is not deemed subject to the person's original intention. And, it is fair to add, we know it is not subject to the original intention, because the person's action has not accomplished the original intention or has placed limits upon the original intention. What is done is wholly determinative of what is originally intended, and that is the case whether the result is that the water is deemed capable or incapable of imparting susceptibility to uncleanness.

2. Yosé at M. Makhsirin 1:5 expresses the contrary view. Water that has been wiped off is detached with approval. But water that has remained on the leek has not conformed to the man's intention, and that intention is shown by what the man has actually done. Accordingly, the water remaining on the leek is not subject to the law, If water be put. The upshot is to reject the view that what is done is wholly determinative of what is originally intended. We sort things out by appeal to nuances of effect. We now see how Judah's view is expressed at M. Makh. 3:6:

A.   If a farmer's olives were located on the roof and rain fell on them—

B.   if he was pleased, then the water that has fallen is under the law, "If water be put," [and therefore imparts susceptibility to uncleanness, in line with Lev. 11:34, 37] [and if not, it is not subject to that law].

C.   R. Judah says, "It is not possible for the farmer not to be pleased on account of the rain. But if he actually stopped up the water-spout or if he shook the olives in the rain, then the water is under the law, 'If water be put, and if not, it is not under the law, 'If water be put.']"

Judah's point here is that we assess the farmer's attitude toward the situation solely in terms of what he actually does. Unless by some concrete action or gesture one is implicated in the wetting down, attitude or intention – which here stands for potentiality, that is, what someone may do by reason of the present attitude – is null.

The upshot is very simple. A central problem in the interpretation of the Mishnah, the foundation-document of Judaism, is to explain this very strange mode of discourse. Specifically, we want to know whether – as I have claimed but not yet demonstrated – its philosophical authorship has chosen a strikingly concrete and unphilosophical manner for the expression of what clearly are abstract and profoundly reflective philosophical positions on the nature of human intention in relationship to action, or, in the broader framework I have composed, the relationship between actuality and potentiality. Clearly, what is required is a sustained exercise of rereading and reinterpretation of the entire Mishnah. It will not suffice to give examples of philosophical issues that arise out of the details of cases. Nor will showing that in a finite number of instances, a given philosophical issue inheres. There is, indeed, a considerable literature of exegesis that works on precisely that matter. But that literature is entirely episodic and notional, and on the strength of available results, we cannot proceed to that characterization of the modes and media of thought of the Mishnah that is required in any effort to assess the philosophical principles of the document. Since the literature that is now in print does not suffice, the entire work has to be done all over again. And that is what I now proceed to undertake.

To begin with, we undertake an exegesis of the entire document in an effort to classify each of its paragraphs. We want to know whether the case exhausts the matter, or whether the case clearly appeals to a generative principle. Once I have shown through detailed exegesis of a number of tractates the facts of the matter, I can proceed to a classification of every paragraph of the Mishnah's sixty-two usable tractates (excluding tratate Avot) in two ways: first, is there a principle that transcends the case? Second, is that principle one of a general philosophical interest? And, finally, I can accurately and on the basis of a sustained inquiry characterize the Mishnah as to the proportions that are of an exemplary and a philosophical order as against the proportions that are limited to cases and the detailed ad hoc application of rules. The issue then is the limits of the practicality of practical reason and the extent of the application of applied logic. My basic hypothesis is that once reason and logic come into play, they also take over and dictate discourse. Practical reason is always reason, and applied logic always an exercise in logic. And, I shall maintain in the final part of the projected study, when reason defines thought, then a program of issues congruent to the potentialities of reason will engage intellect, and that program is best represented, in our frame of reference, by philosophy. But we are a long way from the consideration of that ultimate abstraction.

I have chosen five tractates for this initial inquiry. All are relatively brief. Coming from different divisions, they allow us to dismiss the possibility that a given subject matter will provoke discussion of a philosophical order, while another topic will not. That broader sample guarantees that there is no correlation between modes of thought and themes. For my comments, I limit my remarks to the points of philosophical interest, with a sentence or two, as needed, to clarify what is at stake. For this exercise I follow four prior studies of mine, and one of former students of mine, as follows:

UQSIN: *A History of the Mishnaic Law of Purities.* Volume XX. *Uqsin* (Leiden, 1977: E. J. Brill).

ORLAH: Howard Scott Essner, "The Mishnah Tractate *Orlah:* Translation and Commentary," in William Scott Green, ed., *Approaches to Ancient Judaism* (Chico: Scholars Press for Brown Judaic Studies, 1981) Volume III, pp. 105-148. The translation was revised and corrected by Alan J. Avery-Peck, and is reproduced from Jacob Neusner, *The Mishnah. A New Translation* (New Haven and London: Yale University Press, 1988), pp. 158-166. The outline of the tractate given in Chapter 10 is by Essner and is so signified *ad loc.*

BESAH: *A History of the Mishnaic Law of Appointed Times* (Leiden: E. J. Brill, 1983) Volume IV, pp. 1-57.

QIDDUSHIN: *A History of the Mishnaic Law of Women* (Leiden: E. J. Brill, 1980) Volume IV, pp. 213-265.

MEILAH: *A History of the Mishnaic Law of Holy Things* (Leiden: E. J. Brill, 1980) Volume V, pp. 79-146.

All the translations of Mishnah-passages are copied from my *The Mishnah. A New Translation* (New Haven and London: Yale University Press, 1988). Thanks go to Yale University Press for permission to reproduce my translation. While in some cases I briefly summarize my commentary to the Mishnah, in my *History of the Mishnaic Law*, in many I simply raise without further amplification the questions of philosophy that occupy me here. Readers who wish further clarification of details of passages can refer to the long commentary.

Part Two

FROM REGULATION TO RULE: ARE MISHNAH-TRACTATES UQSIN, ORLAH, BESAH, QIDDUSHIN, AND MEILAH PHILOSOPHICAL?

6

The Plan of Mishnah-Tractate Uqsin

Mishnah-tractate Uqsin deals with problems of the susceptibility to uncleanness of food, including springs and other handles. It carries forward the interests of M. Tohorot 1:1-3:4, in particular by raising some distinctive, but markedly secondary, considerations. Uqsin's most striking trait is the highly ambitious character of its formal and redactional work. Chapters One and Three constitute major redactional efforts, reminiscent of the careful work exhibited in the final chapters of Yadayim, but far more successful in esthetic result. The opening chapter commences with a generalization of fundamental importance, M. 1:1, illustrated twice, first at M. 1:2-4, second at M. 1:6. The closing chapter is still more intricate, as we shall see. It works with two large aggregates of material, M. 3:1-3, concluded at M. 3:9, and M. 3:4-7, to which are joined M. 3:8 and *its* appendix, M. 3:10-11.

The susceptibility of food to uncleanness is treated in two aspects.

First, how do we deal with inedible parts of food? Are they regarded as insusceptible because they are inedible?

To understand the second aspect, we must recall that, in order to impart uncleanness to other things, food must be of the bulk of an egg (and in order to render the human body unfit for heave-offering, food must be of the bulk of half a half-loaf). Now, how do we deal with these same inedible parts when we estimate the bulk or volume of food? Do they "join together" with the edible part to contribute to the requisite bulk for imparting uncleanness? Or, because they are not edible, do we exclude them from the estimate?

The opening unit treats both questions together. Something may be susceptible to uncleanness but not be deemed part of the basic piece of fruit or vegetable when it comes to estimating the bulk of the whole.

We refer, specifically, to a part of the piece of fruit or vegetable which serves as a handle – e.g., a stem or spring – but which does not in any way protect the basic fruit. On the other hand, what does protect the fruit, such as a rind or a husk, both shares in the uncleanness of the fruit and also contributes to its bulk. Accordingly, the basic distinction is between a stem or spring and the shell or husk or rind. This matter is worked out in the first major division of the tractate, a summary of which follows:

I. Food: Handles, Husks –
A. Susceptibility to Uncleanness; B. Joining Together

1:1-6, 2:1-4

1:1   Whatever serves as a handle and not protection is made unclean and imparts uncleanness but does not join together [to form the bulk requisite to impart uncleanness, an egg's bulk]. What is protection but not a handle is made unclean and imparts uncleanness and joins together. What is neither protection nor a handle is not made unclean and does not impart uncleanness.

1:2   Roots of garlic, etc. – lo, these contract uncleanness and impart uncleanness and joint together.

1:3   These contract uncleanness and impart uncleanness but do not join together + various items + repetition of the generalization.

1:4   These do not contract uncleanness and do not convey uncleanness and do not join together.

1:5   All stalks of produce which one threshed in the threshing floor are insusceptible....The sprig of a grape-cluster which is stripped of its grapes is clean. If one left on it a single grape, it is susceptible + two further examples of the same view.

1:6   The stalks of figs, etc., lo, these contract uncleanness and impart uncleanness and join together. The stems...lo, these contract uncleanness and impart uncleanness and do not join together. And the stalks of all other produce do not contract uncleanness and do not impart uncleanness.

2:1   Olives which one pickled with their leaves – the leaves are insusceptible, for one only pickled them for appearance' sake.

2:2   All pits contract uncleanness and impart uncleanness but do not join together + illustrations.

2:3   The pomegranate or watermelon, part of which is rotten – the rotten part does not join together. If it is sound on the sides and rotten in the middle, the sound parts do not join together.

2:4   All rinds contract uncleanness and impart uncleanness and join together.

Once we have discussed "joining together" in the context of the estimation of the bulk of a piece of fruit or vegetable for purposes of imparting uncleanness, we logically turn to the inseparable issue of connection, but from the opposite viewpoint: At what point in the processing of vegetables do the outer leaves no longer "join together," which is to say, at what point is disconnection effected? The second division of the tractate, raising that interesting matter, makes the basic point that when the processing has reached the point at which the disintegration of the piece of vegetable into its parts is irreversible, we deem the parts no longer connected, that is, no longer to constitute a single, whole piece of vegetable, even though they still are physically in one piece. This unit is followed by a miscellany on the susceptibility of plants located in pots. The point is that when plants are in the ground, they are insusceptible to uncleanness; when they are located in utensils, they are susceptible, deemed uprooted or plucked up. What about a pot with a hole, through which a leaf can emerge and rejoin the soil? It is not susceptible. While this little unit falls into the rubric of "susceptibility of foods," the connection is so general, and the details so specific, that it is not possible to regard the set as a prologue to the following unit, all the more so as related to the foregoing. I cannot definitively account for its location here or even for its inclusion in our tractate. My guess is that the point of relevance is in the judgment that once it is possible for a root to effect egress and return to the soil, we deem the plant insusceptible to uncleanness as if the root already had reached the ground, in the theory that the process is irreversible.

II. Food: Connection

2:5-8 (+2:9-10)

2:5   He who chops up produce to cook it, even if he did not cut it through – it is not connected. If he did so to pickle it, etc., it is connected. If he began to take it apart, only the food with which he began is not deemed connected, etc. The nuts and almonds are connected until one has crushed them.

2:6   The shell of a roasted egg is connected until chipped, and one of a boiled egg until crushed; a bone in which is marrow is connected to the marrow until crushed, etc.

2:7   Leaves of produce, when green [edible] join together, and when white, do not join together.

2:8   Leaves of onions, etc., if there is sap in them, are measured as they are. If there is empty space in them, one presses down on the empty space.

2:9   A cucumber which one planted in a pot and which grew and the root of which went outside the pot is insusceptible.

2:10   Utensils of dung and clay, through which roots can penetrate, do
            not render seeds therein susceptible to uncleanness. A pot with a
            hole does not render seeds susceptible to uncleanness.

The third theme of the tractate, like the second, reverts to the opening
unit, this time to its element on the susceptibility of food to uncleanness.
The chapter as a whole exhibits unusual interplay of both redactional,
including formal, and thematic sophistication. We have two major
units, first, M. 3:1-3+9, which surround the second, M. 3:4-7+8, and it is
M. 3:8 which links the theme of M. 3:1-3+9 to its own set. M. 3:10-11,
joined together before inclusion in our chapter, then conclude discussion
of a theme important at M. 3:8, an appendix to M. 3:8 and to the chapter
as a whole. The problem of the chapter (and unit) as a whole is, When
do diverse sorts of food become susceptible to uncleanness: M. 3:1-3+9
deal with the issue of intention and preparation. Something which is
not normally eaten by human beings is not susceptible to uncleanness as
food. But if a person forms the intention to eat it, then it becomes
susceptible as food. Food which is dry is insusceptible to uncleanness
and requires preparation for susceptibility through the intentional
application of liquid, we recall from M. Makh. 1:1. But M. Makh. 1:1
also specifies that food or liquid which imparts uncleanness requires no
preparation to become susceptible. Since it already imparts
uncleanness, there is no need to render it susceptible to receive
uncleanness. M. 3:1+2-3 work out problems in connection with various
sorts of food. M. 3:9 forms a concluding exposition of the rule of M. 3:1,
which M. 3:2-3 have already expounded in great detail, a double-
illustration parallel to M. 1:1+2-4, +6. It is joined to M. 3:8 by its
reference to fish, and so means to link M. 3:8 – with its antecedent
materials – to M. 3:1-3, a truly masterful work of redaction. That other
unit, M. 3:4-7+8, is organized around two redactional principles, first
theme, for M. 3:4-7, then *authority,* for M. 3:8. M. 3:4-7 ask whether
something may be deemed food for one purpose but not for another, e.g.,
food, in that it may be purchased with second-tithe money, which
Scripture declares must be spent solely on the acquisition of edibles; but
not-food, in that it is insusceptible to uncleanness as food. Aqiva
maintains that such a distinction is possible, and Yohanan b. Nuri
denies it. Now the construction itself is so laid out that each authority
is given illustrative cases in support of his principle. M. 33:4, prior to
the statement of the dispute, illustrates the conception of Yohanan b.
Nuri. M. 3:5 states the dispute. M. 3:6 presents the Houses in agreement
on Yohanan b. Nuri's position. Then M. 3:7 gives a rule in accord with
Aqiva's. M. 3:8 is linked, so far as I can see, only by authorities common
to M. 3:7 and 3:8, the Houses and Aqiva, both of whom, we see, are

included in the antecedent materials. At dispute is Judah's conception that what is going to happen is not treated as if it already has happened – a conception attributed to the House of Hillel and to Aqiva at M. 3:8. M. 3:11 presents a dispute on exactly the same matter. M. 3:11 is jointed to M. 3:10 by its theme – bees, their hives, and their honeycombs. The whole has been inserted as an appendix to the chapter because of its connection to M. 3:8. Had M. 3:11 followed M. 3:8, of course, the connection would have proved still firmer, since the issue of when various kinds of food become susceptible to uncleanness as food, or as liquid in particular, faces the Houses in both units.

III. Food – Susceptibility to Uncleanness

3:1-11

3:1-3   There are things which require preparation but do not require intention, intention and preparation, intention and no preparation, no intention and no preparation. + illustrations, 3:2-3.

3:4   Dill once it has imparted its flavor is no longer subject to heave-offering and does not receive uncleanness as food.

3:5   Costus, etc., are purchased with money of second-tithe but do not receive uncleanness as food, so Aqiva. Yohanan b. Nuri: If they are purchased with money of tithe, then why do they not receive uncleanness as food + *vice versa?*

3:6   Unripe figs and grapes – Aqiva declares susceptible, Yohanan b. Nuri: Susceptible when they are liable to tithes. Olives and grapes which have turned hard – House of Shammai declare susceptible, House of Hillel declare insusceptible....And so with regard to tithes [= Yohanan b. Nuri].

3:7   Palm sprout – lo, it is like wood in every respect [clean of food uncleanness] but it is purchased with money of tithe [= Aqiva].

3:8   Fish – from what point do they receive uncleanness? Houses + Aqiva. Branch of a fig tree broken off but attached by bark – Judah declares insusceptible the figs on the branch. *Vs.* sages.

3:9   Fat of carrion of clean beast is not unclean with the uncleanness of carrion, therefore it requires preparation. Fat of carrion of unclean beast is unclean with uncleanness of carrion, therefore it does not require preparation. Unclean fish and locusts require intention in the villages.

3:10   A bee-hive – Eliezer says, it is like the ground + three further rules; sages say, It is not like the ground + three further rules.

3:11   Honeycombs – from what point are they susceptible to uncleanness as a liquid + Houses.

(3:12   Post-Mishnaic postscript.)

We therefore see how the authorship has laid out the themes of the tractate:

I.   Food: Handles, Husks
    A.   Susceptibility of food to uncleanness
    B.   Joining together/connection
II.   Joining together/connection + disconnection (B)
III. Susceptibility of food to uncleanness (IA).

Accordingly, we are given an example of a careful laying out of a dense repertoire of themes and principles, in which the complex opening thought is taken up, element by element, through the unfolding of the tractate.

7

Mishnah Tractate Uqsin
Chapter One

1:1

A. Whatever is a handle but not a protector contracts uncleanness and imparts uncleanness but does not join together

B. [If] it protects even though it is not a handle, it contracts uncleanness and imparts uncleanness and joins together.

C. [If] it is not a protector and not a handle, it does not contract uncleanness and does not impart uncleanness.

What we have here is an essay on the three relationships of substances to one another: wholly distinct, C, wholly mixed and united, B, and partly joined, partly autonomous, A. This is, of course, a theory of mixtures.

The facts that require our attention are simple. If a source of uncleanness touches the handle of an object, the fruit hanging by it becomes unclean; if uncleanness touches the fruit, the handle is affected. But the handle is not included with the fruit to make up the prescribed egg's bulk or the prescribed half a half-loaf's bulk for the reception and transmission of uncleanness. A piece of fruit smaller than that bulk or volume is deemed inconsequential and outside of the system of cultic uncleanness. What serves as a protector of the produce, by contrast, such as a husk or a shell, is deemed wholly part of the piece of fruit and so part of its volume or bulk.

The distinction therefore is between the component of a piece of produce that serves as a handle, and the one that serves as protection, e.g., a shell or a husk. What is a handle is so connected that if the produce becomes unclean, the handle becomes unclean. So the handle is connected both to receive uncleanness from the produce and also to transmit uncleanness to it. On the other hand, if we wish to measure the volume of the produce, so as to determine whether it is of sufficient bulk to contract uncleanness or to transmit uncleanness to other food, we do not include in our measurement that handle of the piece of produce. It is attached, but it is not integral, to the produce. The connection then is not complete. The handle is not deemed wholly mixed together, in its substance, with the produce. On the other hand, parts of the produce that protect the piece of produce, e.g., the husk or the shell, is deemed wholly part of the produce, so that it serves both to receive and transmit uncleanness affecting the produce, and it also serves as part of the produce for the purposes of measurement of the volume of the produce. Finally, what is related to the piece of produce but does not serve as a handle and also does not serve as protection is regarded as completely separate from the produce. It does not transmit uncleanness to it, should it itself become unclean. It does not receive uncleanness from it (unless it actually touches the produce in some extraneous way), and it also is not measured with the produce to determine the volume of the produce.

1:2

A.   The roots of garlic, onions, and leeks, when they are wet,

B.   and the nipple end thereof, whether wet or dry,

C.   and the scape that is close to the bulb,

D.   "the roots of lettuce,

E.   "the long radish, and the round radish,"

F.   the words of R. Meir.

G.   R. Judah says, "The large root of the long radish joins together, but its fibrelike roots do not join together" –

H.   the roots of the mint and of the rue,

I.   and wild herbs and garden herbs which one uprooted to transplant,

J.   and the spine of an ear [of corn] and its husk,

K.   R. Eleazar says, "Also the downy growth" –

L.   lo, these contract uncleanness and impart uncleanness and join together.

1:3

A.   These contract uncleanness and impart uncleanness but do not join together:

B.   The roots of the garlic and onions and leeks when they are dry,

C.   and the scape that is not close to the bulb;

D.   and the branch [handle] from which the grape cluster hangs, a handbreadth on either side,

E.   and the stem of the grape cluster, whatever its length,

F   and the tail of the grape cluster that is stripped [of grapes];

G.   and the stem of the brush of the palm tree to a length of four handbreadths;

H.   and the stalk of an ear [of corn] to a length of three handbreadths;

I.   and the stalks of anything that is reaped, three [handbreadths];

J.   and as to that which is not usually reaped – their stems and their roots, in any measure at all,

K.   and the outer husks of ears of corn –

L.   lo, these contract uncleanness and impart uncleanness but do not join together.

1:4

A.   These do not contract uncleanness and do not convey uncleanness and do not join together:

B.   The roots of stalks of cabbage, and shoots of beet roots, and turnips, those which it is the way to chop off but are uprooted.

C.   R. Yosé declares unclean in the case of all of them, and declares clean in the case of the stalks of cabbages and turnips.

These items simply illustrate the opening generalization and fall into the same philosophical category: the nature of mixtures.

1:5

A.   All stalks of produce which one threshed in the threshing floor are insusceptible to uncleanness.

B.   R. Yosé declares susceptible to uncleanness.

C.   The sprig of a grape cluster which is stripped of its grapes is clean.

D.   [If] one left on it a single grape, it is susceptible to uncleanness.

E.   The fruit stalk of a date palm which is stripped [of its dates] is insusceptible to uncleanness.

F.   [If] one left on it a single date, it is susceptible to uncleanness.

G.   And so with pulse:

H.   A stalk which is stripped is insusceptible to uncleanness.

I.   [If] one left on it a single pod, it is susceptible to uncleanness.

J.   R. Eleazar b. Azariah declares clean in the case of that of the bean, and declares unclean in the case of [other] pulse,

K.   because one wants [to make use of them] in handling them.

Clean/insusceptible, unclean/susceptible refer to the object, that is, the handle, which in no way serves the primary piece of fruit. Hence the basic principle applied expressed at M. 1:1 and applied at M. 1:2-4 is applied once more.

1:6

A.   The stalks of figs and dried figs,

B.   and acorns and carobs,

C.   lo, these contract uncleanness and impart uncleanness and join together.

D.   R. Yosé says, "Also the stem of the gourd."

E.   And the stems of pears and pippins and quinces and medlars,

F.   the stem of the gourd – a handbreadth,

G.   the stem of the artichoke – a handbreadth,

H.   R. Eleazar bar Sadoq says, "Two handbreadths" –

I.   lo, these contract uncleanness and impart uncleanness and do not join together.

J.   And the stalks of all other [produce] do not contract uncleanness and do not impart uncleanness.

This illustrates M. 1:1, reproducing the language of M. 1:1C. The entire chapter forms an essay on the nature of connection, which is to say, the three types of mixtures.

8

Mishnah Tractate Uqsin
Chapter Two

2:1

A. Olives which one pickled with their leaves – they [the leaves] are insusceptible to uncleanness,

B. for one pickled them only for appearance sake.

C. The fine hair on a cucumber and the sprout thereof are insusceptible to uncleanness.

D. R. Judah says, "So long as it is before the merchant, it is susceptible to uncleanness."

The issue of connection is worked out in a different way here. But the point is the same as before. Are the leaves deemed connected in any way? No, they are not, for the reason given at B. Hence they fall into the classification of parts of an object that in no way are deemed mixed with the object itself. The issue of intent is raised as well, as is explicit at B, D. Judah holds that since the merchant wants the fine hair, it is deemed part of the produce. So in assessing what constitutes an intrinsic part of a piece of produce, we take account of the attitude of the owner of the produce. This introduces intentionality into the issue of mixture.

2:2

A. All pits contract uncleanness and impart uncleanness but do not join together.

B. The pit of a soft date, even though it is detached [from the edible part] joins together,

C. and that of the dry [date] does not join together.

D. Therefore the skin around the pit of a dried [date] joins together, and that of the soft does not join together.

E. A pit, part of which is detached –

F.   that which is near the edible part joins together
G.   A bone on which is flesh –
H.   that which is near the edible part joins together
I.   [If] it was on it [the bone] on one side –
J.   R. Ishmael says, "They regard it as if it encompasses it in a ring."
K.   And sages say, "That which is near the edible part joins together."
L.   For example, the savory, marjoram, and thyme.

We carry forward the issue of mixture. Pits fall into the category of objects that are partially joined with, but partially distinct from, the produce, in the classification of stems. While the principle is clear, the cases are somewhat contradictory of the claim that all pits fall into that same category; some do, some do not. The main point is that pits are likely to fall out and are not tightly joined to the produce so do not add to its volume or bulk. The point of Eff. is to introduce the analogy to meat on a bone, which follows the same rule as the flesh and the pit. What if there is meat on one side of the bone only? Sages maintain that the part of the bone near the meat joins together, that is, is treated as part of the meat for purposes of measuring volume and connection. Ishmael asks whether, if we were to take the meat and stretch it, it would go all the way around the bone like a ring? Then even the other side of the bone, where there is no meat, is deemed connected. The issue here then is potentiality. If the meat can potentially spread around the bone, we treat it as though it were spread around the bone.

2:3

A.   The pomegranate or the watermelon, part of which is rotten –
         [what is rotten] does not join together.
B.   [If it is] sound on one side and the other and rotten in the middle,
         it does not join together.
C.   The nipple of the pomegranate joins together.
D.   And its sprouting hair does not join together.
E.   R. Eleazar says, "Even the comb is insusceptible to uncleanness."

What is rotten is not connected to the sound part of the pomegranate and does not serve either as a handle or as a protector. The issue is as above.

2:4

A.   All rinds contract uncleanness and impart uncleanness and join
         together [to make up the requisite bulk to impart uncleanness].
B.   R. Judah says, "There are three skins in an onion:
C.   "(1) The inner one, whether whole or perforated, joins together;
D.   "(2) the middle one, when whole, joins together, and when
         perforated, does not join together;

E.   "(3) and the outer one, one way or the other, is insusceptible to uncleanness."

Here is a classic restatement of the three types of mixtures.

2:5

A.   He who chops up [produce] to cook [it], even if he did not [wholly] cut it through – it is not connected.

B.   [If he did so] to pickle it, to seethe it, or to set it on the table, it is connected.

C.   [If] he began to take [it] apart, the food with which he began is not deemed connected.

D.   The nuts which one strung out on a string, and the onions which one tied into a bunch – lo, they are connected.

E.   [If] he began to take the nuts apart or to peel the onions, it is not connected.

F.   The nuts and the almonds are connected until one has crushed them.

The question of mixtures is joined to the one of intention. If one starts chopping up the produce planning to cook it, the produce is not deemed connected. In cooking the produce must fall apart. If the man began to pull the produce apart, we have no reason to suppose that the process of disconnection will inevitably continue; therefore only the food actually taken apart is deemed disconnected. Hence we dismiss the potentiality of what one may do, even though one's intention is to do exactly that; we take account only of what one actually has done.

2:6

A.   [The shell of] a roasted egg [is connected for uncleanness] until it has been chipped.

B.   And that of a boiled egg – [it is deemed connected for uncleanness] until it is crushed.

C.   A bone in which is marrow is connected until it will be wholly crushed.

D.   [The rind of] a pomegranate which one has cut in two is connected until one will knock it with a stick [to empty it of seeds].

E.   Likewise:

F.   the loose stitches of the laundrymen,

G.   and the garment which is sewn with threads of mixed stuff –

H.   it is connected until one will begin to take it apart.

When the contents of the shell are wholly accessible, then the shell is not connected to the contents, since it no longer protects them, in line with M. 1:1B. The bone is connected to the marrow until it is crushed, the seeds to the rind until actually knocked out. The interesting side is at F-H. Even though the loose stitches do not hold well and potentially will unravel, until they actually have been unravelled by the owner or tailor, they are deemed to connect the parts of the garment.

2:7

> A.   The outer leaves of produce –
> B.   when green, join together; and when white, do not join together.
> C.   R. Eleazar b. Sadoq says, "The white ones join together in the case of the cabbage, because they are food;
> D.   "and in the case of lettuce, since they guard the edible part."

When inedible, the withered greens do not protect the produce or join together with it.

2:8

> A.   The leaves of onions and the shoots of onions –
> B.   if there is sap in them,
> C.   are measured as they are.
> D.   If there is empty space in them, one presses down on their empty space.
> E.   A spongy piece of bread is measured as it is.
> F.   If there is an empty space in it, one presses down on its empty space.
> G.   Calf meat which is swollen,
> H.   and old meat which is shrunken,
> I.   are measured as they are.

What do we measure in reaching the requisite volume for produce to impart uncleanness? What is intrinsic to the produce, but not what is extrinsic. The distinction is entirely familiar.

2:9

> A.   A cucumber which one planted in a pot and which grew and [the root of which] went outside of the pot is insusceptible to uncleanness.
> B.   Said R. Simeon, "What is its character that it should be insusceptible to uncleanness?
> C.   "But that which is susceptible to uncleanness remains in its status of susceptibility to uncleanness, and that which is insusceptible to uncleanness is eaten."

The shoot that grew outside the pot is insusceptible to uncleanness so far as the pot is concerned. It is no longer attached in any way, and that is an issue that derives from our basic principle.

2:10

A.   Utensils of dung and utensils of [unbaked] clay, through which roots can penetrate, do not render seeds [contained therein] susceptible to uncleanness.

B.   A pot with a hole does not render seeds susceptible to uncleanness.

C.   One without a hole renders seeds susceptible to uncleanness.

D.   How large is the measure of the hole?

E.   Sufficient[ly] large so that a small root can go out.

F.   [If] one filled it up with dirt to its brim, lo, it is like a tray which does not have a rim.

Seeds detached from the ground and wet down are susceptible to uncleanness. If the roots can go through the sides, then the seeds or plants are deemed attached to the ground, just as at M. 2:9. Since we do not take account of whether the roots have penetrated but only can penetrate, both at A and, conversely, also at B (the pot with the hole), the issue here is whether the potential is deemed actual, and it is.

9

Mishnah Tractate Uqsin
Chapter Three

3:1

A. There are [things] which require preparation [to be made susceptible to uncleanness] but do not require intention,

B. intention and preparation,

C. intention and no preparation,

D. neither intention nor preparation.

E. All edible foods which are designated for use by man require preparation but do not require intention.

What is subject to susceptibility to uncleanness in the classification of food must be regarded by a human being as suitable for eating, and also must be wet down to be made susceptible. Some things require both what is called "intention," meaning, the decision of a human being to regard the food as susceptible, and also "preparation," which means, wetting down, some one, some the other, some neither. The consideration of intention involves whether or not people usually eat the substance. If they do, no further intention is needed. If not, then before the substance can be deemed susceptible to uncleanness as food, there must be distinct, human intention to consume it as food. So both intention and preparation are required for substances that are not usually eaten by human beings, on the one side, but also not unclean in and of themselves, on the other.

3:2

A. He who cuts off [flesh] from man and from beast and from a wild animal and from fowl,

B. from the carrion of an unclean bird,

C. and fat in the villages,

D. and all other produce of the field,

E.   except for truffles and fungus–

F.   R. Judah says, "Except for wild leeks, purslane, and asphodel" –

G.   R. Simeon says, "Except for cardoon" –

H.   R. Yosé says, "Except for acorns" –

I.   lo, these require intention and preparation.

3:3

A.   The carrion of an unclean beast located anywhere,

B.   and the carrion of clean fowl in the villages

C.   require intention but do not require preparation.

D.   The carrion of a clean beast located anywhere,

E.   and the carrion of clean fowl,

F.   and fat in the markets

G.   do not require intention or preparation.

H.   R. Simeon says, "Also: the [carcass of] a camel, rabbit, cony, and pig."

What requires intention is food not usually consumed by human beings. Carrion of unclean beasts is not usually eaten. Those items that do not require preparation are the ones that impart uncleanness of food on their own and impart uncleanness to other food. No further preparation is needed. The carrion of clean beasts is eaten. That of clean fowl and fat in the markets is eaten; someone will eat it, if not a Jew. They are therefore deemed always ready for human consumption, and also do not require preparation.

3:4

A.   Dill, once it has imparted its flavor in the cooking pot, is no longer subject to heave-offering and does not receive uncleanness as food.

B.   Sprouts of the service tree and of candytuft and leaves of arum do not receive uncleanness as food until they are sweetened.

C.   R. Simeon says, "Also: those of colocynth are like them."

Once dill has imparted its flavor, it has carried out that for which it is intended and is no longer susceptible to uncleanness as food. The sprouts are bitter and inedible, but can be sweetened; when they are sweetened, they are susceptible.

3:5

A.   "Costus, and amomum, and the principal spices, crowfoot, and asafoetida, and black pepper, and lozenges of safflower

B.   "are purchased with money of [second] tithe,

C.   "but do not receive uncleanness as food," the words of R. Aqiba.

D.   Said to him R. Yohanan b. Nuri, "If they are purchased with money of [second] tithe, then why do they not receive uncleanness as food? If they do not receive uncleanness as food, then they also should not be purchased with the money of [second] tithe."

Money received in exchange for food in the status of second tithe and brought to Jerusalem must be used for food. Aqiba deems spices as food for that purpose, but not as food in regard to susceptibility to uncleanness. Yohanan says that things can be one thing or the other but not both.

3:6

A. Unripe figs and grapes –

B. R. Aqiba declares susceptible to uncleanness as food.

C. R. Yohanan b. Nuri says, "[That is the case] when they reach the time of liability to tithes."

D. Olives and grapes which have turned hard –

E. The House of Shammai declare susceptible to uncleanness.

F. And the House of Hillel declare insusceptible to uncleanness.

G. Black cumin –

H. The House of Shammai declare insusceptible.

I. And the House of Hillel declare susceptible.

J. And so [with regard to the question of whether it is liable to] tithes [do they disagree].

The issue is in line with Yohanan b. Nuri's views.

3:7

A. The palm sprout –

B. lo, it is like wood in every respect,

C. except that it is purchased with money of [second] tithe.

D. Unripened dates are food, but are free of tithes,

The issue is in line with Aqiba's views. Here is something which is classified as not-food but which may be purchased with the designated funds.

3:8

A. Fish – from what point do they receive uncleanness?

B. The House of Shammai say, "When they are caught."

C. And the House of Hillel say, "When they die."

D. R. Aqiba says, "If they could live."

E. The branch of a fig tree which was broken off but was still attached by its bark –

F. R. Judah declares clean.

G. And sages say, "If it can live."

H. Grain which was uprooted and is attached even by a small root is insusceptible to uncleanness.

The susceptibility of fish states in concrete ways the issue of whether we deem what must happen as if it already has happened, as at E-G+H. The House of Shammai hold that while living things are insusceptible, since the fish, once caught, will inevitably perish, it is deemed as if dead now, and susceptibility to uncleanness as food begins as soon as the fish is in the net. The House of Hillel is given the view that what is inevitably going to happen is not deemed to have happened until it actually will have taken place. Aqiba goes a step further and adds that the fish must not only be dead, but must be irreversibly dead.

3:9

A.   Fat of [the carrion of] a clean beast is not unclean with the uncleanness of carrion.

B.   Therefore it requires preparation.

C.   Fat [of the carrion of] an unclean beast is unclean with the uncleanness of carrion.

D.   Therefore it does not require preparation.

E.   Unclean fish and unclean locusts require intention in the villages.

We find ourselves back in the elucidation of M. 3:1.

3:10

A.   A beehive –

B.   R. Eliezer says, "Lo, it is (1) like the ground;

2. "and they write a prosbol depending on it;

3. "and it does not receive uncleanness [when standing] in its place;

4. "and he who scrapes honey from it on the Sabbath is liable for a sin-offering."

C.   And sages say, "It is (1) not like the ground;

2. "and they do not write a prosbol depending on it;

3. "and it does receive uncleanness [when standing] in its place;

4. "and he who scrapes honey from it on the Sabbath is free."

3:11

A.   Honeycombs – from what point are they susceptible to uncleanness as liquid?

B.   The House of Shammai say, "When one will smoke out [the bees therefrom]."

C.   And the House of Hillel say, "When one will have broken [the honeycombs to remove the honey] ."

M. 3:10 has been tacked on as an introduction to M. 3:11. The issue is the conflict between potentiality and actuality, as has been spelled out above, in Chapter Five, and is in line with M. 3:8. As soon as we have smoked the bees out, even before the honeycombs have been broken and the honey removed, the honey is susceptible, because it is inevitable that the honeycombs will be broken, so they are regarded as though they have already been broken and therefore are liquid. The opposite view is that the honeycombs enter the category of liquid only when they have been broken.

10

The Plan of Mishnah Tractate Orlah

By Howard Scott Essner

The broad topic of this tractate is the biblical prohibition against the consumption and the use of the fruit of a tree in the first three years of the tree's growth. It is based on a single biblical verse: *When you come to the land and plant any kind of tree for food, you shall treat it as forbidden. For three years it will be forbidden, it will not be eaten* (Lev. 19:23). The fourth-year fruit, like Second Tithe, is to be brought to Jerusalem and eaten there. For this reason, the laws concerning the fourth-year fruit are located in M. Maaser Sheni.

The tractate has no problematic; no generative principle shapes the way the tractate approaches its subject matter. Indeed, it is difficult to speak of a "tractate" at all, if by tractate we mean a systematic approach to a single subject. What we have instead are three loosely connected chapters (with a fourth, small concluding unit), each with its own subject matter and clearly defined inner logic. The three chapters are, for the most part, complete unto themselves. They have in common only a broad thematic concern and a loose redactional relationship.

The first unit's task is to clarify the biblical verse by defining some of its terms. First (M. 1:1-2), it defines what is meant by a "fruit tree," i.e., which trees are liable to the prohibition. It presents two definitions. First, a tree is liable because a man uses it for food (M. 1:1). If he uses it for another purpose, it is not liable. Second, a tree is defined as a fruit tree simply because it bears fruit (M. 1:2). The chapter next turns to the question of planting (M. 1:3-5). Specifically, it wants to know whether replanting an old tree is considered to be a new planting, so that the old tree is liable. It also discusses whether grafting vines and sinking shoots are considered to be like planting a tree. Finally, it defines "fruit" by asking whether certain stages of growth of fruit, for example, unripe berries, and certain parts of fruit, for example, the fruit-pits, are liable.

The second chapter deals with the problem of what happens when prohibited produce is mixed with permitted produce. The chapter is completely unrelated to the first. The *'orlah*-prohibition is not the central concern of the chapter; it is dealt with only as one of many analogous agricultural prohibitions. In fact, the chapter could have been placed in any number of tractates in this Order. (Tosefta for this chapter is located in T. Terumot.) The chapter outlines the procedure for neutralizing the effect of prohibited produce in a mixture. The general principles are stated in M. 2:1 and M. 2:4. The rest of the chapter contains a series of rules that elaborate the general principles.

The third unit (M. 3:1-8) discusses the prohibition of the use of *'orlah*-fruit. It is interested in the problem of mixtures: in this case, what happens when an item in which *'orlah*-fruit is used is mixed with permitted items. But this unit has a principle that shapes its discussion and which Chapter Two does not know. The unit assumes that any item that is separate and distinct cannot be neutralized in a mixture. The issue is whether it is man's view of the item or its natural state which determines its distinctiveness. This problem is presented in a series of disputes that runs throughout the unit.

The concluding unit (M. 3:9) closes the tractate by raising two new issues: the resolution of doubts and the legal basis for the extension of biblical prohibitions outside of the Land of Israel.

Let us now review the tractate in outline.

I. Definition of Biblical Terms:

1:1-5, 7-9
A.   Fruit tree: 1:1-2
    1:1   Tree is liable if it is used for food
    1:2   Tree is liable if it bears fruit
B.   Planting: 1:3-5
    1:3-4   Status when replanted determined by condition of tree
    1:5   Sunken shoot: uprooted tree takes status of sunken shoot
C.   Fruit, status of parts: 1:7-9
    1:7-8   twelve items
    1:9   thin branch is used, early berries not used

II. Mixtures of Forbidden and Permitted Produce:

1:6, Chapter Two
A An orchard of permitted and forbidden saplings is prohibited: 1:6
B. Procedure for neutralizing forbidden produce in a mixture: 2:1-3
    2:1   heave-offering: a ratio of one hundred to one 'orlah-fruit: two hundred to one
    2:2-3   one type of forbidden fruit combines with common fruit to neutralize other type of forbidden fruit
C. Mixtures not neutralized: 2:4-7
    2:4-5   forbidden seasoning and leaven not neutralized
    2:6   forbidden produce mixed with same kind of permitted
    2:7   forbidden produce mixed with different kind of permitted
D. Mixtures of forbidden and permitted leaven in dough: 2:8-9, 11-12
    2:8   both mixed in before dough rises: dough is forbidden
    2:9   dough rises with permitted, then forbidden falls in: Sages: dough is permitted; Simeon: forbidden
    2:11-12 not enough of either to leaven; Sages: permitted; Eliezer: according to first type to fall in
E. Different seasonings combine in a mixture: 2:10
F. Vessels greased with clean, then unclean oil: 2:13
G. Mixtures with three components: 2:14-17
    2:14   leaven of heave-offering, diverse kinds and permitted: forbidden to nonpriests, permitted to priests
    2:15   seasoning of heave-offering, diverse kinds permitted
    2:16   meat from Most Holy Things, Remnant or refuse, permitted
    2:17   meat from Most Holy Things, Lesser Holy Things and common: forbidden to unclean persons, permitted to clean

III. Prohibition Against the Use of 'Orlah-Fruit:

3:1-8
A. Forbidden dye and weaving: 3:1-3
    3:1   garment dyed with forbidden dye is burnt, if mixed with others; Sages: neutralize; Meir: burnt
    3:2   one string dyed with forbidden dye woven in garment; Sages: neutralized; Meir: burnt
    3:3   use of wool of firstling forbidden
B. Fire made from coals from 'orlah-fruit: 3:4-5
    3:4   food cooked on forbidden fire is burnt
    3:5   bread baked on forbidden fire is burnt
C. Mixtures of items made with 'orlah-fruit: 3:6-8
    3:6   bunches of fenugrek
    3:7-8   Meir: item sold separately not neutralized in mixture; Sages: only six items not neutralized

IV. Resolution of Doubts:

3:9
A.   Doubtful fruit prohibited in Land of Israel, permitted elsewhere: 3:9A-J
B.   Extension of biblical prohibitions outside of the Land: 3:9K-M

11

Mishnah Tractate Orlah
Chapter One

Translated by
Howard Scott Essner and Alan J. Avery-Peck

1:1

    A.   One who plants [a fruit tree] as a fence or for lumber –

    B.   [the tree] is exempt from [the restriction of] orlah [Lev. 19:23-24].

    C.   R. Yosé says, "Even [if] he said '[The side of the tree facing] inward [facing toward the fields, is intended] for food, and [the side of the tree facing] outward [facing away from the field, is intended] as a fence,'

    D.   "[the side of the tree facing] inward is subject [to the restriction of orlah], and [the side of the tree facing] outward is exempt."

The tree is subject to the prohibition if the produce is used for food, not so if it is used for lumber. The power of intention, unaccompanied by action, is sufficient in Yosé's view, to exempt part of the tree from the taboo.

1:2

    A.   When our fathers came to the Land [of Israel],

    B.   [if] he found [a fruit tree already] planted,

    C.   it was exempt [from the restriction of orlah].

    D.   [If] he planted [a fruit tree],

    E.   even though they had not [yet] conquered [all of the Land],

    F.   it was subject.

    G.   He who plants [a fruit tree] for public [use] –

    H.   it is subject [to the restriction of orlah].

    I.   R. Judah exempts.

    J.   (1) One who plants [a fruit tree] in the public domain,

       (2) and a gentile who planted [a fruit tree],

       (3) and a robber who planted [a fruit tree],

       (4) and he who plants [a fruit tree] in a boat,

       (5) and that [fruit tree] which sprouts by itself [without being planted] –

K.   [the tree] is subject to [the restriction of] orlah.

The intention for public use of the tree suffices to remove it from the taboo. The rule, J.5, that a tree that sprouts by itself is exempt, is weighty. It means that the taboo is invoked only where by a deliberate action a farmer has planted the tree and intends to use the produce. If the tree grows on its own, it falls outside of the system. Consequently, the working of the fundamental system is precipitated by the intentionality of the farmer in planting the tree. Another factor is the insistence that the tree be planted on the farmer's own land, in the land of Israel. If it is planted by a robber, it does not count; if in a boat, likewise.

1:3

A.   A tree which was uprooted together with the clump of earth [surrounding its roots],

B.   [or a tree which] a river swept away together with the clump of earth [surrounding its roots] –

C.   if it is able to live [from the clump alone and is replanted], it is exempt [from the restriction of orlah].

D.   But if not [if it could not live without being replanted], it is subject [after it is replanted, as if it were a new tree].

E.   (1) [If] its clump of earth was separated from it,

       (2) [if] the plough shook it and exposed its roots,

       (3) or [if a man] shook it and repaired it with soil –

F.   if it is able to live [from the soil remaining around its roots], it is exempt.

G.   But if not, it is subject.

The status of the uprooted tree depends upon whether or not it is a new planting. If the tree is able to live from the clump of earth alone, it is not considered a new planting. This is the case even if the tree has already been replanted. Therefore only the possible, and not the actual, survival is taken into account (Essner, p. 114).

1:4

A.   [As for] a tree which was uprooted, [but] a root remained [in the ground],

B.   [should the tree be replanted] it is exempt [from the restriction of orlah, for it is deemed the same old tree] –

C.   How thick need the root be?

D.   R. Gamaliel says in the name of R. Eleazar b. Judah of Bartotha, "As [thick as] a weaver's stretching pin."

Since the tree can live in its present condition even when it is replanted it is not considered to have been planted anew. The dimensions necessary for a root from which a tree may live are given. The issue of potential survival is in play then, not the actualities of the case.

1:5
A.   [As for] a tree which was uprooted, and a sunken shoot [remained] there, and it [the tree] draws sustenance from it [the shoot] –

B.   the old [tree] returns to the status of the sunken shoot [and is subject to the restrictions of orlah].

C.   If he sunk a shoot year after year,

D.   and [the shoot] broke off [from the tree],

E.   he counts it [the years of prohibition under the law of orlah] from the time at which it broke off.

F.   Grafting of vines and regrafting of the grafted part,

G.   even if he sunk them as shoots in the ground,

H.   are permitted [the new graftings are not subject to the restriction of orlah].

I.   R. Meir says, "If he grafted in a place in which its [the vine's] growth is healthy,

J.   "it is permitted [not subject];

K.   "but in a place in which its growth is poor

L.   "it is prohibited [subject]."

M.   And so a sunken shoot which is broken off and which is filled with fruit, if [the fruit] increased by one two-hundredth part,

N.   all of the fruit is prohibited [under the restriction of orlah].

This is a simple problem of taxonomy. Is the sunken shoot which was a branch of a tree and was trained downward and partially buried in the ground a new tree, governed by its own status as to the orlah-taboo, or is it part of the original tree? Even though it grows its own roots, so long as it is attached to the tree, it is in the same status as the original tree. If it is uprooted and lives from the sunken shoot, the tree is now independent of the original tree. We do not take account of the potential of the shoot to maintain itself. The issue of taxonomy is addressed in a different way in connection with grafting, Fff. The status of the grafts runs parallel to that of the sunken shoots; since they are connected to the vine and live from it, their status is that of the vine, even if one trains the grafts like the sunken roots and they can live off their own roots (Essner, p. 117).

1:6

A.   [As for] a sapling [subject to the restriction] of orlah, or [a sapling prohibited under the laws] of diverse kinds in a vineyard, which was mixed together with [permitted] saplings –

B.   behold, this one may not pick [fruit from any of the trees],

C.   If he picked,

D.   [the forbidden produce] is neutralized in [a ratio of] one [part of forbidden fruit] to two hundred parts of permitted fruit].

E.   And this is so provided that he does not purposely [pick the produce in order to have it neutralized].

F.   R. Yosé says, "Even [if] he purposely picks [the produce],

G.   "it is neutralized in two hundred and one."

The issue is one of mixtures. If we have prohibited fruit mixed with permitted fruit, e.g., fruit from an orlah-tree with fruit from mature trees, then we neutralize one part of prohibited fruit in two hundred parts of permitted. That is the point at which the presence of the prohibited fruit is null by reason of its immateriality.

1:7

A.   (1) Leaves, (2) young sprouts, (3) sap of vines and (4) budding berries [of vines] are permitted [for use] under [the laws of] orlah, the Fourth Year [Lev. 19:24] and the Nazirite vow [Num. 6:1-8].

B ..   But they are forbidden [for use] under [the prohibition of] the Asherah [a tree used in idol worship; Dt. 7:5].

C.   R. Yosé says, "The budding berry is forbidden, because it is a fruit."

D.   R. Eliezer says, "He who curdles milk with the sap of [a tree subject to] orlah –

E.   "[the milk] is forbidden [under the law of orlah]."

F.   Said R. Joshua, "I have heard explicitly that one who curdles milk with the sap of the leaves [of an orlah tree, for] with the sap of the roots [of an orlah tree] –

G.   "[the milk] is permitted [not in the status of orlah].

H.   "[But he who curdles milk] with the sap of unripe figs [of an orlah tree] –

I.   "[the milk] is forbidden, because the [figs] are fruit."

1:8

A.   (5) Defective grapes, (6) grape pips, (7) grape skins, (8) wine [made] from them, (9) the rind of a pomegranate and (10) its young bud, (11) walnut shells and (12) fruit pits are forbidden [for use] under [the restrictions of] orlah, the Asherah, and the Nazirite vow.

B.   But they are permitted under [the prohibition of] the Fourth Year.

C. And fallen unripe fruit is forbidden in all cases [under the prohibitions of orlah, the Fourth Year, the Asherah, and the Nazirite vow].

Only the fruit of the tree is liable to the laws of orlah. What is not part of the fruit is permitted. The sap, D., imparts its status to the entire mixture. At issue between Eliezer and Joshua is the classification of the sap of the leaves and of the roots and the like. The materials of M. 1:8 all are parts of the fruit and therefore forbidden under the taboo; all are used in the production of wine and are forbidden to a Nazirite.

1:9
A. R. Yosé says, "They may plant a young shoot of [an] orlah [tree], but they may not plant a walnut of [an] orlah [tree], because [the walnut] is fruit [and subject to the restrictions of orlah],

B. "And they may not graft with [a young shoot of] early date berries of [an] orlah [tree]."

The same consideration applies here: what is like the fruit is in the status of the fruit, and what is not is not.

12

Mishnah Tractate Orlah
Chapter Two

Translated by
Howard Scott Essner and Alan J. Avery-Peck

2:1

A.　(1) Heave-offering, (2) heave-offering of the tithe separated from produce about which there is a doubt whether or not it already was tithed, (3) dough offering and (4) firstfruits are neutralized in one hundred and one [one hundred parts of common produce neutralizes the effect of one part of any of these offerings].

B.　And [these different offerings] join together [to comprise the quantity of forbidden produce which renders forbidden a mixture with permitted produce].

C.　And it is necessary to remove [from the mixture, for the priest, a quantity of produce equal to that of the offering which was lost in the common produce].

D.　(5) Orlah [fruit] and [fruit prohibited under the laws of] (6) diverse kinds in a vineyard are neutralized in [a ratio of] one [part of either of these] to two hundred [parts of permitted produce].

E.　And they join together.

F.　But it is not necessary to remove [a like quantity of produce from the mixture] –

G.　R. Simeon says, "Orlah [fruit] and diverse kinds do not join together [to create the quantity of forbidden produce which renders forbidden permitted produce with which they are mixed]."

H.　R. Eliezer says, "They join together [if together] they impart flavor [to the permitted food with which they are mixed],

I.　"but not [in other cases, so as to render] the mixture forbidden."

It is possible to absorb a quantity of a substance of one kind within the body of a quantity of a substance of another classification, so that the mixture is complete, and the traits of the larger quantity of the substance are imparted to the mixture as a whole. Exact proportions are given here: one hundred to one for the items at 2:1A, two hundred to one, for 2:1D. The point about "joining together" is of course fundamental; that is what is accomplished.

2:2

A.   Heave-offering neutralizes orlah [fruit with which it is mixed], and orlah [fruit] neutralizes heave-offering [with which it is mixed].

B.   How so?

C.   [This occurs in the case of a batch of heave-offering which fell into [a batch of common produce so as to yield a total of] one hundred [*seahs*],

D.   and afterward three kabs [one-half seah] of orlah [fruit], or three kabs of [fruit prohibited by] diverse kinds in a vineyard fell [into the mixture].

E.   This is [a case in] which heave-offering neutralizes orlah [fruit], and orlah [fruit] neutralizes heave-offering [such that the final mixture is in the status of common produce].

From our viewpoint, the important rule is as before, that complete mixtures are possible through the vast preponderance of one body of material over another. That is not only the case in liquids, but also in solids.

2:3

A.   (1) Orlah [fruit] neutralizes [fruit prohibited under the law of] diverse kinds in a vineyard, (2) [fruit prohibited under the law of diverse kinds in a vineyard neutralizes orlah [fruit], and (3) orlah [fruit] neutralizes [other] orlah [fruit].

B.   How so?

C.   [This occurs in the case of] a seah of orlah [fruit] which fell into two hundred [seahs of permitted fruit],

D.   and afterward a little more than a seah of orlah [fruit] or a little more than a seah of [fruit prohibited under the law of] diverse kinds in a vineyard fell [into the mixture].

E.   This is [a case in] which orlah [fruit] neutralizes [fruit prohibited under the law of] diverse kinds in a vineyard, and [fruit prohibited under the law of diverse kinds in a vineyard neutralizes orlah [fruit], and orlah [fruit] neutralizes [other] orlah [fruit].

One type of prohibited fruit may combine with common produce to neutralize a different type of prohibited fruit.

2:4

A.   Whatever [forbidden produce] leavens, spices, or is mixed in sufficient quantity [with common food],

B.   whether [the forbidden produce is] heave-offering, orlah or [produce forbidden as] diverse kinds in a vineyard –

C.   [the resultant dish] is forbidden.

D.   And the House of Shammai say, "[Whatever leavens, etc.], also conveys uncleanness [in the mixture]."

E.   But the House of Hillel say, "R does not convey uncleanness, unless it is an egg's bulk [in quantity]."

2:5

A.   Dositheus of Kefar Yatmah was one of the disciples of the House of Shammai and he said, "I have heard [a tradition] from Shammai the Elder, who said, "'It does not convey uncleanness unless it is an egg's bulk [in quantity].'"

2:6

A.   And [with reference] to what did they say, "Whatever leavens, spices or is mixed [etc.,]" yields a strict ruling [in that the mixture is forbidden even if it contains sufficient permitted produce to neutralize the forbidden]?

B.   [They said it with reference to the case of] one kind [of produce] mixed with [produce of its] same kind.

C.   [And with reference to what did they say, "Whatever leavens, etc." yield [both] a lenient and a strict ruling?

D.   [They said it with reference to the case of] one kind [mixed] with a different kind.

E.   How so? [How does the law yield a strict ruling in the case of like mixed with like, B]?

F.   Leaven of wheat [in the status of heave-offering] which fell into wheat dough [which is common produce],

G.   and there is enough of it [the leaven] to leaven [the dough],

H.   whether there is [a quantity of heave-offering which is] neutralized in one hundred and one [parts of common produce], or whether there is not [so little heave-offering as is] neutralized in one hundred and one –

I.   it is forbidden.

J.   [If] there is not [so little heave-offering as is] neutralized in one hundred and one [parts of common produce],

K.   whether there is enough of it to leaven [the dough], or whether there is not enough of it to leaven [the dough] –

L.   it is forbidden [= strict ruling].

2:7

A.   "To yield both a lenient and a strict ruling [in the case of] one kind [of produce mixed with produce of] its same kind [= M. 2:6C-D]." – How so?

B.   For example, pounded beans [which are heave-offering] which were cooked with lentils [which are common produce],

C.   and there are [enough] of them [the pounded beans] to give a flavor [to the lentils],

D.   whether there is [little enough heave-offering] to be neutralized in one hundred and one, or whether there is not [so little heave-offering as is] neutralized in one hundred and one –

E.   it is forbidden [= strict ruling].

F.   [If] there is not [enough] of them to impart flavor [to the lentils],

G.   whether there is [so little heave-offering as is] neutralized in a hundred and one, or whether there is not [little enough heave-offering] to be neutralized in a hundred and one –

H.   [the mixture] is permitted [as common food, = lenient ruling].

When the prohibited produce imparts its character to the permitted, such that even though small in volume, it affects the whole, then we regard the prohibited as paramount, with the result that the whole is deemed prohibited. We take account of what serves to leaven or flavor the food.

2:8

A.   Leaven of common produce which fell into dough,

B.   and there is enough of it to leaven [the dough],

C.   and afterwards [but before the dough had risen] leaven of heave-offering or of diverse kinds in a vineyard fell in,

D.   and there is enough of [this leaven] to leaven [the dough] –

E.   [the dough] is forbidden [under the restrictions pertaining to heave-offering or diverse kinds].

2:9

A.   [As regards] leaven of common produce which fell into dough

B.   and leavened it,

C.   and afterward leaven of heave-offering or leaven of diverse kinds in a vineyard fell in,

D.   and there is enough of this [leaven] to leaven [the dough] –

E.   [the dough] is forbidden.

F.   R. Simeon permits.

If the leaven of a prohibited variety has fallen into the dough but is not needed to raise that dough, the dough is still forbidden. The mixture is nonetheless affected. Simeon distinguishes only in detail.

2:10

A.   [As regards] spices –

B.   [If] two or three [different] types [of prohibitions pertain] to one kind [of spice], or to three [distinct] kinds [of spices] –

C.   it is forbidden,

D.   for [the spices] join together [to render forbidden that which they flavor].

E.   R. Simeon says, "Two or three different types [of prohibitions which pertain] to one kind [of spice], or two [different] kinds [of spices subject] to one type [of prohibition] do not join together [to render forbidden the food which they flavor]."

Here we treat as a common mixtures spices that are subject to diverse prohibitions. Since all fall into the category of forbidden spice, all serve to joint together, even though the flavor each forbidden spice is different from that of the other forbidden spices. The upshot is that the spices work together to flavor the mixture, and all of the flavor derives from prohibited spices, even though the prohibitions affecting the diverse spices are not of the same classification.

2:11

A.   Leaven of common produce and [leaven] of heave-offering which fell into dough,

B.   [and there is] not enough of either to leaven [the dough],

C.   [but] they combined and leavened [it] –

D.   R. Eliezer says, "I rule [on the status of the dough] according to the last [leaven which fell in]."

E.   But sages say, "Whether the prohibited [leaven] fell in first or last, it does not render [the dough] prohibited unless there is enough of it to leaven [by itself] ."

2:12

A.   Yoezer of the Birah was one of the disciples of the House of Shammai, and he said, "I asked Rabban Gamaliel the Elder who was standing at the Eastern Gate [about the rule of M. 2:11A-C], and he said, "'It does not render [the dough] prohibited unless there is enough of it to leaven [by itself].'"

2:13

A.   [As regards leather] garments [such as sandals] which one greased with unclean oil and then greased with clean oil,

B.   or garments which one greased with clean oil and then greased with unclean oil –

C.   R. Eliezer says, "I rule [on the status of cleanness of the garments] according to the first [oil used]."

D.   But sages say, "According to the last [oil used]."

Prohibited and common leaven fall into the dough, each in a quantity insufficient to leaven the dough. Together they leaven it. How do we sort out the status of the dough? Eliezer maintains that the leaven that completed the requisite volume of leavening imparts its status to all of the leaven, hence to the dough as a whole. Sages prohibit the dough only when the leaven that is prohibited by itself suffices. M. 2:13 is tacked on for thematic reasons.

2:14

A. Leaven of heave-offering and [leaven] of diverse kinds in a vineyard which fell into dough,

B. [and] there is not enough of either to leaven [the dough],

C. but they joined together and leavened [it] –

D. [the dough] is forbidden to non-priests and permitted to priests.

E. R. Simeon permits [it both to] non-priests and priests.

2:15

A. [As for] spices of heave-offering and [spices] of diverse kinds in a vineyard which fell into a pot,

B. [and] there is not enough of either to season [the food in the pot],

C. but they joined together and seasoned it –

D. [the food] is forbidden to non-priests and permitted to priests.

E. R. Simeon permits [it both to] non-priests and priests.

2:16

A. [As regards] a piece [of flesh] of Most Holy Things [which is permitted to priests but forbidden to non-priests], of refuse [which is forbidden to priests and non-priests alike; Lev. 7:15], and of remnant [which is forbidden to priest and non-priest alike; Lev. 7:16] [which alone were not of sufficient quantity to flavor other food, but] which [together] were cooked with [other, permitted] pieces [of flesh], and flavored them –

B. [the dish] is forbidden to non-priests and permitted to priests.

C. R. Simeon permits [it to both] non-priests and priests.

2:17

A. Flesh of Most Holy Things [which is forbidden to non-priests; M. Zeb. 5:4] and flesh of Lesser Holy Things [which is permitted to clean priests and non-priests; M. Zeb. 5:6-8] which were cooked [with a quantity of] ordinary flesh sufficient to neutralize either of the types of meat alone but not together –

B. [the resultant dish] is forbidden to those who are unclean and permitted to those who are clean [it is deemed to have the status of Lesser Holy Things].

The issue is the same as above. The mixtures now are of substances that are permitted to one group of people and forbidden to another, priests, non-priests. We have three components in the mixture, one top of food forbidden to both, one forbidden to one and permitted to the other, one permitted to both parties. Such a mixture is permitted to the group

which may eat the second component but forbidden to the ground that
may not (Essner, p. 125).

13

Mishnah Tractate Orlah
Chapter Three

Translated by
Howard Scott Essner and Alan J. Avery-Peck

3:1

A.   A garment which one dyed with [dye made from] rinds of orlah [fruit] is to be burned.

B.   [If] it was confused with other [permitted garments] –

C.   "All are to be burned," the words of R. Meir.

D.   But sages say, "It is neutralized in [a ratio of] one [forbidden garment] to two hundred [permitted ones]."

3:2

A.   One who dyes a sit's length [of thread] in [dye made from] rinds of orlah [fruit] and wove it into a garment,

B.   but it is not known which [of the garment's threads] it is –

C.   R. Meir says, "The garment must be burned."

D.   But sages say, "It is neutralized in [a ratio of] one [forbidden thread] to two hundred [permitted ones]."

3:3

A.   One who weaves into a garment a sit's length of wool from a firstling

B.   the garment must be burned.

C.   And [if he weaves] a Nazirite's hair or hair from the firstborn of an ass [Ex. 13:13] into a sack –

D.   the sack must be burned.

E.   But in the case of [hair from other] Holy Things, it renders [the object into which it is woven] sanctified [prohibited] in any quantity whatsoever [even less than a sit's length].

3:4
A.   Food which one cooked [in an oven fired] with rinds of orlah [fruit] must be burned.
B.   [If the food] was mixed with other [food], it is neutralized in [a ratio of one [part of forbidden food] to two hundred [parts of permitted food].

3:5
A.   An oven which they fired with rinds of orlah [fruit], and in which one baked bread –
B.   the bread is to be burned.
C.   [If the bread] was mixed with other [loaves of permitted bread] it is neutralized in [a ratio of] one [forbidden loaf] to two hundred [permitted loaves].

3:6
A.   Whoever had bunches of fenugreek that are [prohibited under the laws of] diverse kinds in a vineyard –
B.   [the bunches] must be burned.
C.   [If the bunches] were mixed with other [permitted bunches] –
D.   "All must be burned,'" the words of R. Meir.
E.   And sages say, "They are neutralized in [a ratio of] one [forbidden bunch] to two hundred [permitted bunches]."

3:7
A.   For R. Meir would say, "Whatever normally is counted [when being sold] renders [other food mixed with it] sanctified [forbidden, so that all of the food in the mixture must be burned]."
B.   But sages say, "Only six foods render [other foods] sanctified.
C.   And Aqiba says, "Seven [foods render others forbidden]."
D.   And these are the [sages' six foods]: (1) nuts from Perekh, (2) pomegranates from Baddan, (3) sealed jars [containing forbidden wine], (4) beet shoots, (5) cabbage stalks and (6) Greek gourds.
E.   R. Aqiba says, "Also (7) loaves [of bread] of a householder."
F.   To those [among these items] to which the [restrictions of] orlah are applicable [D1-3], the [restrictions of] orlah [apply].
G.   To that to which the prohibition of diverse kinds in a vineyard is applicable [D4-6, E7], the prohibition of diverse kinds in a vineyard [applies].

3:8
A.   [If] (1) the nuts were split, (2) the pomegranates cut open, (3) the jars [of wine] opened, (4) the gourds cut into, or (5) the loaves broken into, they are neutralized in [a ratio of] one [part of forbidden produce] to two hundred [parts of permitted produce].

We continue with the matter of the disposition of mixtures, making the point once more than there can be neutralization when the volume of what is permitted vastly outweighs the volume of what is prohibited. Neutralization here is at a ratio of two hundred to one. M. 1-3 deals with dye from orlah-fruit, M. 3:4-5 with food, M. 3:6-8 general principles. Meir takes the view that any prohibited item that is defined as distinct cannot be neutralized in a mixture. Sages differ on all but six items. Meir holds that what can be counted out, one by one, cannot be mixed with something else. Only those items that man through his action defines as discrete and separate cannot be neutralized (Essner, p. 143). Sages list items that have something special in their nature, not in the way that man treats them, and that is what makes them distinct (Essner).

3:9

A. [Fruit about which there is] a doubt [whether or not it is in the status] of orlah –

B. [if it is] in the Land of Israel [the fruit in question] is forbidden [deemed to have the status of orlah].

C. But in Syria [the fruit] is permitted [not in the status of orlah].

D. And outside of the Land [of Israel], one may go down [to the orchard] and purchase [such fruit],

E. provided that he does not see him [the seller] pick [the fruit].

F. [As to] a vineyard which was planted with vegetables [which are of diverse kinds], and outside of [this vineyard] vegetables [of like kinds] are sold –

G. [if it is] in the Land of Israel [the produce] is forbidden [under the law of diverse kinds].

H. But in Syria, it is permitted,

I. And outside of the Land [of Israel], one may go down and buy [this produce],

J. provided that he [the Israelite] does not pick [it] with his hand.

K. [Consumption] in any locale [of] produce on behalf of which the omer has not yet been offered is forbidden by Scripture.

L. And the [prohibition against eating produce which is] orlah [applies outside of the Land of Israel] by law.

M. And [the prohibition against planting together] diverse kinds [in a vineyard applies outside of the Land of Israel] by authority of the scribes.

We classify cases of doubt in accord with an established principle, the area in which the produce is grown that is subject to doubt. The principle is that we work matters out by appealing to a criterion of differentiation: the location of the produce that is subject to doubt forming one set of the grid's lines, the stringency or leniency of the ruling, the other. Then matters are easy to sort out, as at B, C, D.

14

The Plan of
Mishnah Tractate Besah

Also called Yom Tob, this tractate deals with one topic only, the preparation of food on the festival-day. Scripture states that it is permitted to prepare food on the festival-day. That seems to be the clear sense of Ex. 12:16, which refers to Passover:

> On the first day you shall hold a holy assembly, and on the seventh day a holy assembly; no work shall be done on those days; but what every one must eat, that only may be prepared by you.

Now Mishnah's authorities quite reasonably assume that what is permitted on the festival-days of Passover is equally permitted on other festival-days, that is, also Pentecost and Tabernacles' first and seventh day as well. Since one may prepare food on the first and seventh days of Passover, it follows that one may do so on the other equivalent days. Mishnah prefers to speak in general terms, supplying rules which apply to a number of distinct occasions, and that is its purpose here.

In point of fact the generative conceptions are rather subtle, and, as we have come to expect, clearly appear to come to closure prior to the bulk of the exegetical and expository work of the tractate itself. Self-evidently, these rules do not derive from Scripture. So far as Scripture is concerned, there is no possibility to generate rules such as those governing how one may cook food. Yet from the very opening dispute of the tractate, on the status of an egg born on a festival, we are faced with a set of disputes and rules which take for granted a rich corpus of unexamined, but consistently applied and unanimously affirmed, rules on just such matters. The issues are, first, that food for use on the festival must be available and subject to designation (in fact or at least in potentiality) prior to the festival. Second, one may (or may not) carry on the preparation of food on the festival in precisely the way in which he may do so on an ordinary day. Third, one may (or may not) carry on preparation of what is required for the preparation of food, that is, secondary and tertiary sorts of acts of labor, in the way in which one may do so on an ordinary day, and fourth one may (or may not) do such acts of labor at all. Clearly the tractate is troubled by restrictive conceptions and distinctions, e.g., between actually preparing food and acts of labor required for preparing food but not directly pertaining thereunto; acts of labor indirectly involved with that same process; and so on. The analogy of the Sabbath is everywhere in the shadows, as M. 5:2 makes explicit. That analogy is drawn long before the tractate begins.

The exegesis of the tractate is made more difficulty still by the failure to take up one at a time, and spell out, the logical potentialities of the several operative principles. In general we are used to a logical, not merely topical, procedure. By the usual procedure one thing is discussed at length at one time, then succeeded by some other topic. We expect that a given principle will be fully worked out and articulated in a clearly defined frame of discourse. But here the diverse principles alluded to above are presented in two successive sequences, and even then, in neither one are they clearly separated from one another and laid out fully and clearly.

First of all, there is a set of materials organized around the names of specific authorities. This is somewhat in the manner of Mishnah tractate Eduyyot, but by no means so chaotic as Eduyyot. These materials formed around named authorities run through the several principles just now listed, as well as others. Positions on them, or on their application, are assigned to the Houses of Shammai and Hillel, and to some other earlier authorities. The fact that to each of the Houses is assigned each of the possible contradictory positions on some of the principles hardly makes exegesis easy. Then, in the subsequent units, the tractate runs through exactly the same principles, now in a somewhat more typical and orderly way. Still, there is a miscellaneous character to the whole, and one may make a case for a more extensive differentiation among the several units of the tractate than I offer in the following outline.

I. Preparing Food on the Festival-Day.

1:1-5:7
A.   The Houses and other authorities: 1:1-2:10.
      1:1   An egg born on the festival-day – the House of Shammai say, It
              may be eaten. House of Hillel: It may not. The egg is (not)

	deemed ready prior to the festival for use on the festival, since the dam is (not) ready as well.
1:2	He who slaughters a wild beast or fowl on the festival – House of Shammai: One may dig up dirt and cover the blood. House of Hillel: He must have dirt ready for that purpose. One may (not) do deeds on the festival which are secondary to the preparation of food. The work may (not) be done in the usual fashion.
1:3	House of Shammai: They do not move a ladder form one dovecot to another. House of Hillel permit. One may (not) do deeds on the festival which are tertiary to the preparation of food.
1:4	Amplification of M. 1:3.
1:5-6	The House of Shammai: They do not remove cupboard doors on the festival (to get at the food). House of Hillel permit. House of Shammai: They do not take up a pestle to hack meat on it. House of Hillel permit. Secondary actions in connection with the preparation of food are (not) permitted.
1:7-9	House of Shammai: Spices are crushed in a wooden crusher – House of Hillel: In the normal way. Food may (not) be prepared in the usual way on the festival. Qualification: One prepare on the festival food for use afterward.
1:10	They send clothing for use on the festival. Whatever they may use on the festival-day do they send.
2:1	On a festival which coincided with Friday a person should not do cooking to begin with on Friday for purposes of the Sabbath. But he prepares food for the festival-day, and if he leaves something over for the Sabbath, that is all right. Or he prepares a cooked dish on Thursday and relies on it for preparing food on Friday for use on the Sabbath. Cf. M. 2:6-7.
2:2-3	If the festival came on Sunday, the House of Shammai say, They immerse everything on Friday. The House of Hillel: Utensils on Friday but human beings on Saturday. Not relevant to the festival. Cf. M. 2:6-7.
2:4-5	House of Shammai say: On festivals they bring peace-offerings and do not lay hands on them and do not offer whole-offerings. There is no food produced by whole-offerings. Only offerings which produce food may be offered on the festival. House of Hillel: They bring all sorts and lay hands. House of Shammai: A person may heat water for his feet only if it also is suitable for drinking. House of Hillel permit.
2:6-7	In three rulings does Gamaliel impose the more stringent ruling, in accord with the House of Shammai, and in three the lenient rulings. They do not cover up hot food on the festival for use on the Sabbath (*vs.* M. 2:1); do not put together a candlestick (for use in lighting up a meal), and do not bake bread into large loaves.

2:8-10   In three matters does Eleazar b. 'Azariah permit and sages
           prohibit: They curry cattle on a festival-day, and on a festival-day
           they grind pepper in a pepper-mill in the normal way.

3:1   They do not catch fish, etc. Non-essential acts may not be done,
           even though they are relevant to the preparation of food.
           (General principle: Whatever lacks some phase of the process of
           hunting is prohibited.)

B.   Designating food before the festival for use on the festival: 3:2-3:8

3:2   Nets for trapping a wild beast, fowl, or fish, which one set on the
           eve of the festival-day – one should not take what is caught there
           in on the festival, unless he knows for sure the creature was
           caught before the festival.

3:3   A beast on the point of death one should not slaughter unless
           there is time to roast and eat a bit of its meat on the festival-day
           itself.

3:4   A firstling which fell into a pit.

3:5   A domesticated beast which died – one should not move it from
           where it is located.

3:6   They do not buy shares in a beast to begin with on the festival-
           day. But they take shares on the eve and may then slaughter it on
           the festival-day.

3:7   They do not whet a knife on the festival-day.

3:8   Filling measures on the festival-day.

C.   Doing actions connected with preparing food on a festival-day in a
      different manner from ordinary days. Other restrictions: 54:1-5:2

4:1   He who brings jars of wine does not bring them in a basket or
           hamper but brings them on his shoulder.

4:2   They do not take pieces of wood from the walls of a *sukkah* but
           from wood nearby (since the *sukkah* was not available for
           supplying wood before the festival-day, but only on the eighth day
           when it is not longer needed for the festival of Sukkot).

4:3   They do not chop firewood from beams or from a beam which
           broke on the festival-day. They do not chop wood in an ordinary
           way.

4:4   They do not open a hole in a lump of clay for use as a lamp for
           thereby one makes a utensil.

4:5   They do not break clay utensil to roast a fish thereon.

4:6   Eliezer: A person takes a wood-splinter to pick at his teeth. That
           is so even though the splinter is not designated for that purpose.

4:7   They do not produce fire from wood, stones, earth, or liquid.

5:1   They let down pieces of produce through a hatchway on the
           festival, but not on the Sabbath.

5:2   Concluding generalization: For any act for which people are
           liable on grounds of Sabbath rest, optional acts or acts of religious
           duty on the Sabbath, they are liable on the festival, except for the

preparation of food, which is allowed on the festival and not allowed on, the Sabbath.

D. Appendix: 5:3-7.

5:3-5   What a person owns is in his status so far as the Sabbath limit is concerned.

5:6   The same consideration. A person's property is in his own status.

5:7   The same matter.

We see clearly that the tractate is not organized around the exposition of principles and the exegesis of rules which express those principles. Nor is the thematic structure clearly revealed.   Indeed, even the outline suggests somewhat greater order than is in fact the case.   There is at A a clearcut redactional preference for presenting materials organized around the names of authorities, the Houses, Gamaliel, and Eleazar b. 'Azariah.   The ideas of the Houses and the Yavnean authorities, however, are diverse and miscellaneous, though, it is clear, principally relevant to our tractate.   The next unit has as its general theme the principle that one is expected to designate in advance of the festival food which he will prepare thereon.   If one in an emergency wishes to slaughter an animal which was not designated, he must be able to eat some bit of it while it is still the festival.   The third unit, C, has as its principal (but, alas, not sole) theme the notion that on the festival one must do even licit deeds in a way somewhat different from ordinary, so as to take cognizance of the holiness of the festival-day.   But not all the rules express that notion.   then there is a concluding generalization which implies we have had a far more carefully arranged tractate than has been the case, and a brief appendix, linking the festival to the Sabbath and so underlining the main point of the antecedent generalization.

15

Mishnah Tractate Besah
Chapter One

1:1

A. An egg which is born on the festival-day –

B. the House of Shammai say, "It may be eaten [on that day]."

C. And the House of Hillel say, "It may not be eaten."

D. The House of Shammai say, "[A minimum of] leaven in the volume of an olive's bulk, and [a minimum of] what is leavened in the volume of a date's bulk [are prohibited on Passover (Ex. 13:7)]."

E. And the House of Hillel say, "This and that are [prohibited in the volume of] an olive's bulk."

1:2

A. He who slaughters a wild beast or fowl on the festival –

B. the House of Shammai say, "He digs with a shovel and covers up [the blood (Lev. 17:13)]."

C. And the House of Hillel say, "He should not slaughter [at all],

D. "unless he had dirt ready [for covering up the blood] while it was still day[light on the day preceding the festival]."

E. But they concur that if he actually did slaughter, he may dig with a mattock and cover up [the blood],

F. and that the ashes of the oven are deemed to have been made ready [on the preceding day, and they too may be used for covering up the blood].

1:3

A. The House of Shammai say, "They do not move a ladder from one dovecot to another.

B. "But one may lean it from one window to another"

C. And the House of Hillel permit [moving it].

D.   The House of Shammai say, "One may not take [pigeons for slaughtering on the festival-day] unless he [physically touched and] stirred them up while it was still day."

E.   And the House of Hillel say, "One may stand [at a distance] and say, 'This one and that one I shall take.'"

At stake in the matter of the chicken, M. 1:1, is whether we regard what is going to happen as though it already has happened, or whether we interpret a potentiality as tantamount to an actuality. The House of Shammai take the latter position, the House of Hillel, the former. The problem is simple. It is permitted on the festival-day to slaughter a chicken and to prepare it for eating on that same day. What is the law having to do with an egg born on the festival-day? The House of Shammai classify the egg under the rule governing the dam. The dam is deemed ready, so is the egg. The House of Hillel regard the egg as distinct from the dam. When it is born, it follows its own rule. The egg was not available prior to the festival, so, it is not permitted on the festival itself. There was no prior act of designation or preparation of the egg for use on the holy day. At M. 1:2 we deal with whether or not one's intent, as to preparation of food for the festival-day, covers acts that are ancillary to the actual cooking, which is permitted. The House of Shammai say that whatever is associated with the preparation of food is deemed to have been covered by the general intention of cooking food, and the House of Hillel insist that the concrete act of intentionality cover every detail of what is to be done on the festival-day. The same issue occurs at M. 1:3.

1:4

A.   [If] one designated black ones and found white ones,

B.   white ones and found black ones,

C.   two and found three –

D.   they are prohibited.

E.   [If he designated] three and found two, they are permitted.

F.   [If he designated pigeons] in the nest and found them in front of the nest, they are prohibited.

G.   But if there are only those particular birds there, lo, these are permitted.

Pigeons to be used on the festival must be designated in advance. The ones that are designated must assuredly be the ones that are actually taken.

1:5

A.   The House of Shammai say, "They do not remove cupboard doors on the festival."

B.   (1) And the House of Hillel permit (2) even putting them back.

C. The House of Shammai say, "They do not take up a pestle to hack meat on it."

D. And the House of Hillel permit [doing so].

E. The House of Shammai say, "They do not place a hide before the tread [as a doormat],

F. "nor may one lift it up,

G. "unless there is an olive's bulk of meat on it."

H. And the House of Hillel permit.

I. The House of Shammai say, "They do not take out into public domain a minor, a *lulab*, or a scroll of the Torah."

J. And the House of Hillel permit.

1:6

A. The House of Shammai say, "They do not bring dough offering and priestly gifts to the priest on the festival-day,

B. "whether they were raised up the preceding day or on that same day."

C. And the House of Hillel permit.

D. The House of Shammai said to them, "It is an argument by way of analogy:

E. "The dough offering and the priestly gifts [Dt. 18:3] are a gift to the priest, and heave-offering is a gift to the priest.

F. "Just as [on the festival-day] they do not bring heave-offering [to a priest], so they do not bring these other gifts [to a priest]."

G. Said to them the House of Hillel, "No. If you have stated that rule in the case of heave-offering, which one [on the festival] may not designate to begin with, will you apply that same rule concerning the priestly gifts, which [on the festival] one may designate to begin with?"

We take up secondary actions connected with the preparation of food. The House of Hillel regard such actions as permissible, and the House of Shammai impose a narrow interpretation on what is permitted. The issue is the power of intentionality. If the purpose is to get at food in the cupboard, we may take off and even replace the doors. The point of each dispute is the same, only the details shift. The same reasoning as at M. 1:5E-H applies to M. 1:6. If there is food on the hide, then the hide may be handled by reason of that food. The Hillelites permit handling the hide and stretching it, even if there is no food connected with it, to encourage the people to slaughter beasts for festival use without risk of the hide. So the basic action, which is permitted, of cooking, extends to a range of actions quite unconnected with cooking.

1:7 1

A. The House of Shammai say, "Spices are crushed in a wooden crusher,

B. "and salt in a cruse and with a wooden pot stirrer."

C.   And the House of Hillel say, "Spices are crushed in the usual way, in a stone pestle, and salt in a wooden pestle."

1:8.

A.   He who picks out pulse on a festival-day –

B.   the House of Shammai say, "He makes his selection of food and eats it [right away]."

C.   And the House of Hillel say, "He makes his selection in his usual way, [putting it down using] his lap, a basket, or a dish;

D.   "but not [using] a board, sifter, or sieve [and preparing a large quantity, for the next day]."

E.   Rabban Gamaliel says, "Also: he swills and separates the husks."

1:9

A.   The House of Shammai say, "They send on the festival-day only [prepared] portions of [food] ."

B.   And the House of Hillel say, "They send domestic beasts, wild beasts, and fowl,

C.   "whether alive or already slaughtered."

D.   They send wine, oil, fine flour, and pulse,

E.   but not grain.

F.   And R. Simeon permits [sending] even grain.

The issue is whether one may act only in an ordinary way, M. 1:7, or even in an unusual way. The House of Shammai, M. 1:8, want the person to nibble but not make an ordinary meal. The Hillelites allow eating in a normal way, just as at a meal. M. 1:9 has the Shammaites take the view that the food must be ready for consumption on the festival-day; the House of Hillel regard it as adequate if the food is potentially edible on that day. The basic issue remains just as before. It concerns whether the scriptural reference to cooking is taxonomic and exemplary or ad hoc and exclusionary, as I shall explain in Chapter Thirty-Two.

1:10

A.   They send clothing, whether sewn or not [yet] sewn,

B.   and even though there are diverse kinds [linen and wool] in them,

C.   if they are needed for use on the festival.

D.   But [they do not send] a nail-studded sandal or an unsewn shoe.

E.   R. Judah says, "Also: Not a white shoe,

F.   "because it requires a craftsman['s work, to put on the blacking],"

G.   This is the governing principle: Whatever may be used on the festival-day do they send.

The inclusionary principle is at work, turning the case into a rule, G, of the broadest possible leniency.

16

Mishnah Tractate Besah
Chapter Two

2:1

A.   On a festival which coincided with the eve of the Sabbath [Friday] –

B.   a person should not do cooking to begin with on the festival-day [Friday] for the purposes of the Sabbath.

C.   But he prepares food for the festival-day, and if he leaves something over, he has left it over for use on the Sabbath.

D.   And he prepares a cooked dish on the eve of the festival-day [Thursday] and relies on it [to prepare food on Friday] for the Sabbath as well.

E.   The House of Shammai say, "Two dishes."

F.   And the House of Hillel say, "A single dish."

G.   But they concur in the case of fish and the egg [cooked] on it, that they constitute two dishes.

H.   [If] one ate [the dish intended for the Sabbath] or it was lost, one should not cook another in its stead in the first instance.

I.   But if he left over any amount at all of it, he relies on it for the Sabbath.

The issue is the relationship between cooking on the Sabbath, which is permitted, and preparing food on the festival solely for use on the Sabbath, which is not permitted. If one should do so, then he or she will have violated the sanctity particular to the festival-day itself. If, on the other hand, if one prepares food specifically for the festival but leaves some over, the food may be eaten on the next day, which is the Sabbath. One may also prepare food in advance of the festival-Sabbath sequence and use it also for the Sabbath. On the strength of the dish prepared in advance, on Thursday, one may continue on the festival-day itself to prepare food for use on the Sabbath. To begin

127

with, one may not prepare food on the festival for the Sabbath, so one cannot begin to do cooking on the festival-day for use on the Sabbath. But if one has begun the cooking-process before that time, he or she may continue to do so.

2:2

A.   [If the festival-day] coincided with the day after the Sabbath [Sunday],

B.   the House of Shammai say, "They immerse everything before the Sabbath."

C.   And the House of Hillel say, "Utensils [are to be immersed] before the Sabbath.

D.   "But man [may immerse] on the Sabbath [itself]."

2:3

A.   And they concur that they effect surface contact between water [which is unclean], contained in a stone utensil [which is insusceptible to uncleanness, with the water of an immersion pool] in order to render [the unclean water] clean.

B.   But they do not immerse [unclean water in an unclean utensil which contains it].

C.   And they immerse [utensils if they are to be changed] from one use to another use,

D.   or [at Passover] from one association [joined to make use of a single Passover lamb] to another [such] association.

The point of M. 2:2 is that a human being may immerse on the Sabbath, since this is a mode of Sabbath-enjoyment. I see no philosophical point inhering in that rule. M. 2:2 serves to introduce M. 2:3, and this again deals with the issue of classification: union, partial union, utter separation. The Houses concur at M. 2:3A concerning the immersion of water on the festival or Sabbath. Unclean water can be made clean in an immersion-pool of requisite size, and since this is for drinking, the water may be purified on the festival-day. But we may not immerse an unclean vessel, in line with M. 2:2, along with the unclean water. Therefore a utensil insusceptible to uncleanness, a stone utensil, is to be used. Now the point pertinent to union is that merely effecting contact between the surface of the unclean water and the surface of the water of an immersion pool effects the requisite purification. M. 2:3 introduces the issue of intention and how it affects immersion. If one plans to use utensils in connection with unconsecrated food and then decides to use them in connection with food in the status of heave-offering, he or she has to immerse once again what are now, in fact, cultically clean utensils.

2:4

A.   The House of Shammai say, "[On a festival] they bring peace-offerings, but they do not lay hands on them.

B.   "But [they do] not [bring] whole-offerings [at all]."

C.   And the House of Hillel say, "They bring peace-offerings and whole-offerings,

D.   "and they lay hands on them."

2:5

A.   The House of Shammai say, "A person may not heat water for his feet,

B.   "unless it also is suitable for drinking.

C.   And the House of Hillel permit.

D.   A man may [to begin with] make a fire and heat himself by it.

2:6

A.   In three rulings does Rabban Gamaliel impose the more stringent ruling, in accord with the opinion of the House of Shammai:

B.   (1) They do not cover up hot food on the festival-day for use on the Sabbath.

C.   (2) And they do not put together a candlestick on the festival-day.

D.   (3) And [on a festival] they do not bake bread into large loaves but only into small ones.

E.   Said Rabban Gamaliel, "Never in my father's house did they bake bread into large loaves, but only into small ones."

F.   They said to him, "What shall we make of your father's house? For they imposed on themselves a strict rule, while imposing a lenient rule for all Israelites,

G.   "so that [Israelites] may bake large loaves and thick cakes."

2:7

A.   Also: he gave three rulings to impose a lenient opinion:

B.   (1) They sweep between the couches,

C.   (2) And they put spices on the fire on the festival-day.

D.   (3) And they prepare a kid roasted whole on Passover night.

E.   But sages prohibit [in all three instances].

2:8

A.   In three matters does R. Eleazar b. Azariah permit and do sages prohibit:

B.   (1) One's cow goes forth [on the Sabbath] with a strap which is between her horns [cf. M. Shab, 4:5];

C.   they curry cattle on a festival-day;

D.   and [on a festival-day] they grind pepper in its pepper mill [in the normal manner].

E.   R. Judah says, "They do not curry cattle on the festival-day,

F.   "because doing so makes a wound.

G.   "But they may comb them."
H.   And sages say, "They do not curry them.
I.   "Also: they do not comb them."

Once more the House of Shammai make distinctions that the House of Hillel do not recognize, just as at M. 1:1. The House of Shammai permit bringing peace-offerings on the festival-day, because the sacrificer eats part of the animal that is sacrificed, but other aspects of the rite may not be carried on. Since whole-offerings yield no food for the sacrificer (or for the priest for that matter), these are not permitted at all. The House of Hillel permit all manner of deeds that are connected with the preparation of food, including heating water for drinking; and that is the case even when the deeds have nothing to do with food-preparation at all. M. 2:6, 7, 8 remain within the same framework of issues and need not detain use.

2:9

A.   A pepper mill is susceptible to uncleanness by reason of constituting three distinct sorts of utensil:
B.   because it forms a receptacle,
C.   and because it is a metal utensil,
D.   and because it constitutes a sieve.

2:10

A.   A child's wagon is susceptible to midras uncleanness,
B.   and may be handled on the Sabbath,
C.   but may be dragged [on the Sabbath] only over other articles [e.g., matting].
D.   R. Judah says, "No utensils may be dragged, except for a wagon, because it presses down [the earth, and does not break through the surface]."

Eleazar b. Azariah allows food prepared in the normal way, rejecting the conception of the House of Shammai in that regard. The three parts of a pepper-mill, M. 2:9, are susceptible to uncleanness on three distinct counts, and if one part breaks, the others remain susceptible each on its own count.

17

Mishnah Tractate Besah
Chapter Three

3:1

A.   They do not catch fish in a vivarium on a festival-day.

B.   And they do not cast food for them.

C.   But they do catch a wild beast or fowl from a vivarium.

D.   And they do cast food for them.

E.   Rabban Simeon b. Gamaliel says, "Not all vivaria are equivalent."

F.   This is the operative principle: Whatever lacks some phase of the process of hunting is prohibited [to be caught], but whatever does not lack some phase of the process of hunting is permitted [to be caught].

We now work through exclusions from the principle that the preparation of food is permitted. Hunting may not be done; it falls outside the classification of food-preparation.

3:2

A.   Nets for trapping a wild beast, fowl, or fish, which one set on the eve of the festival-day –

B.   one should not take [what is caught therein] out of them on the festival-day,

C.   unless one knows for sure that [creatures caught in them] were trapped on the eve of the festival-day.

D.   M'SH B: A gentile brought fish to Rabban Gamaliel, and he said, "They are permitted. But I do not want to accept them from him."

The act of intention must be particular to the thing that is going to be eaten. The general intention of eating what is trapped does not suffice; these particular items must be designated, just as at M. 1:1.

3:3

A.   A beast on the point of death one should not slaughter

B.   unless there is a sufficient interval on the [festival-day] to eat of it an olive's bulk of flesh which has been roasted.

C.   R. Aqiba says, "Even an olive's bulk of raw meat from the place at which the beast is slaughtered [will sufficel."

D.   [If] one has slaughtered it in the field, he should not bring it in on a pole or barrow.

E.   But he may bring it in by hand, limb by limb.

The remission of the prohibition depends on the possibility of actually eating some of the meat on the festival-day itself. This then imposes an important qualification on the basic rule.

3:4

A.   A firstling which fell into a pit –

B.   R. Judah says, "Let an expert climb down and examine it. If it bears a blemish, let one bring it up and slaughter it [on the festival]. And if not, he should not slaughter it."

C.   R. Simeon says, "Any [beast,] the blemish of which has not been discerned while it is still day [before the festival] – this is not [deemed] to be in the category of that which is ready [for festival use] while it is still day before the festival."

The important consideration is at C, which again imposes a limitation on the remission.

3:5

A.   A domesticated beast which died – one should not move it from where it is located.

B.   M'SH W: They asked R. Tarfon about such a case and about a dough-offering which had contracted uncleanness. So he went into the study house and asked.

C.   They told him, "One should not move them from where they are located."

These items may not be moved because they may not be used, a refinement of the foregoing rules.

3:6

A.   They do not take shares in a beast to begin with on the festival-day.

B.   But they take shares in it on the eve of the festival, and they then slaughter and divide it among themselves [on the festival-day itself].

C.   R. Judah says, "One may weigh out meat in the balance with a utensil or in the balance with the chopper."

D.   And sages say, "They do not use scales at all."

3:7

A They do not whet a knife on the festival-day,

B. but one draws it over another [knife].

C. A person should not say to a butcher, "Weigh out a denar's worth of meat for me."

D. But he slaughters [the beast], and they divide it up among themselves.

3:8

A A person says to his fellow, "Fill up this utensil for me,"

B. but not with a measure.

C. R. Judah says, "If it was a utensil which served as a measure, he should not fill it up [either]."

D. M'SH B: Abba Saul b. Botnit would fill up his measuring cups on the eve of a festival and hand them over to purchasers on the festival itself.

E Abba Saul says, "Also on the intermediate days of the festival one does so,

F. "because of the clearness of measure."

G. And sages say, "Also on an ordinary day one does so, because of the exactness of the measure [not filled in haste].

H. A person goes to a storekeeper whom he usually patronizes and says to him, "Give me onions and nuts by number."

I. For that is in any case how a householder counts out [these same things] in his own home.

Taking shares in the beast is part of the process of preparing it for eating, and the other prohibited items are not part of that process. The same consideration is operative throughout.

18

Mishnah Tractate Besah
Chapter Four

4:1

A.   He who [on a festival] brings jars of wine from one place to another should not bring them in a basket or hamper.

B.   But he brings them on his shoulder or [carrying them] before him.

C.   And so too: he who takes straw should not hang the hamper over his back.

D.   But he brings it [carrying it] in his hand.

E.   And they break into a stack of chopped straw but not into wood stacked in the storage hut.

On the festival-day those activities involved in the preparation of food that may be done must be carried out in an extraordinary way.

4:2

A.   They do not take pieces of wood from [the roof or walls of] a sukkah, but [they do] from that [wood] which is near it.

B.   They bring pieces of wood –

C.   from the field – from [that wood] which has been gathered together,

D.   and from the outer area [near the town] – even from [that wood] which has been scattered about.

E.   What is the 'outer area' [to which reference is made]?

F.   "Any area near the town," the words of R. Judah.

G.   R. Yosé says, "Any area into which people enter with a key,

H.   "and even that which is inside the Sabbath limit."

One may not dismantle the hut to get wood for cooking but may gather wood from what is nearby.

4:3

A.   They do not chop firewood either from beams

135

B.   or from a beam which broke on the festival-day.

C.   And they do not chop wood with an ax, saw, or sickle,

D.   but [only] with a chopper.

E.   A hut full of produce, [which was] blocked up, but which was damaged [so that one now unexpectedly has access to the produce through the breach –

F.   one takes produce out through the breach.

G.   R. Meir says, "Also: One makes a breach to begin with and removes produce."

The beams have not been designated and made ready before the festival for use as firewood for cooking on the festival. The produce at E is always designated for eating, so breaking into the hut does not violate the sanctity of the festival, since it is an act of destruction relevant in preparing food.

4:4

A.   They do not open up a hole [in a lump of clay for use as a lamp],

B.   because one thereby makes a utensil.

C.   And one does not make charcoal on a festival-day.

D.   And they do not chop a wick into two.

E.   R. Judah says, "One severs it with a flame between two lamps. [Having set each end into a lamp, he lights the wick in the middle]."

4:5

A.   They do not break a clay utensil or cut a piece of paper

B.   to roast a salt fish thereon.

C.   And they do not clear out the ashes of an oven or stove.

D.   But they level them down.

E.   And they do not bring two jars together to set a pot on them.

F.   And they do not prop up a pot with a chip,

G.   and so is the rule for a door.

H.   And they do not lead a domestic beast with a staff on the festival-day.

I.   And R. Eleazar b. R. Simeon permits [doing so].

The limitations concern what may not be done in connection with food preparation; all these items are unnecessary or excessive.

4:6

A.   R. Eliezer says, "A person takes a wood splinter which may be before him to pick at his teeth.

B.   "And he sweeps up what is in the courtyard to make a fire.

C.   "For whatever is located in the courtyard is deemed available for use [before the festival begins]."

D.   And sages say, "He sweeps up what is before him [in the house] to make a fire."

4:7

A.   They do not produce fire [on the festival-day] from wood, stones, earth [sulphur], or liquid.

B.   And they do not heat tiles white – hot to roast on them.

C.   And further did R. Eliezer say, "A man takes up a position at the storage hut on the eve of the Sabbath in the seventh year and says, 'From this [produce] I shall eat tomorrow."

D.   And sages say, "[He may do so only] if he makes a mark and says, 'From this place up to that place [shall I take produce to eat tomorrow].'"

Eliezer, M. 4:6A, permits using what is not designated in advance for that particular purpose. Eliezer accepts the conception of designation even when it is in the most general terms, so M. 4:7.

19

Mishnah Tractate Besah
Chapter Five

5:1

A.   They let down pieces of produce through a hatchway on the festival,

B.   but not on the Sabbath.

C.   And they cover up pieces of produce with utensils against dripping liquid.

D.   And so [may they cover up] jugs of wine or oil.

E.   And they place a utensil under a spout [to catch dripping rain] on the Sabbath.

On the festival-day, produce may be protected from spoilage, something that on the Sabbath is prohibited.

5:2

A.   For (1) any act for which [people] are liable on grounds of Sabbath rest, for (2) optional acts, or for (3) acts of religious duty, on the Sabbath,

B.   are they liable in regard to the festival-day.

C.   And these are the acts for which people are liable by reason of Sabbath rest:

D.   (1) they do not climb a tree, (2) ride a beast, (3) swim in water, (4) clap hands, (5) slap the thigh, (6) or stamp the feet.

E.   And these are the acts [for which people are liable] by reason of optional acts:

F.   (1) they do not sit in judgment, (2) effect a betrothal, (3) carry out a rite of *halisah*, (4) or enter into levirate marriage.

G.   And these are the acts [for which people are liable] by virtue of acts of religious duty:

H.   (1) they do not declare objects to be sanctified, (2) make a vow of valuation, (3) declare something to be herem, (4) or raise up heave-offering or tithe.

I.   All these actions on the festival have they declared [to be culpable], all the more so [when they are done] on the Sabbath.

J.   The sole difference between the festival and the Sabbath is in the preparation of food alone.

5:3

A.   Domestic cattle and utensils [belonging to a person] are in the status of the owner [himself and restricted to the same limits].

B.   He who hands over his domestic beast to his son or to a shepherd – lo, they are in the status of the owner.

C.   Utensils set aside for use of one of the brothers in a household – lo, they are in his same status.

D.   And those not set aside [for use of a particular person], lo, they are in the status of [the brothers as a whole], so they may go to the place [to which all the brothers may go].

5:4

A.   He who borrows a utensil from his fellow on the eve of the festival – it is in the status of the one who borrows [the utensil].

B.   [If he borrows it] on the festival-day, it is in the status of the one who lends.

C.   A woman who borrowed from her girl friend spice, water, or salt for her dough – lo, they are in the status of the two of them.

D.   R. Judah declares exempt in the case of water,

E.   for it is of no substance.

5:5

A.   A burning coal is in the status of its owner.

B.   But the flame [may go] anywhere.

C.   A burning coal belonging to the sanctuary is subject to the laws of sacrilege.

D.   But a flame is neither available for common use nor subject to the laws of sacrilege [if it is subjected to common use].

E.   He who takes out a burning coal to the public domain is liable.

F.   [But if he takes out] a flame, he is exempt.

G.   A cistern belonging to an individual – [its water] is in the status of that individual.

H.   But if it belongs to the residents of that town, [its water] is in the status of the residents of that town.

I.   And one belonging to those who came up from Babylonia is in the status of the person who draws water from it.

5:6

A.   He whose pieces of fruit [produce] were located in another town,

B. and the residents of that town prepared an erub so as to bring him some of his produce –

C. [nonetheless] they should not bring it to him.

D. But if he made the erub [in his own behalf],

E. his pieces of produce are in his own status.

5:7

A. He who invited guests to his house –

B. they should not take away portions of food in their hand,

C. unless he had given them possession of their portions on the eve of the festival-day.

D. They do not give drink to field animals or slaughter them.

E. But they give drink and slaughter household animals.

F. What are household animals?

G. Those that spend the night in town.

H. Field animals?

I. Those that spend the night in [distant] pastures.

The sole difference between the festival and the Sabbath is as stated, and that is the point of this interesting taxonomy. But the place in the intellectual program of the tractate is not negligible, as I shall point out in Chapter Thirty-Two. The extension, M. 5:3-5, 6, 7, clarifies the classification, as to location, of various objects that may or may not be shifted or move on the Sabbath or on the festival alike.

20

The Plan of
Mishnah Tractate Qiddushin

A secondary and derivative tractate, openly citing *verbatim* or imitating pericopae of other tractates, Qiddushin shows what Mishnah looks like when it cannot avoid a theme but has nothing to say about said theme. We ring the changes on all the familiar topics, e.g., matters of doubt and the effect and limitations of testimony given by a person about himself or herself and about someone else as well. We review pericopae relevant in general theme – e.g., modes of acquisition of various persons and objects – but in no way pertinent to the topic of our tractate in particular. We have a fair amount of *aggadah*, lacking any particular point for our tractate. In all, before us is a vast and important topic, the consecration of a woman through betrothal to a particular man. But we turn out to consider not a single genuinely fresh and significant idea, even of a legalistic sort. This is a failed tractate indeed. Clearly someone wanted a tractate on betrothals, even though he and his coworkers had very little to put into such a tractate. Equally clearly, it is not Scripture which necessitated or even generated it, since Scripture's reference to the matter of betrothals scarcely appears to have been utilized by our tractate.

What does make a perceptible impact upon Qiddushin is Gittin, Ketubot, and Yebamot, which contribute to the slight tractate before us, directly, in the form of some few pericopae, or indirectly, in the form of significant ideas on the organization of the topic. Gittin lays out the theme of writs of divorce in terms of delivering the writ, preparing it, and stipulations contained within it. Similarly, Qiddushin takes up procedures of betrothal. Its special interest is not in the writ, let alone sexual relations, either of which effects betrothal, but in the donation to the girl of a token of money as a symbol of her betrothal. The tractate opens with a vast construction on rules of acquisition, filling the whole of Chapter One. This construction is developed in its own framework and addresses the topic before us only in the opening rule, M. 1:1. But it serves as an excellent introduction to the shank of the tractate, Chapters Two and Three, because it specifies those ways in which a girl is betrothed. They are three: money, writ, or sexual relations, of which only the first is taken seriously. When at I.B, we turn to the spelling out of the way in which an exchange of money, or something of value, serves, we are given a set of rulings along the lines of Gittin. That is, just as at Gittin we take account of (1) the intervention of an agent, (2) the making of stipulations, (3) impaired writs of divorce, and then (4) attention to matters of doubt in writs of divorce, so now we do the same with regard to betrothals. After a very brief reprise of the issues of agency and stipulations, we turn to impaired betrothals, due to insufficient funds, ineligible candidates for betrothal, use of funds not belonging to the groom, and impaired agency. The unit on procedures of betrothal, I.B, ends with two pericopae primary to other tractates, Gittin and Ketubot. Likewise when we deal with impaired betrothals, I.C, we proceed to a very impressive appendix on stipulations and conditions drawn from the model of M. Gittin 7:5. At the end of the shank comes the expected unit on doubts, I.E.

The tractate's other unit deals with the question of castes within the Israelite community. These are of two sorts, children deriving from impaired marriages, II.A, and "historical" castes, II.B. There is then a miscellany, II.C, which I simply cannot explain. To be sure, its opening entry, M. 4:8, is relevant to the interests of II.A, B. But the next are not, and they clearly have a more suitable location in unit I. At the end comes a homiletical conclusion, a favorite device of those who worked on the redaction of this order and therefore an appropriate redactional flourish.

I. Betrothals.

1:1-3:11
A Rules of Acquisition: 1:1-10
  1:1-6   A woman is acquired [as a wife] in three ways, and acquires [freedom for] herself [as a free agent] in two ways. She is acquired through money, writ, or sexual intercourse, and acquires herself through a writ of divorce or the husband's death. There are six entries on human beings, women and slaves, and three on animals, real estate and movables.
  1:7-8   Five part construction on liability of men and women to various sorts of commandments. 1:8: Appendix to M. 1:7.

1:9-10   Continuation of foregoing: Commandments applicable both in the Land and abroad and only in the Land. Homiletical

B. Procedures of Betrothal: Agency, Value, Stipulations: 2:1-5

2:1   Procedure of betrothal. (1) Use of an agent. (2) The use of money: How much.

2:2-3   The use of money or something equivalent to money in value, continued. Six parts. (3) Stipulations and conditions in the process of betrothal. six parts.

2:4   Use of an agent, modeled on M. Git. 6:3

2:5   Stipulations in betrothals, borrowed from M. Ket. 7:7.

C. Impaired Betrothal: 2:6-3:1

2:6   Impaired betrothal: insufficient funds.

2:7   Impaired betrothal: ineligible woman.

2:8   Impaired betrothal: Use of what does not belong to the prospective groom.

2:9-10   Continuation of foregoing.

3:1   Impaired agency: The agent betrothes the girl for himself. Stipulations of time and their effect upon betrothals.

D. Stipulations: 3:2-6

3:2-3 + 4 "Behold you are betrothed to me on condition that I pay you two hundred *zuz*," – stipulations and conditions, modeled on M. Git. 7:5. Six part construction.

3:5   Stipulations and conditions, six part construction.

3:6   Continuation of foregoing theme.

E. Doubts: 3:7-11

3:7   Cases of doubt in betrothals: "I betrothed my daughter and don't know to whom I have betrothed her."

3:8   Father's testimony on status of daughter is believed when he has the power to do what he says he has done. Triplet.

3:9   Case of doubt in betrothals: father's testimony.

3:10-11 Conflicting testimony in betrothals, parallel to M. Yeb. 15:5-7

II. Castes for the Purposes of Marriage.

3:12-4:11

A The Status of the Offspring of Impaired Marriages: 3:12-13

3:12-13 Four part construction: Where there is valid betrothal and no transgression, the offspring follows the status of the male. Valid betrothal but transgression: The offspring follows the status of the inferior party. If a woman cannot betrothe this man but may betrothe some other, the offspring is a *mamzer*. If she has no right to betrothe any Israelite, the offspring is in the status of the woman (= slave-girl or gentile-girl).

B. Castes and Intermarriage: 4:1-7

4:1-3   Ten castes came up from Babylonia. Which ones may intermarry with which other castes.

4:4-5   He who marries a priest-girl has to investigate her genealogy for four generations of mothers, and Levite- or Israelite-girl, one

4:6-7   Daughter of a male of impaired priestly stock is invalid for marriage into the priesthood for all time. Daughter of an Israelite married to a woman of impaired priestly stock – his daughter is valid for marriage into the priesthood. Dispute on this topic.

C. Miscellany: 4:8-11

4:8   He who says, "This, my son, is a *mamzer*" is not believed. Rerun of M. 3:8.

4:9   He who gave power to his agent to accept tokens of betrothal for his daughter but then himself went and betrothed her (pair of triplets). Agency and doubts.

4:10-11   Four-part construction on testimony of status of wife and children from overseas.

D. Homiletical Conclusion: 4:12-14

4:12   A man should not remain alone with two women, but a woman may remain alone with two men.

4:13-14   An unmarried man may not teach scribes. Other rules on unmarried men, also on being alone with women.

21

Mishnah Tractate Qiddushin
Chapter One

1:1

A. A woman is acquired [as a wife] in three ways, and acquires [freedom for] herself [to be a free agent] in two ways.

B. She is acquired through money, a writ, and sexual intercourse.

C. Through money:

D. The House of Shammai say, "For a denar or what is worth a denar"

E. And the House of Hillel say,"For a perutah or what is worth a perutah."

F. And how much is a perutah?

G. One eighth of an Italian issar

H. And she acquires herself through a writ of divorce and through the husband's death.

I. The deceased childless brother's widow is acquired through an act of sexual relations.

J. And acquires [freedom for] herself through a rite of halisah and through the levir's death.

1:2

A. A Hebrew slave is acquired through money and a writ.

B. And he acquires himself through the passage of years, by the Jubilee year, and by deduction from the purchase price [redeeming himself at this outstanding value (Lev. 25:50-51)].

C. The Hebrew slave girl has an advantage over him.

D. For she acquires herself [in addition] through the appearance of tokens [of puberty].

E. The slave whose ear is pierced is acquired through an act of piercing the ear [Ex. 21:5].

F. And he acquires himself by the Jubilee and by the death of the master.

1:3

A.   A Canaanite slave is acquired through money, through a writ, and through usucaption.

B.   "And he acquires himself through money paid by others and through a writ [of indebtedness] taken on by himself," the words of R. Meir.

C.   And sages say, "By money paid by himself and by a writ taken on by others,

D.   "on condition that the money belongs to others."

1:4

A.   "Large cattle are acquired through delivery, and small cattle through lifting up," the words of R. Meir and R. Eleazar.

B.   And sages say, "Small cattle are acquired through an act of drawing."

1:5

A.   Property for which there is security is acquired through money, writ, and usucaption.

B.   And that for which there is no security is acquired only by an act of drawing [from one place to another].

C.   Property for which there is no security is acquired along with property for which there is security through money, writ, and usucaption.

D.   And property for which there is no security imposes the need for an oath on property for which there is security.

1:6

A.   Whatever is used as payment for something else,

B.   once this one has effected acquisition [thereof] –

C.   the other has become liable for what is given in exchange.

D.   How so?

E.   [If] one exchanged an ox for a cow, or an ass for an ox,

F.   once this one has effected acquisition, the other has become liable for what is given in exchange.

G.   The right of the Most High is effected through money, and the right of ordinary folk through usucaption.

H.   One's word of mouth [dedication of an object] to the Most High is equivalent to one's act of delivery to an ordinary person.

The six entries on human beings, and three on acquiring property – live, real, movable – set forth the nine categories in the order dictated by the pertinent traits listed in the successive predicates.

1:7

A.   For every commandment concerning the son to which the father is subject – men are liable, and women are exempt.

B.   And for every commandment concerning the father to which the son is subject, men and women are equally liable.

C.   For every positive commandment dependent upon the time [of year], men are liable, and women are exempt.

D.   And for every positive commandment not dependent upon the time, men and women are equally liable.

E.   For every negative commandment, whether dependent upon the time or not dependent upon the time, men and women are equally liable,

F.   except for not marring the corners of the beard, not rounding the corners of the head (Lev. 19:27), and not becoming unclean because of the dead (Lev. 21:1).

1:8

A.   [The cultic rites of] laying on of hands, waving, drawing near, taking the handful, burning the incense, breaking the neck of a bird, sprinkling, and receiving [the blood]

B.   apply to men and not to women,

C.   except in the case of a meal-offering of an accused wife and of a Nazirite girl, which they wave.

We now place into correct order men and women in relationship to various religious duties.

1:9

A.   Every commandment which is dependent upon the Land applies only in the Land,

B.   and which does not depend upon the Land applies both in the Land and outside the Land,

C.   except for *orlah* and mixed seeds [Lev. 19:23, 19:19].

D.   R. Eliezer says, "Also: Except for [the prohibition against eating] new [produce before the *omer* is waved on the sixteenth of Nisan] [Lev. 23:14]."

The land is now placed into hierarchical relationship with other lands.

1:10

A.   Whoever does a single commandment – they do well for him and lengthen his days.

B.   And he inherits the Land.

C.   And whoever does not do a single commandment – they do not do well for him and do not lengthen his days.

D.   And he does not inherit the Land.

E.   Whoever has learning in Scripture, Mishnah, and right conduct will not quickly sin,

F.   since it is said, "And a threefold cord is not quickly broken" (Qoh. 4:12).

G.   And whoever does not have learning in Scripture, Mishnah, and
        right conduct has no share in society.

This item is tacked on because of the reference to the Land, B, D. The
homily has no taxonomic interest in the way that the other pericopes
do, but it of course places into correct order those who do, and do not,
conform to the Torah.

22

Mishnah Tractate Qiddushin
Chapter Two

2:1

A. A man effects betrothal on his own or through his agent.

B. A woman becomes betrothed on her own or through her agent.

C. A man betrothes his daughter when she is a girl on his own or through his agent.

D. He who says to a woman, "Be betrothed to me for this date, be betrothed to me with this,"

E. if [either] one of them is of the value of a perutah, she is betrothed, and if not, she is not betrothed.

F. "By this, and by this, and by this" –

G. if all of them together are worth a perutah, she is betrothed, and if not, she is not betrothed.

H. [If] she was eating them one by one, she is not betrothed,

I. unless one of them is worth a perutah. "

The opening generalization, M. 2:1A-B is a clear hierarchization, in this case, treating as equal, in respect to betrothal, the woman and the man. Both may use an agent or act on their own. M. 2:1D-I proceed to establish the rule of connection or mixture as it pertains to this case. Specifically, the requirement that there be an exchange of something of value, as indicated worth a penny, is met if the diverse items that are handed over are joined together in context, and it is not met if these items, each of insufficient value, are not so joined together in context as to constitute a gift of requisite value. The conception of joining together or connection is worked out now in terms of contiguity, e.g., "if all of them together...," and "if she was eating them one by one...."

2:2

A. "Be betrothed to me for this cup of wine," and it turns out to be honey –

B. "...of honey," and it turns out to be of wine,

C. "...with this silver denar," and it turns out to be gold,

D. "...with this gold one," and it turns out to be silver –

E. "...on condition that I am rich," and he turns out to be poor –

F. "...on condition that I am poor," and he turns out to be rich –

G. she is not betrothed.

H. R. Simeon says, "If he deceived her to [her] advantage, she is betrothed."

2:3

A. "...on condition that I am a priest," and he turns out to be a Levite,

B. "...on condition that I am a Levite," and he turns out to be a priest,

C. "...a Netin," and he turns out to be a mamzer,

D. "...a mamzer, " and he turns out to be a Netin,

E. "...a town dweller," and he turns out to be a villager,

F. "...a villager," and he turns out to be a town dweller,

G. "...on condition that my house is near the bath," and it turns out to be far away,

H. "...far," and it turns out to be near:

I. "...on condition that I have a daughter or a slave girl who is a hairdresser'" and he has none,

J. "...on condition that I have none," and he has one;

K. "...on condition that I have no children," and he has;

L. "...on condition that he has," and he has none –

M. in the case of all of them, even though she says, "In my heart I wanted to become betrothed to him despite that fact," she is not betrothed.

N. And so is the rule if she deceived him.

What is at stake is not only that stated conditions of a contract must be met, which is hardly a proposition of profound philosphical interest, but the intervention of intention or attitude in such conditions, that is, Simeon's conception. M. 2:3 then presents the contrary view, that intention or attitude plays no role at all.

2:4

A. He who says to his messenger, "Go and betroth Miss So-and-so for me, in such-and-such a place,"

B. and he went and betrothed her for him in some other place,

C. she is not betrothed.

D. [If he said,] "...lo, she is in such-and-such a place,"

E. and he betrothed her in some other place,

F. lo, she is betrothed.

2:5

A.   He who betroths a woman on condition that she is not encumbered by vows,

B.   and she turns out to be encumbered by vows –

C.   she is not betrothed.

D.   [If he married her without specifying and she turned out to be encumbered by vows, she goes forth without collecting her marriage contract.

E.   ...on condition that there are no blemishes on her, and she turns out to have blemishes, she is not betrothed.

F.   [If he married her without specifying and she turned out to have blemishes, she goes forth without collecting her marriage contract.

G.   All blemishes which invalidate priests [from serving in the Temple] invalidate women.

The language at M. 2:3 does not treat the location of the women as operative, that at M. 2:4 does. The philosophical point is spelled out in Chapter Thirty-Two. At M. 2:5 the consideration is whether or not an intention or attitude has formed part of the initial stipulation.

2:6

A.   He who betroths two women with something worth a perutah,

B.   or one woman with something worth less than a perutah,

C.   even though he sent along [additional] presents afterward,

D.   she is not betrothed,

E.   since he sent the presents later on only because of the original act of betrothal [which was null].

F.   And so in the case of a minor who betrothed a woman.

The action later on is performed in reliance upon the original, but null, agreement. We interpret the intention as defined by the initial action, which was null; that is, he only gave the gifts because he thought they were going to a woman to whom he was already betrothed. Then we do not say that he has meant by the gifts to complete the initial transaction of betrothal.

2:7

A.   He who betroths a woman and her daughter,

B.   or a woman and her sister, simultaneously –

C.   they are not betrothed,

D.   WM'SH B: Five women, including two sisters, and one gathered figs, and they were theirs, but it was Seventh-Year produce. And [someone] said, "Lo, all of you are betrothed to me in virtue of this basket of fruit," and one of them accepted the proposal in behalf of all of them –

E.   And sages ruled, "The sisters [in the group of five] are not
         betrothed."

I see no philosophical issue at M. 2:7A-C. But the case and ruling, M.
2:7D-E, indicate that the agreement of one of the sisters has no bearing
upon the attitude of the others. In that detail, the case is congruent
with the foregoing.

2:8

A.   He [who was a priest] who betroths a woman with his share [of the
         priestly gifts], whether they were Most Holy Things or Lesser Holy
         Things –
B.   she is not betrothed.
C.   [If one did so] with food in the status of second tithe,
D.   "whether inadvertently or deliberately, he has not effected
         betrothal," the words of R. Meir.
E.   R. Judah says, "If he did so inadvertently, he has not effected
         betrothal. If he did so deliberately, he has effected betrothal."
F.   And in the case of that which has been dedicated:
G.   "If he did so deliberately, he has effected betrothal, and if he did
         so inadvertently, he has not effected betrothal," the words of R.
         Meir.
H.   R. Judah says, "If he did so inadvertently, he has effected
         betrothal. If he did so deliberately, he has not effected betrothal."

Since the priest does not own Holy Things, he cannot use his share to
betrothe a woman. We turn to interstitial problems. Food in the status
of second tithe is consecrated and so does not wholly belong to the
farmer. Meir therefore says it cannot be used in the way it has been
used. Judah says that if the man did so inadvertently, it is an act of
betrothal made in error and null; but if it was done deliberately, it is
valid, since the food in part belongs to the owner. The next case
reverses the positions, because if the man did so deliberately, he has
deconsecrated or secularized the object and so may make use of it. If
inadvertently, he has not deconsecrated the object. Judah says that
only if one inadvertently treats something holy as though it were
profane does he remove the status of sanctity from said object and so
commit sacrilege. And once he has committed sacrilege and
deconsecrated the object, he may use it for his secular purpose. So the
entire discussion here rests upon the attitude and engagement of the
man.

2:9

A.   He who betrothed a woman with (1) orlah fruit, (2) with fruit which
         was subject to the prohibition against Mixed Seeds in a vineyard,
         (3) with an ox which was to be stoned, (4) with a heifer the neck of

which was to be broken, (5) with birds set aside for the offering of a mesora, (6) with the hair of a Nazir, (7) with the firstborn of an ass, (8) with meat mixed with milk, (9) with unconsecrate animals [meat] which had been slaughtered in the courtyard [of the Temple] –

B.   she is not betrothed.

C.   [If] he sold them off and betrothed a woman with the money received in exchange for them, she is betrothed.

2:10

A.   He who consecrated a woman with food in the status of heave-offering, tithe, or gifts [to be given to the priest], purification water, purification ash –

B.   lo, this woman is betrothed,

C.   and even if she is an Israelite.

The items of M. 2:9A must be destroyed and cannot be used for benefit, so they are valueless to the woman. But if one received money for them, M. 2:9C, then that money, though it is in the status of the objects themselves, still has value to the woman and so she is betrothed. But the issue here is not the woman's attitude but the objective status of the object she has received, since she can have deemed the prohibited things of M. 2:9A to have value and that fact has no bearing. The point of M. 2:10 is that since an Israelite may dispose of the things that are listed in M. 2:10A, giving them to any priest of his choosing, he has sufficient domain over them to use them as tokens of betrothal.

23

Mishnah Tractate Qiddushin
Chapter Three

3:1

A. He who says to his fellow, "Go and betroth Miss So-and-so for me," and he went and betrothed her for himself —

B. she is betrothed.

C. And so: He who says to a woman, "Lo, you are betrothed to me after thirty days [have passed]," and someone else came along and betrothed her during the thirty days —

D. she is betrothed to the second party.

E. [If] it is an Israelite girl betrothed to a priest, she may eat heave-offering.

F. [If he said,] "...as of now and after thirty days," and someone else came along and betrothed her during the thirty days,

G. she is betrothed and not betrothed.

H. [If it is either] an Israelite girl betrothed to a priest, or a priest girl betrothed to an Israelite, she should not eat heave offering.

Here we really do have a case of the potential and the actual. If the man says, "You are betrothed after thirty days," do we take account of that potential action? No, we do not do so. If someone came along in the stated period and actually betrothed the woman, we do not consider what was supposed to have happened at the end of the month. A potential action is null in the face of a reality.

3:2

A. He who says to a woman, "Behold, you are betrothed to me, on condition that I pay you two hundred zuz," —

B. lo, this woman is betrothed, and he must pay [her what he has promised].

C. "...on condition that I pay you within the next thirty days," and he paid her during the thirty days, she is betrothed.

D.   And if not, she is not betrothed.

E.   "...on condition that I have two hundred zuz," lo, this woman is betrothed, and [if] he has that sum.

F.   "...on condition that I shall show you two hundred zuz, "

G.   lo, this woman is betrothed, and [if] he will show her that sum.

H.   But if he showed her the money on the table of a money-changer, she is not betrothed.

3:3

A.   "...on condition that I have a kor's space of land,"

B.   lo, this woman is betrothed, and [if] he has it.

C.   "...on condition that I have that land in such – and – such a place,"

D.   if he has it in that place, she is betrothed, and if not, she is not betrothed.

E.   "...on condition that I show you a kor's space of land,"

F.   lo, this woman is betrothed, and [if] he will show it to her,

G.   But if he showed her [land] in a plain [which was not his], she is not betrothed.

3:4

A.   R. Meir says, "Any condition which is not stated as is the condition of the sons of Gad and the sons of Reuben [that is, in both negative and positive formulations], is no condition,

B.   "since it says, And Moses said to them, 'If the children of Gad and the children of Reuben will pass over (Num. 32:29). And it is written, And if they will not pass over armed (Num. 32:20)."

C.   R. Hananiah b. Gamaliel says, "The matter had to be stated in just that way, for if not, it would have been implied that even in the Land of Canaan they would not inherit land."

M. 3:2 is clear that we expect the condition to be met, and we take for granted the man's intention is to meet that condition. The point at M. 3:2H is that the language of the man is understood to signify that he has that amount of capital at his disposal, not that he will merely show the money.

3:5

A.   He who betroths a woman and said, "I was thinking that she is a priest, and lo, she is a Levite," "...a Levite, and lo, she is a priest,"

B.   "A poor girl, and lo, she is a rich girl," "A rich girl, and lo, she is a poor girl,"

C.   lo, she is betrothed,

D.   for she has not deceived him.

E.   He who says to a woman, "Lo, you are betrothed to me after I convert to Judaism," or "after you convert,"

F.   "...after I am freed'" or "after you are freed,"

G.   "...after your husband died," or "...after your sister dies,"

H.   after your levir will have performed the rite of removing the shoe with you –

I.   she is not betrothed.

J.   And so he who says to his fellow, "If your wife gives birth to a girlchild, lo, [the baby] is betrothed to me" – she is not betrothed.

K.   If the wife of his fellow indeed was pregnant and the foetus was discernible, his statement is confirmed, and if she produced a girlchild, the baby is betrothed.

3:6

A.   He who says to a woman, "Lo, you are betrothed to me, on condition that I speak in your behalf to the government'" or, "That I work for you as a laborer,"

B.   [if] he spoke in her behalf to the government or worked for her as a laborer, she is betrothed.

C.   And if not, she is not betrothed.

D.   "...on condition that father will concur,"

E.   [if] father concurred, she is betrothed. And if not, she is not betrothed.

F.   [If] the father died, lo, this woman is betrothed.

G.   [If] the son died, they instruct the father to state that he does not concur.

At M. 3:5A-D, we set a limit to the matter of attitude or intention. If the woman has not deceived the man, then the mere fact that he intended to marry a woman of the priestly caste and discovers that he has not done so does not change anything. She bears no responsibility for the misinformation, and his intention by itself is not a consideration. M. 3:5Eff. turns to the matter of what is potential. We do not take account of the things that may or even must come about, e.g., conversion or death. The same is so at J-K, but not that the potentiality is a firm one, K, and we do consider it effective. M. 3:6 goes over the ground of M. 3:2-3.

3:7

A.   "I have betrothed my daughter, but I don't know to whom I have betrothed her,"

B.   and someone came along and said, "I have betrothed her,"

C.   he is believed.

D.   [If] this one said, "I betrothed her," and [at the same time], that one said, "I betrothed her," both of them give her a writ of divorce.

E.   But if they wanted, one of them gives her a writ of divorce and one of them consummates the marriage.

3:8

A.   "I have betrothed my daughter," "I have betrothed her and I have accepted her writ of divorce when she was a minor "

B.   and lo, she is yet a minor –

C.   he is believed.

D.   "I betrothed her and I accepted her writ of divorce when she was a minor," and lo, she is now an adult –

E.   he is not believed.

F.   "She was taken captive and I redeemed her," whether she is a minor or whether she is an adult,

G.   he is not believed.

H.   He who said at the moment of his death, "I have children," is believed.

I.   [If he said,] "I have brothers," he is not believed.

J.   He who betroths his daughter without specification – the one past girlhood is not taken into account.

3:9

A.   He who has two groups of daughters by two wives [in succession], and who said,

B.   "I have betrothed my oldest daughter, but I do not know whether it is the oldest of the older group or the oldest of the younger group, or the youngest of the older group, who is also older than the oldest of the younger group" –

C.   "all of them are prohibited [to marry without a writ of divorce], except for the youngest of the younger group," the words of R. Meir.

D.   R. Yosé says, "They are all permitted, except for the oldest of the older group."

E.   "I betrothed my youngest daughter, but I do not know whether it was the youngest of the younger group, or the youngest of the older group, or the oldest of the younger group, who is younger than the youngest of the older group" –

F.   "all of them are prohibited except for the oldest of the older group," the words of R. Meir,

G.   R. Yosé says, "All of them are permitted, except for the youngest of the younger group."

Cases of doubt are resolved in accord with simple principles. At M. 3:7 we work out uncontested testimony. If someone alleges that he has betrothed the daughter and there is no contrary allegation, and there is reason to believe the man, we do so. If there is contested testimony, we accept both to the degree that each must divorce the woman. Where the father, M. 3:8, has the power to do what he says he has done, we believe him. Where not, we do not believe him. M. 3:9 makes the same point as M. 3:8, but in a somewhat complicated case.

3:10

A.   He who says to a woman, "I have betrothed you,"

B.   and she says, "You did not betroth me"

C.　　he is prohibited to marry her relatives, but she is permitted to marry his relatives.

D.　　[If] she says, "You betrothed me," and he says, "I did not betroth you,"

E.　　he is permitted to marry her relatives, and she is prohibited from marrying his relatives.

F.　　"I betrothed you'"

G.　　and she says, "You betrothed only my daughter'"

H.　　he is prohibited from marrying the relatives of the older woman, and the older woman is permitted to marry his relatives.

I.　　He is permitted to marry the relatives of the young girl, and the young girl is permitted to marry his relatives.

3:11

A.　　"I have betrothed your daughter,"

B.　　and she says, "You betrothed only me,"

C.　　he is prohibited to marry the relatives of the girl, and the girl is permitted to marry his relatives.

D.　　He is permitted to marry the relatives of the older woman, but the older woman is prohibited from marrying his relatives.

Here we have conflicted testimony. We believe each party, to the limit of his testimony; but the one does not affect the status of the other.

3:12

A.　　In any situation in which there is a valid betrothal and no commission of a transgression, the offspring follows the status of the male,

B.　　What is such a situation?

C.　　It is the situation in which a priest girl, a Levite girl, or an Israelite girl was married to a priest, a Levite, or an Israelite.

D.　　And any situation in which there is a valid betrothal, but there also is the commission of a transgression, the offspring follows the status of the impaired [inferior] party.

E.　　And what is such a situation?

F.　　It is a widow married to a high priest, a divorcée or woman who has undergone the rite of halisah married to an ordinary priest, a mamzer girl, or a Netin girl married to an Israelite, an Israelite girl married to a mamzer or a Netin.

G.　　And in any situation in which a woman has no right to enter betrothal with this man but has the right to enter into betrothal with others, the offspring is a mamzer.

H.　　What is such a situation?

I.　　This is a man who had sexual relations with any of those women prohibited to him by the Torah.

J.   But any situation in which a woman has no right to enter into
        betrothal with this man or with any other man – the offspring is in
        her status.
K.   And what is such a situation?
L.   It is the offspring of a slave girl or a gentile girl.

3:13

A.   R. Tarfon says, "Mamzerim can be purified [from the taint of
        bastardy].
B.   "How so?
C.   "A mamzer who married a slave girl –
D.   "the offspring is a slave girl.
E.   "[If] he then freed him, the son turns out to be a free man."
F.   R. Eliezer says,"Lo, this is a slave who also is in the status of a
        mamzer."

This classification seems to me not to make any point of philosophical
interest or even relevance.   The propositions at hand are rules
particular to the data before us, not principles that are subject to
generalization and extension to other kinds of cases altogether.

24

Mishnah Tractate Qiddushin
Chapter Four

4:1

A. Ten castes came up from Babylonia: (1) priests, (2) Levites, (3) Israelites, (4) impaired priests, (5) converts, and (6) freed slaves, (7) mamzers, (8) Netins, (9) "silenced ones" [*shetuqi*], and (10) foundlings.

B. Priests, Levites, and Israelites are permitted to marry among one another.

C. Levites, Israelites, impaired priests, converts, and freed slaves are permitted to marry among one another.

D. Converts, freed slaves, mamzers, Netins, "silenced ones," and foundlings are permitted to marry among one another.

4:2

A. And what are "silenced ones"?

B. Any who knows the identity of his mother but does not know the identity of his father.

C. And foundlings?

D. Any who was discovered in the market and knows neither his father nor his mother.

E. Abba Saul did call a "silenced one" [*shetuqi*] "one who is to be examined" [*beduqi*].

4:3

A. All those who are forbidden from entering into the congregation are permitted to marry one another.

B. R. Judah prohibits.

C. R. Eliezer says, "Those who are of certain status are permitted to intermarry with others who are of certain status.

D. "Those who are of certain status and those who are of doubtful status, those who are of doubtful status and those who are of certain status, those who are of doubtful status and those who are of doubtful status –

E.   "it is prohibited."

F.   And who are those who are of doubtful status?

G.   The "silenced one," the foundling, and the Samaritan.

The ten genealogical castes are classified by the defined traits, M. 4:2, 3, and hierarchized as to the forming of marital groups, with Nos. 1-3 one such group, 2-6, a second, and 5-10, a third. The consequences of the classification then are spelled out at M. 4:3.

4:4

A.   He who marries a priest girl has to investigate her [genealogy] for four [generations, via the] mothers, who are eight:

B.   (1) her mother, and (2) the mother of her mother, and (3) the mother of the father of her mother, and (4) her mother, and (5) the mother of her father, and (6) her mother, and (7) the mother of the father of her father, and (8) her mother.

C.   And in the case of a Levite girl and an Israelite girl, they add on to them yet another [generation for genealogical inquiry].

4:5

A.   They do not carry a genealogical inquiry backward from [proof that one's priestly ancestor has served] at the altar,

B.   nor from [proof that one's Levitical ancestor has served] on the platform,

C.   and from [proof that one's learned ancestor has served] in the Sanhedrin.

D.   And all those whose fathers are known to have held office as public officials or as charity collectors – they marry them into the priesthood, and it is not necessary to conduct an inquiry.

E.   R. Yosé says, "Also: He who was signed as a witness in the ancient archives in Sepphoris."

F.   R. Haninah b. Antigonos says, "Also: Whoever was recorded in the king's army."

4:6

A.   The daughter of a male of impaired priestly stock is invalid for marriage into the priesthood for all time.

B.   An Israelite who married a woman of impaired priestly stock – his daughter is valid for marriage into the priesthood.

C.   A man of impaired priestly stock who married an Israelite girl – his daughter is invalid for marriage into the priesthood.

D.   R. Judah says, "The daughter of a male proselyte is equivalent to the daughter of a male of impaired priestly stock."

4:7

A.   R. Eliezer b. Jacob says, "An Israelite who married a female proselyte – his daughter is suitable for marriage into the priesthood.

B.   "And a proselyte who married an Israelite girl – his daughter is valid for marriage into the priesthood.

C.   "But a male proselyte who married a female proselyte – his daughter is invalid for marriage into the priesthood.

D.   "All the same are proselytes and freed slaves, even down to ten generations – [the daughters cannot marry into the priesthood],

E.   "unless the mother is an Israelite."

F.   R. Yosé says, "Also: A proselyte who married a female proselyte: his daughter is valid for marriage into the priesthood."

The responsibility for not violating caste restrictions rests on the male. The male who marries has to make sure that the woman is suitable for marriage to him, and this is done by investigating the genealogies of the mother and the grandmother on the mother's side and the same on the father's, as spelled out, so M. 4:4-5. At M. 4:6-7 the point is made that the male of impaired priestly stock cannot produce a daughter who may marry into the priesthood, but a female of impaired stock marries an ordinary Israelite, and the daughter, now an Israelite, may marry into the priesthood. The impairment passes on through the male line without limit.

4:8

A.   He who says, "This, my son, is a mamzer" is not believed.

B.   And even if both parties say concerning the foetus in the mother's womb, "He is a mamzer," they are not believed.

C.   R. Judah says, "They are believed."

The father cannot discredit the offspring.

4:9

A.   He who gave the power to his agent to accept tokens of betrothal for his daughter, but then he himself betrothed her –

B.   if his came first, his act of betrothal is valid.

C.   And if those of his agent came first, his act of betrothal is valid.

D.   And if it is not known [which came first], both parties give a writ of divorce.

E.   But if they wanted, one of them gives a writ of divorce, and one consummates the marriage.

F.   And so: A woman who gave the power to her agent to accept tokens of betrothal in her behalf, and then she herself went and accepted tokens of betrothal in her own behalf –

G.   if hers came first, her act of betrothal is valid.

H.   And if those of her agent came first, his act of betrothal is valid.

I.   And if it is not known [which of them came first], both parties give a writ of divorce.

J.   But if they wanted, one of them gives a writ of divorce and one of them consummates the marriage.

The important point is that once the power of attorney is given, it is valid and cannot be retracted without explicit action. Then first come, first served.

4:10

A.   He who went along with his wife overseas, and he and his wife and children came home,

B.   and he said, "The woman who went abroad with me, lo, this is she, and these are her children" –

C.   he does not have to bring proof concerning the woman or the children.

D.   [If he said,] "She died, and these are her children,"

E.   he does bring proof about the children,

F.   But he does not bring proof about the woman.

4:11

A.   [If he said], "I married a woman overseas. Lo, this is she, and these are her children,"

B.   he brings proof concerning the woman, but he does not have to bring proof concerning the children.

C.   "...she died, and these are her children,"

D.   he has to bring proof concerning the woman and the children.

We deal with an ascending sequences of doubt. In the first case, the woman is there and so too the children. In the second, we do not have the wife, but we do have the children. In the third, both the wife and the children are unknown, but the wife is available for interrogation. In the fourth, all four are unknown. The main point is that if the woman is confirmed as genealogically valid for the man, then the status of the woman is established as well.

4:12

A.   A man should not remain alone with two women, but a woman may remain alone with two men.

B.   R. Simeon says, "Also: One may stay alone with two women, when his wife is with him.

C.   "And he sleeps with them in the same inn,

D.   "because his wife keeps watch over him."

E.   A man may stay alone with his mother or with his daughter.

F.   And he sleeps with them with flesh touching.

G.   But if they [the son who is with the mother, the daughter with the father] grew up, this one sleeps in her garment, and that one sleeps in his garment.

4:13

A. An unmarried man may not teach scribes.

B. Nor may a woman teach scribes.

C. R. Eliezer says, "Also: He who has no wife may not teach scribes."

4:14

A. R. Judah says, "An unmarried man may not herd cattle.

B. "And two unmarried men may not sleep in the same cloak."

C. And sages permit it.

D. Whoever has business with women should not be alone with women.

E. And a man should not teach his son a trade which he has to practice among women.

F. R. Meir says, "A man should always teach his son a clean and easy trade. And let him pray to him to whom belong riches and possessions.

G. "For there is no trade which does not involve poverty or wealth.

H. "For poverty does not come from one's trade, nor does wealth come from one's trade.

I. "But all is in accord with a man's merit."

J. R. Simeon b. Eleazar says, "Have you ever seen a wild beast or a bird who has a trade? Yet they get along without difficulty. And were they not created only to serve me? And I was created to serve my Master. So is it not logical that I should get along without difficulty? But I have done evil and ruined my living."

K. Abba Gurion of Sidon says in the name of Abba Gurya, "A man should not teach his son to be an ass driver, a camel driver, a barber, a sailor, a herdsman, or a shopkeeper. For their trade is the trade of thieves."

L. R. Judah says in his name, "Most ass drivers are evil, most camel drivers are decent, most sailors are saintly, the best among physicians is going to Gehenna, and the best of butchers is a partner of Amalek."

M. R. Nehorai says, "I should lay aside every trade in the world and teach my son only Torah. For a man eats its fruits in this world, and the principal remains for the world to come. But other trades are not that way. When a man gets sick or old or has pains and cannot do his job, lo, he dies of starvation. But with Torah it is not that way. But it keeps him from all evil when he is young, and it gives him a future and a hope when he is old. Concerning his youth, what does it say? They who wait upon the Lord shall renew their strength (Is. 40:31). And concerning his old age what does it say? 'He shall still bring forth fruit in old age' (Ps. 92:14). And so it says with regard to the patriarch Abraham, may he rest in peace, 'And Abraham was old and well along in years, and the Lord blessed Abraham in all things' (Gen. 24:1). We find that the patriarch Abraham kept the entire Torah even before it was revealed, since it says, 'Since Abraham obeyed my voice and kept my charge, my commandments, my statutes, and my laws' (Gen. 26:5)."

These items are clear as given. They express attitudes, e.g., toward women and various traces, Torah-study and the like, but contain no principles that can guide the analysis of unrelated cases.

25

The Plan of Mishnah Tractate Meilah

While presenting its share of arid, wholly formal constructions, Meilah also raises profound and interesting questions about the nature of the sacred. It asks, for example, about the status of that sacred object or substance which has been subjected to sacrilege, pointing out that, if we punish a person for the commission of sacrilege, then we must treat that which has been subjected to it as secular. It raises issues of agency and, concommitantly, responsibility for an action, joining these issues to the matter of inadvertence. Third, it goes over profound matters of the metaphysics of the cult, familiar at Zebahim and Menahot, and shows the inner logic of several possible positions. These are only three items of its program of inquiry. The tractate unfolds with appropriate attention to matters of form and formal redaction, so that it is the intellectual and aesthetic apogee of our division.

Let us consider first of all the topic, the matter of sacrilege. As usual, Maimonides (*Trespass* 1:1-3, Lewittes, pp. 411-412) provides a fine introduction:

1:1   It was forbidden for a private person to make any profane use of the hallowed things of the Lord, both of things that were offered upon the Altar and of things hallowed for the repair of the Temple. Anyone who made such use of hallowed things of the Lord to the extent of a *perutah* committed a trespass.

1:2   Parts of offerings that became permitted to be eaten – such as flesh of a sin-offering or a guilt-offering after its blood has been sprinkled, or the Two Loaves after the sprinkling of the blood of the Two Lambs – were not included in the law of trespass. Even if a nonpriest ate of these or similar things, inasmuch as some persons were permitted to enjoy them, anyone who enjoyed them did not commit a trespass. Even if hallowed things of this kind became unfit and forbidden to be eaten, as long as there had

169

been a time when they were permitted, the penalty for trespass was not incurred because of them.

1:3   Anyone who willfully committed trespass incurred flogging and had to pay in full the amount by which he had diminished the value of the holy thing. The admonition against such trespass was inferred from the Scriptural verse: *Thou mayest not eat within thy gates the tithe of thy corn...nor any of thy vows* (Deut. 12:17); and it was learned from oral tradition that this was an admonition to one who would eat from the flesh of a burnt-offering, since it belonged wholly to the Lord. The same admonition applied to every other holy thing which belonged to the Lord alone, whether it was of the things hallowed for the Altar or of the things hallowed for the repair of the Temple: if anyone enjoyed therefrom a use worth a *perutah*, he incurred flogging.

If one committed a trespass unwittingly, he was required to pay for what he had enjoyed plus an additional fifth. He also was required to bring a ram worth two *sela'* and offer it as a guilt-offering, and atonement was made for him. This was the offering known as "the guilt-offering of trespasses." For it is said: *If anyone commit a trespass, and sin through error, in the holy things of the Lord, then he shall bring his forfeit unto the Lord, a ram without blemish...for a guilt-offering. And he shall make restitution for that which he hath done amiss in the holy thing, and shall add the fifth part thereto*, etc. (Lev. 5:15, 16). Paying the principal and an additional fifth together with bringing the offering was a positive commandment.

The tractate is unusually cogent. Its two principal units properly arrange, first of all, rules on the applicability of the laws of (1) sacrilege to *sacrifices*, then, with a necessary prologue, principles of (2) sacrilege of *Temple property*.

I. Sacrilege of Sacrifices in Particular.

1:1-3:8
A   When the laws of sacrilege apply to a sacrifice: 1.1-4

1:1   The laws of sacrilege apply to a sacrifice which has never been subjected to the private use of the priest but has always remained the possession of the altar. They cease to apply to a sacrifice which at some point has belonged to the priests. If the blood is properly tossed, the laws of sacrilege are suspended. But if not, they remain in effect; this is Joshua's view.

1:2-3   Meat of Most Holy Things which went forth beyond the veils before the tossing of the blood – Eliezer: The laws of sacrilege apply [because the tossing of the blood does not affect the meat]. 'Aqiba: The laws of sacrilege do not apply [since the blood has been properly tossed in regard to part, if not all, of the meat].

1:4 A deed having to do with the blood in the case of Most Holy Things produces a ruling which is lenient and one which is stringent. But in the case of Lesser Holy Things, the whole result is to impose a stringent ruling. Before the tossing of the blood, Lesser Holy Things are not subject to the laws of sacrilege.

B. Stages in the status of an offering: 2:1-9

2:1-9 The point at which the laws of sacrilege apply to various sacrifices, the point at which the sacrifice may be made invalid by a *Tebul Yom*, the point at which the prohibitions of refuse, remnant, and uncleanness are invoked, and the point at which the laws of sacrilege no longer apply.

2:1-5 Animal offerings.

2:6-9 Meal- and incense-offerings.

C. Cultic property which is not subject to sacrilege but which also is not to be used for non-cultic purposes: 3:1-8

3:1-2 Sin-offerings which are left to die because they cannot serve the purpose for which they were designated and cannot serve another purpose. Nazirite's offering: coins set aside for that purpose cannot be used for secular purposes but are not subject to sacrilege.

3:3 Cultic material which at one point is not subject to the laws of sacrilege but which at some other is subject to them.

3:4-5 Ashes of the inner altar, birds too young or too old, which are not subject to sacrilege but which also cannot be used for secular purposes.

3:6 The status of materials dedicated to the Temple or the altar which cannot be used for the altar but the value of which can serve for the upkeep of the Temple: such materials are subject to the laws of sacrilege. Exemplifications.

3:7-8 Roots of trees growing from secular property to the Temple property. He who sanctifies a forest: the law of sacrilege applies to the whole of it. But if the Temple treasurers purchase wood, the laws of sacrilege do not apply to the chips or the foliage.

II. Sacrilege of Temple Property in General.

4:1-6:6

A. Sacrilege has been committed only when the value of a *perutah* of Temple property has been used for secular purposes. The joining together of diverse objects for the purpose of reaching the *perutah's* value: 4:1-2(+3-6)

4:1 Things consecrated for the altar join together to form the requisite volume or value – a *perutah's* worth – to be subject to the laws of sacrilege.

Things consecrated for the upkeep of the house join together.

Things consecrated for the altar and things consecrated for the upkeep of the house join together.

4:2   Five things in a burnt-offering join together [to form the requisite volume for liability to sacrilege].

[4:3-6   All forms of refuse join together. All forms of remnant join together. All forms of carrion join together, etc. Joshua: General principle. 4:4 Refuse and remnant do not join together, etc.

4:5   All foodstuffs join together to render the body invalid at a volume of half a half-loaf of bread, etc. 4:6 *'Orlah*-fruit and diverse kinds of the vineyard join together.]

B.   Sacrilege is defined by the one who does it, or by the thing to which it is done: 5:1-2

5:1-2   He who derives benefit to the extent of a *perutah's* value from that which is consecrated, even though he did not cause deterioration through use, has committed an act of sacrilege, so 'Aqiba. Sages: Anything which is not subject to deterioration through use, once one has derived benefit from it, he has committed an act of sacrilege. Anything which is subject to deterioration through use, one has not committed an act of sacrilege unless he has caused deterioration through use.

If one has derived benefit to the extent of half a *perutah* and caused deterioration to the extent of half a *perutah*, he has not committed an act of sacrilege – until he will derive benefit to the extent of a *perutah* or cause deterioration to the extent of a *perutah*.

C.   Sacrilege effects the secularization of sacred property: 5:3-5

5:3   One does not commit sacrilege after another has done so to the same object, except for a beast or a utensil of cultic service, since in these latter cases the object cannot be secularized.

Rabbi: Anything which is not subject to redemption is subject to a case of sacrilege following sacrilege.

5:4   If one took a stone or beam from what is consecrated, lo, he has not committed an act of sacrilege. If he gave it to his fellow, he has done it. But his fellow has not done it. Thus: Sacrilege applies only where there is enjoyment of consecrated property to the extent of a *perutah's* worth.

5:5   What one has eaten and what his fellow has eaten join together, and even over an extended period of time.

D.   Agency in effecting an act of sacrilege: 6:1-5(+)

6:1   If the agent carried out his errand and thereby inadvertently committed an act of sacrilege, the householder is responsible. If the agent did not carry out his errand, then he is responsible and the householder is exempt.

6:2   An agent who is not subject to responsibility, e.g., a minor, who carried out his errand leaves the householder responsible. If the agent did not carry out his errand, then the storekeeper becomes responsible, since the householder is not, for the inadvertent act of sacrilege.

6:3   If one gave a *perutah* and said to the agent, "With half bring lamps and with half wicks," and he went and brought lamps for the whole of it, both of them – householder and agent – are not held responsible, since by neither has an act of sacrilege to the extent of a *perutah* been committed. Half of what the householder instructed has been done, half not.

6:4   If he gave the agent two *perutot* and said, "Bring me an *etrog*," and he went and brought him one for a *perutah* and a pomegranate for one, both are liable for an act of sacrilege. Judah: The householder has not committed an act of sacrilege, for his instructions have not been carried out.

6:5   He who deposits coins with a money-changer, if bound up – the money-changer should not make use of them. Therefore if they were consecrated and he paid them out, he has committed an act of sacrilege.

[6:6   A *perutah* which has been consecrated which fell into a purse containing other money, as soon as one has paid out the first coin, he has committed an act of sacrilege, so 'Aqiba. Sages: Only when the last coin has been paid out has he committed an act of sacrilege. 'Aqiba: The first coin may be that which is consecrated.]

Beginning with the most basic rules affecting sacrifices, the tractate first attends to the question of when an object becomes susceptible to the laws of sacrilege. The second unit then asks about property, not solely animal-sacrifices, the value of which has been consecrated for the altar or for the upkeep of the Temple, but which is not sacrificed in the narrow sense.

The sacrifice is subject to sacrilege so long as that which renders the sacrifice permitted for priestly use has not been properly offered up (M. Zeb. Chapter Two). Secondary issues do not affect that primary principle. The opening unit then provides a very handsome construction, detailing the point at which various sacrifices and offerings become, and cease to be, subject to the laws of sacrilege. Finally we turn to cultic property which is not subject to the laws of sacrilege, on the one hand, but which also cannot be used for secular purposes, on the other. The second unit, turning to Temple property in general, first establishes the fact that sacrilege has been committed only when Temple property to the value of a *perutah* has been used for secular purposes. The matter of 'joining together' to reach that value forthwith is raised, with extraneous materials on the same question appended. The second major consideration, II.B., is, as stated, a very interesting inquiry, based upon the facts provided by II.A., the importance of the *perutah's* value. If something sacred has been used for secular purposes, once we punish the act of sacrilege, we also treat the object as no longer sacred, a logical position. We turn, next, to the matter of agency, with the important consideration that the sacrilege under discussion in our tractate is that which is done inadvertently. The problems of the final unit can be phrased in terms other than the particular facts of our tractate, so we have moved, as we see, from issues particular to the cult and altar to those which are general and, in principle, in no way limited to the matter of sacrilege at all. This is yet another indication of the remarkable care with which the tractate has been formed.

26

Mishnah Tractate Meilah
Chapter One

A. Most Holy Things which one slaughtered in the south [side of the altar] –

B. the laws of sacrilege apply to them.

C. [If] one slaughtered them in the south and received their blood in the north,

D. in the north and received their blood in the south,

E. [if] one slaughtered them by day and tossed the blood by night,

F. by night and tossed the blood by day,

G. or [if] one slaughtered them [with the intention of eating that which is usually eaten or offering up that which is usually offered up] outside of their proper time or outside of their proper place –

H. the laws of sacrilege apply to them.

I. A general principle did R. Joshua state: "Whatever has had a moment of availability to [for use by] the priests – the laws of sacrilege do not apply thereto.

J. "And [whatever] has not [yet] had a moment of availability to the priests – the laws of sacrilege do apply thereto."

K. What is that which has had a moment of availability to the priests?

L. That which [after the proper tossing of the blood] has been left overnight, and that which has been made unclean, and that which has gone forth [beyond the veils].

M. And what is that which has not [yet] had a moment of availability to the priests?

N. That which has been slaughtered [with improper intention to eat that which is usually eaten or to offer up that which is usually offered up] outside of its proper time or outside of its proper place,

O.   and that, the blood of which invalid men have received or tossed.

The laws of sacrilege apply to a sacrifice that has never been available for the private use of the priest but has always remained in the domian of the altar. They no longer apply once a sacrifice has at some point belonged to the priests. Joshua maintains that the proper tossing of the blood is the operative consideration. If Most Holy Things, A-B, are invalidated by being slaughtered at the southern side of the altar, rather than at the northern side, which is the correct place, they nonetheless are subject to the laws of sacrilege. Even though sacrifices are invalidated, they remain consecrated and therefore unavailable for priestly use. C-H go over the same ground. Joshua frames matters in terms of availability to the priests but the point is the same. Whatever for a single moment has been permissible for priestly use, that is, whatever sacrifice has had its blood properly tossed, even though afterward invalidated for some reason, is not subject to the laws of sacrilege. The offering has fallen into the domain of the priests. This is illustrated at K-L, in each of which points the offering for a moment was correctly in the domain of the priests, the blood having been properly tossed.

1:2

A.   The meat of Most Holy Things which went forth [beyond the veils] before the tossing of the blood –

B.   R. Eliezer says, "The laws of sacrilege apply to it. And they are not liable on its account because of violation of the laws of refuse, remnant, and uncleanness."

C.   R. Aqiba says, "The laws of sacrilege do not apply to it. Truly are they liable on its account because of violation of the laws of refuse, remnant, and uncleanness."

D.   Said R. Aqiba, "Now, lo, he who separates a sin-offering which is lost, and separated another in its stead, and afterward the first turns up, and lo, both of them are available –

E.   "is it not so that just as its blood exempts its flesh [from the laws of sacrilege], so it exempts the flesh of its fellow?

F.   "Now if [the proper tossing of its blood has exempted the flesh of its fellow from being subject to the laws of sacrilege, is it not logical that it should exempt its own flesh?"

1:3

A.   The sacrificial parts of Lesser Holy Things which went forth [beyond the veils] before the tossing of the blood –

B.   R. Eliezer says, "The laws of sacrilege do not apply to them. And they are not liable on their account because of violation of the laws of refuse, remnant, and uncleanness."

C. R. Aqiba says, "The laws of sacrilege do apply to them. And they are liable on their account because of violation of the laws of refuse, remnant, and uncleanness."

If the blood is properly tossed, then the meat is available to the priests and the laws of sacrilege no longer apply. What if, before the blood is tossed, some of the meat is taken out of the courtyard and invalidated, but then the blood is tossed? Has there been a moment when the priests have actually had a right to said meat? No, Eliezer maintains, and therefore the laws of sacrilege continue to apply, but the meat is not subject to the rules of refuse, remnant, and uncleanness, which we invoke for meat that is valid and available. The tossing of the blood has no affect upon flesh that has been invalidated; there never has been a moment of availability to the priests. Aqiba holds that the tossing of the blood does serve to remove the meat from being subject to the laws of sacrilege, even though the meat is invalid as an offering. Liability to the laws of refuse, remnant, and uncleanness pertains. It is possible in principle for tossing the blood to remove from liability to the laws of sacrilege meat that itself cannot be offered on the altar. We ignore the potentiality of offering the meat; it is not a consideration; we attend only to the actuality of the tossing of the blood. Aqiba's argument invokes the case of two sin-offerings, one lost, then found, another designated as a sin-offering instead of the lost one. Both are in the same status. Slaughtering both, we offer one of them as a sin-offering. This one then exempts the meat of the other from the laws of sacrilege, even though the blood of the other has not been tossed and is not going to be tossed, and even though the other cannot be offered up at all, since it is in the status of a duplicate sin-offering. Tossing the blood has the effect of removing from liability to the laws of sacrilege the invalid meat of the second offering. The case here is parallel. The tossing of the blood is valid, serving as it does that portion of the meat that has not been removed from the courtyard; that same tossing serves for the invalid meat that has been taken out of the courtyard as well.

1:4

A. A deed having to do with the blood in the case of Most Holy Things produces a ruling which is lenient and one which is stringent.

B. But in the case of Lesser Holy Things, the whole [tendency] is to impose a stringent ruling.

C. How so?

D. Most Holy Things before the tossing of the blood –

E. the laws of sacrilege apply to the sacrificial parts and to the meat [which is for the priests].

F.   After the tossing of the blood, the laws of sacrilege apply to the sacrificial parts but they do not apply to the flesh.

G.   On account of this and on account of that are they liable because of violation of the laws of refuse, remnant, and uncleanness.

H.   But in the case of Lesser Holy Things, the whole [tendency] is to impose a stringent ruling – how so?

I.   Lesser Holy Things before the tossing of the blood –

J.   the laws of sacrilege do not apply either to the sacrificial parts or to the flesh.

K.   After the tossing of the blood, the laws of sacrilege apply to the sacrificial parts, but they do not apply to the flesh.

L.   On account of this and on account of that they are liable because of violation of the laws of refuse, remnant, and uncleanness.

M.   It turns out that a deed having to do with the blood in the case of Most Holy Things produces a ruling which is lenient and one which is stringent, but in the case of Lesser Holy Things, the whole [tendency) is to impose a stringent ruling.

Lesser Holy Things are not subject to the laws of sacrilege at all until the blood has been tossed. At that point the portions of the animal that are burned up on the altar (the sacrificial portions) become subject to the laws of sacrilege. Now, we know, M. 1:1, with the sprinkling of the blood, meat of Most Holy Things ceases to be liable to the laws of sacrilege. Before the blood is tossed, the whole of Most Holy Things is subject to the laws of sacriledge, but not the flesh, which the priests may eat. Before the tossing of the blood, no part of Lesser Holy Things is subject to the laws of sacrilege. But afterward, as at M, the laws of sacrilege do apply to part of the meat. Hence we have the upshot spelled out at M. Where the laws yield a strict rule for the one, they yield a lenient rule for the other, and vice versa.

27

Mishnah Tractate Meilah
Chapter Two

2:1

   A.   The sin-offering of fowl –

   B.   the laws of sacrilege apply to it once it [the bird] has been sanctified [designated as a sin-offering].

   C.   [When] its head has been severed, it is rendered fit to be made invalid by a *tebul-yom* and by one whose rites of atonement have not yet been completed and by being left overnight.

   D.   [When] its blood has been tossed, they are liable on its account because of violation of the laws of refuse, remnant, and uncleanness.

   E.   And sacrilege does not apply to it [any longer].

2:2

   A.   The burnt-offering of fowl –

   B.   the laws of sacrilege apply to it once it has been sanctified.

   C.   [When] its head has been severed, it is rendered fit to be made invalid by a *tebul-yom* and by one whose rites of atonement have not yet been completed and by being left overnight.

   D.   [When] its blood has been squeezed out, they are liable on its account because of violation of the laws of refuse, remnant, and uncleanness.

   E.   And the laws of sacrilege apply to it until it is taken out to the ash heap.

2:3

   A.   Cows which are to be burned and goats which are to be burned –

   B.   the laws of sacrilege apply to them once they have been sanctified.

C.   [When] they have been slaughtered, they are rendered fit to be
       made invalid by a *tebul-yom* and by one whose rites of atonement
       have not yet been completed and by being left overnight.

D.   [When] their blood has been tossed, they are liable on their
       account because of violation of the laws of refuse, remnant, and
       uncleanness.

E.   And the laws of sacrilege apply to them in the ash heap until the
       meat is reduced to cinders.

2:4

A.   The burnt-offering –
B.   the laws of sacrilege apply to it once it has been sanctified.
C.   [When] it has been slaughtered, it is rendered fit to be made
       invalid by a *tebul-yom* and by one whose rites of atonement have
       not yet been completed and by being left overnight.
D.   [When] its blood has been tossed, they are liable on its account
       because of violation of the laws of refuse, remnant, and
       uncleanness.
E.   And the laws of sacrilege do not apply to its hide.
F.   But it will be taken out to the ash heap.

2:5

A.   A sin-offering, and a guilt-offering, and communal sacrifices of
       peace offerings –
B.   the laws of sacrilege apply to them once they have been
       sanctified.
C.   [When] they have been slaughtered, they are rendered fit to be
       made invalid by a *tebul-yom* and by one whose rites of atonement
       have not yet been completed and by being left overnight.
D.   [When] their blood has been tossed, they are liable on their
       account because of violation of the laws of refuse, remnant, and
       uncleanness.
E.   The laws of sacrilege do not apply to the meat.
F.   But the laws of sacrilege apply to the sacrificial parts until they are
       taken out to the ash heap.

2:6

A.   The Two Loaves –
B.   the laws of sacrilege apply to them once they have been
       sanctified.
C.   [When] they have formed a crust in the oven, they have been
       rendered fit to be made invalid by a *tebul-yom* and by one whose
       rites of atonement have not yet been completed and to have
       slaughtered the animal sacrifice [which pertains to them (Lev.
       23:18)] on their account.
D.   [When] the blood of the lambs has been tossed, they are liable on
       their account because of violation of the laws of refuse, remnant,
       and uncleanness,

E.   But sacrilege does not apply to them.

2:7

A.   The shewbread –

B.   the laws of sacrilege apply to it once it has been sanctified.

C.   [When] it has formed a crust in the oven, it has been rendered fit to be made invalid by a *tebul-yom* and by one whose rites of atonement have not yet been completed and to be laid out on the table.

D.   [When] the dishes of incense have been offered, they are liable on its account because of violation of the laws of refuse, remnant, and uncleanness.

E.   And sacrilege does not pertain to it [any longer].

2:8

A.   Meal-offerings –

B.   the laws of sacrilege apply to them once they have been sanctified.

C.   [When] they have been sanctified in a utensil, they are rendered fit to be made invalid by a *tebul-yom* and by one whose rites of atonement have not yet been completed and by being left overnight.

D.   [When] the handful [of the meal-offering] has been offered, they are liable on their account because of violation of the laws of refuse, remnant, and uncleanness.

E.   And the laws of sacrilege do not apply to the residue. But the laws of sacrilege apply to the handful [of the meal-offering itself] until it is taken out to the ash heap.

2:9

A.   The handful, the frankincense, the incense, the meal-offerings of priests, and the meal-offering of the anointed priest, and the meal-offering which accompanies drink-offerings [M. Zeb. 4:3] –

B.   the laws of sacrilege apply to them once they have been sanctified.

C.   [When] they have been sanctified in a utensil, they are rendered fit to be made invalid by a *tebul-yom* and by one whose rites of atonement have not yet been completed and by being left overnight.

D.   And they are liable on their account because of violation of the laws of remnant and because of violation of the laws of uncleanness.

E.   But the prohibition of refuse does not apply to them.

F.   This is the general principle: For whatever is subject to that which renders the offering permitted are they not liable on account of violation of the laws of refuse, remnant, and uncleanness until what renders the offering permitted has been properly offered.

G.   And for whatever is not subject to that which renders the offering
          permitted, once it has been sanctified in a utensil are they liable
          on account of the violation of the laws of remnant, and on account
          of violation of the laws of uncleanness.

H.   But the law of refuse does not apply to it [at all].

There are four stages that are set forth: susceptibility to sacrilege, at
which the process commences; susceptibility to being invalidated by a
person not wholly in a state of cleanness but also not unclean;
susceptibility to the prohibitions of refuse, remnant, and uncleanness;
the end of susceptibility to sacrilege altogether. The first five items
cover animal offerings, the last four, meal- and incense-offerings. In
each instance, after telling us that when the item to be offered up has
been designated for its sacred purpose, hence, sanctified, it is subject to
the laws of sacrilege, that is, the commencement of the process, the
passage proceeds to make these points. Once the sacrifice has been
made, meaning, the animal killed, the sacrifice is subject to being made
invalid by a *tebul-yom*, that is, one who has immersed for an
uncleanness but has to await sunset for the completion of the process of
atonement and purification. Second, once the blood is tossed, the
prohibitions of refuse, remnant, and uncleanness, are invoked; the priest
of course is responsible in these matters, and he has a right to the meat
of the offerings in classes that yield a priestly portion. Then when the
beast is burned up or otherwise removed from the process, the laws of
sacrilege no longer apply.

28

Mishnah Tractate Meilah
Chapter Three

3:1

A. (1) The offspring of a sin-offering, and (2) the substitute of a sin-offering, and (3) a sin-offering, the owner of which died, are left to die.

B. [The sin-offering] (1) which became superannuated, or (2) which was lost, or (3) which turned out to be blemished,

C. if [this is] after the owner has effected atonement,

D. is left to die, and does not impart the status of substitute [to an animal designated in its stead].

E. And it is not available for enjoyment but is not subject to the law of sacrilege.

F. And if [this is] before the owner has effected atonement,

G. it is put out to pasture until it suffers a blemish, then is sold, and with its proceeds he [the owner] brings another, and it does impart the status of substitute [to an animal designated in its stead].

H. And it is subject to the law of sacrilege.

3:2

A. He who sets aside coins for his Nazirite offering[s] [Num. 6:14] a he-lamb as a burnt-offering, a ewe-lamb as a sin-offering, a ram as a peace-offering –

B. they [the coins] are not available for benefit.

C. But they [the coins] are not subject to the laws of sacrilege, because they [the sacrifices] are appropriate to be offered wholly as peace-offerings [Lesser Holy Things, not subject to sacrilege before the blood is tossed].

D. [If] he died,

E. [if] they were not designated [for their particular, respective purposes], they fall [to the Temple treasury] as a freewill-offering.

F.   [If] they were designated [for their particular, respective purposes], the money set aside for the sin-offering is to go to the Salt Sea.

G.   They are not available for benefit, but they are not subject to the laws of sacrilege.

H.   [With] the money set aside for the burnt-offering, they are to bring a burnt-offering.

I.   And [with] the money set aside for peace-offerings, they are to bring peace-offerings.

J.   And they are eaten for one day [M. Zeb. 5:6] and do not require bread [Num. 6:19].

M. 3:1C-D makes the point that the animal left to die is not to be used for secular purposes; but it also is not subject to the law of sacrilege, since it is not designated for offering on the altar and therefore is not sanctified. The same rule works itself out at M. 3:2. The coins are for one Nazirite's offering; they cannot be used for any other purpose. But they also are not subject to the laws of sacrilege.

3:3

A.   R. Simeon says, "Blood is subject to a lenient law at the outset and to a strict law at the end, and the drink-offerings are subject to a strict rule at the outset and to a lenient rule at the end.

B.   "The blood at the outset: the laws of sacrilege do not apply to it.

C.   "[When] it has gone forth to the Qidron Brook, the laws of sacrilege apply to it.

D.   "Drink-offerings at the outset: the laws of sacrilege apply to them.

E.   "[When] they have gone forth to the pits, the laws of sacrilege do not apply to them."

Before blood is tossed on the altar, it is not subject to the laws of sacrilege. The remnants of the blood are used for manure. There is no payment for sacrilege. The drink-offerings are subject to the laws of sacrilege. When they flow down to the foundations, they cease to be so.

3:4

A.   The ashes [of the incense] of the inner altar and [of the wicks that remain] of the candelabrum –

B.   are not available for benefit, but the laws of sacrilege do not apply.

C.   He who sanctifies the ash to begin with

D.   the laws of sacrilege apply to it.

E.   (1) Turtledoves which have not yet reached their maturity and (2) pigeons which have become superannuated

F.   are not available for benefit, but the laws of sacrilege do not apply.

G. R. Simeon says, "Turtledoves which have not yet reached their maturity – the laws of sacrilege apply to them. But pigeons which have become superannuated are not available for benefit, but the laws of sacrilege do not apply"

Unlike the ashes of the outer altar, the ashes of the inner altar and of the wicks, once removed from the inner altar, no longer are deemed holy. They cannot be used, but they also are not subject to the laws of sacrilege, and from our perspective that interstitial classification is what is of interest.

3:5

A. The milk of animal sacrifices and the eggs of turtledoves are not available for benefit, but the laws of sacrilege do not apply to them.
B. Under what circumstances?
C. In the case of what is made holy for the use of the altar.
D. But in the case of what is made holy for the upkeep of the Temple house –
E. [If] one has sanctified a chicken, the laws of sacrilege apply to it and to its egg.
F. [If he sanctified] an ass, the laws of sacrilege apply to it and to its milk.

3:6

A. Whatever is appropriate for [use on] the altar but not for the upkeep of the house,
B. for the upkeep of the house and not for the altar,
C. not for the altar and not for the upkeep of the house –
D. the laws of sacrilege apply thereto.
E. How so?
F. [If] one sanctified (1) a hole full of water [B], (2) a dung heap full of dung [C], (3) a dovecote full of pigeons [A], (4) a tree covered with fruit, (5) a field full of herbs –
G. the laws of sacrilege apply to them and to what is in them.
H. But if he sanctified (1) a hole, and afterward it filled with water, (2) a dungheap, and afterward it was filled with dung, (3) a dovecote, and afterward it was filled with pigeons, (4) a tree and afterward it filled with fruit, (5) a field and afterward it was filled with herbs –
I. "the laws of sacrilege apply to them, but the laws of sacrilege do not apply to what is in them," the words of R. Judah.
J. R. Simeon says, "He who sanctifies a field and a tree – the laws of sacrilege apply to them and to what grows in them,
K. "for they are the offspring of that which has been consecrated."
L. The offspring of the tithe of cattle may not suck from [a beast that is] tithe [of cattle].

M.   And others donate [their beasts] thus [on condition that, if the
            tithe of their cattle should be a female beast, its milk should not
            be deemed consecrated but should be available for its offspring].
N.   The offspring of a consecrated beast should not suck from
            consecrated beasts.
O.   And others donate their beasts thus.
P.   Laborers should not eat of dried figs which have been
            consecrated.
Q.   And so: A cow should not eat of vetches which have been
            consecrated.

Eggs and milk, M. 3:5, cannot be offered on the altar and are not subject
to the laws of sacrilege. But if sanctified for the use of the Temple
("upkeep of the Temple house") then the value is consecrated, and then
the laws of sacrilege apply. Here we distinguish among consecrated
things between what can serve on the altar, which is physically holy
in its own corpus, and what cannot, which is holy only as to its value.
The conundrum at M. 3:6 then works on this same secondary distinction.

3:7

A.   [If] the roots of a privately owned tree come into consecrated
            ground,
B.   or those of a tree which is consecrated come into privately owned
            ground,
C.   they are not available for enjoyment, but they are not subject to
            the laws of sacrilege.
D.   A well which gushes forth from a field which is consecrated – [the
            water] is not available for enjoyment, but the laws of sacrilege do
            not apply.
E.   [If] it went outside of the field, they derive benefit from it.
F.   Water which is in a golden jar –
G.   is not available for benefit but is not subject to the laws of
            sacrilege.
H.   [If] one put it into a glass, the law of sacrilege applies to it.
I.   The willow branch [set beside the altar] is not available for benefit
            but is not subject to the law of sacrilege.
J.   R. Eleazar b. R. Sadoq says, "The elders would take some of it for
            their lulabs. "

3:8

A.   A nest which is up at the top of a tree which has been consecrated
B.   is not available for benefit, but is not subject to the law of
            sacrilege.
C.   And that which is on an asherah tree –
D.   one may flick it off with a reed.
E.   He who sanctifies a forest –
F.   the law of sacrilege applies to the whole of it.

G.   And the Temple treasurers who bought wood –

H.   the laws of sacrilege apply to the wood.

I.   But the laws of sacrilege do not apply to the chips and [they do] not [apply] to the foliage.

If roots spread from unconsecrated to consecrated ground or vice verse, one may not make use of the tree, but the tree also is not subject to the law of sacrilege, since it does not wholly fall into the domain of the Temple. At M. 3:8 the nest is built of wood and leaves deriving from unconsecrated property, but the tree is consecrated, so the nest may not be used, yet another interstitial case.

29

Mishnah Tractate Meilah
Chapter Four

4:1
A. Things consecrated for the altar join together with one another [for making up the requisite quantity – a *perutah's* worth – to be subject to] the law of sacrilege,

B. and to impose liability on their account for transgression of the laws of refuse, remnant and uncleanness.

C. Things consecrated for the upkeep of the house join together with one another [in regard to sacrilege].

D. Things consecrated for the altar and things consecrated for the upkeep of the house join together [for making up the quantity to be subject to] the law of sacrilege.

The minimum volume required for invoking the law of sacrilege is of the value of a *perutah*. A misappropriate of less than that in value is null, since one cannot value so paltry a thing.

4:2
A. Five things in a burnt-offering join together [to form the requisite volume for liability to sacrilege]: (1) the meat, (2) the forbidden fat, (3) the fine flour, (4) the wine, and (5) the oil.

B. And six in the thank-offering [join together]: (1) the meat, (2) the forbidden fat, (3) the fine flour, (4) the wine, (5) the oil, and (6) the bread.

C. (1) Heave-offering, and (2) heave-offering of tithe, and (3) heave-offering of tithe of demai, and (4) dough-offering, and (5) first fruits join together

D. to impose a prohibition and to impose liability to the added fifth on their account.

4:3

A.   All forms of refuse join together.

B.   All forms of remnant join together.

C.   All forms of carrion join together.

D.   All forms of creeping things join together.

E.   The blood of a creeping thing and its flesh join together.

F.   A general principle did R. Joshua state, "All things that are alike in the [duration of] uncleanness of each and in the requisite measure of each join together.

G.   "[If they are alike] (1) in [duration of] uncleanness but not in requisite measure, (2) in requisite measure but not in [duration of] uncleanness, (3) neither in [duration of] uncleanness nor in requisite measure,

H.   "they do not join together [to form the volume that is necessary to convey uncleanness]."

4:4

A.   Refuse and remnant do not join together, because they are of two [different] categories.

B.   The creeping thing and carrion,

C.   and so too, carrion and the flesh of a corpse –

D.   do not join together with one another to impart uncleanness,

E.   even in accord with the lesser of the two of them,

F.   Food which has been made unclean by a Father of Uncleanness and that which has been made unclean by an Offspring of Uncleanness join together to impart uncleanness in accord with the lesser remove of uncleanness of the two of them.

4:5

A.   All foodstuffs join together –

B.   to render the body invalid, at a volume of half a half – loaf of bread;

C.   in the case of food, two meals for an erub [M. Erub. 8:21],

D.   in the volume of an olive's bulk to impart uncleanness as food,

E.   in the volume of a fig's bulk in connection with removal [from one domain to another on] the Sabbath [M. Shab. 7:4],

F.   and in the volume of a date's bulk [for the volume prohibited for eating] on the Day of Atonement [M. Yom. 8:2].

G.   All liquids join together –

H.   to render the body invalid, at a volume of a quarter-log;

I.   and for the mouthful [which it is forbidden to drink] on the Day of Atonement.

4:6

A.   Orlah-fruit and diverse kinds of the vineyard join together.

B.   R. Simeon says, "They do not join together."

C. Cloth and sacking, sacking and leather, leather and matting join together with one another.

D. R. Simeon says, "That is because they are suitable to be made unclean as that which is used for sitting [with moshab uncleanness]."

The basic principle throughout is simple: what belongs in the same category joins together, what does not does not join together. Thus: "All things that are alike in the [duration of] uncleanness of each and in the requisite measure of each join together. [If they are alike] (1) in [duration of] uncleanness but not in requisite measure, (2) in requisite measure but not in [duration of] uncleanness, (3) neither in [duration of] uncleanness nor in requisite measure, they do not join together [to form the volume that is necessary to convey uncleanness]."

30

Mishnah Tractate Meilah
Chapter Five

5:1
A.   "He who derives benefit to the extent of a *perutah's* value from that which is consecrated,

B.   "even though he did not cause deterioration [through use of it],

C.   "has committed an act of sacrilege," the words of R. Aqiba.

D.   And sages say, "Anything which is subject to deterioration through use – he has not committed an act of sacrilege unless he has caused deterioration through use.

E.   "But anything which is not subject to deterioration through use – once he has derived benefit from it, he has committed an act of sacrilege."

F.   How so?

G.   [If a woman] put a chain around her neck,

H.   a ring on her finger,

I.   drank from the cup of gold [M. Tam. 3:4B, used for water for the animal to be offered as the whole-offering of the day],

J.   once she has derived benefit from it, she has committed an act of sacrilege.

K.   [If a man] put on a shirt,

L.   covered himself with a cloak,

M.   used an ax to split wood –

N.   he has not committed sacrilege unless he has caused deterioration through use.

O.   [If] he pulled wool out of a sin-offering [lamb] when it was alive, he has committed an act of sacrilege only if he has caused deterioration.

P.   But if this was after it was dead, once he has made use of it, he has committed an act of sacrilege.

193

5:2

A.   [If] one derived benefit to the extent of a half-*perutah* and caused
         deterioration to the extent of a half-*perutah,*

B.   or [if] he derived benefit to the extent of a *perutah* from one thing
         and caused deterioration to the extent of a *perutah* in some other
         thing –

C.   lo, this one has not committed an act of sacrilege –

D.   until he will derive benefit to the extent of a *perutah* and [or]
         cause deterioration to the extent of a *perutah* in the very same
         thing.

Aqiba holds that sacrilege depends upon the user, not the thing used. In
Aqiba's view, therefore, the consideration of deterioration through use
of the object is null.   Sages maintain that if there has been
deterioriation, there has been sacrilege, and that is without regard to
whether or not the person who has caused the deterioration has
derived benefit from the object.

5:3

A.   One does not commit sacrilege after another has committed
         sacrilege [in the same thing] in the case of consecrated things,

B.   except for a beast or a utensil or service.

C.   How so [B]?

D.   [If] he rode on a beast and his fellow came along and rode on it
         and yet another came and rode on it –

E.   drank from the golden cup [M. 5:11] and his fellow came along
         and drank from it, and yet a third party came along and drank
         from it –

F.   pulled wool out of a sin-offering [M. 5:10], and his fellow came
         along and pulled wool from the sin-offering, and yet a third came
         along and pulled wool from the same sin-offering –

G.   all of them have committed an act of sacrilege.

H.   Rabbi says, "Anything which is not subject to redemption is
         subject to a case of sacrilege following sacrilege."

5:4

A.   [If] one took a stone or a beam from what is consecrated, lo, this
         one has not committed an act of sacrilege.

B.   [If] he gave it to his fellow, he has committed an act of sacrilege.

C.   But his fellow has not committed an act of sacrilege.

D.   [If] he built it into the structure of his house, lo, this one has not
         committed an act of sacrilege –

E.   until he actually will live under it [and enjoys its use] to the extent
         of a *perutah's* worth.

F.   [If] he took a *perutah* of consecrated money, lo, this one has not
         committed an act of sacrilege.

G.   [If] he gave it to his fellow, he has committed an act of sacrilege.

H.   But his fellow has not committed an act of sacrilege.

I.   [If] he gave it to a bath keeper, even though he did not take a bath, he has committed an act of sacrilege.

J.   For he [the bath keeper] says to him, "Lo, the bath is open to you. Go in and take a bath."

M. 5:3 holds that something may be subject to sacrilege or not; once it is profaned it cannot then be subjected to another act of sacrilege, since it no longer falls into the category of the sacred. But what cannot leave the status of sanctification can be subjected to successive acts of sacrilege. At M. 5:4, the same point important at M. 5:1-2 is repeated. Only the one who enjoys the benefit of the *materia sacra* is deemed liable to the penalty for violating the sacred status of the materials.

5:5

A.   What he has eaten and what his fellow has eaten,

B.   what he has used and what his fellow has used,

C.   what he has eaten and what his fellow has used,

D.   what he has used and what his fellow has eaten

E.   join together with one another –

F.   and even over an extended period of time.

The issue of connection or mixture is restated. Everything in the same classification joins together to form the requisite volume.

31

Mishnah Tractate Meilah
Chapter Six

6:1

A. The agent who carried out his errand [and thereby inadvertently committed an act of sacrilege] –

B. the householder [who appointed the agent is responsible and] has committed the act of sacrilege.

C. [If the agent] did not carry out his errand [in committing an act of sacrilege],

D. the agent [is responsible and inadvertently] has committed the act of sacrilege.

E. How so?

F. [If] he said to him, "Give out meat to the guests," but he gave them liver,

G. "Liver," and he gave them meat –

H. the agent has committed the act of sacrilege.

I. [If] he said to them, "Give them one piece each," and he [the agent] said, "Take two each," but they took three each,

J. all of them are guilty of committing an act of sacrilege.

K. [If] he said to him, "Bring [such and such a thing] from the window," or, "From the chest," and he brought it to him,

L. even though the householder said, "I meant only from here," and he brought it from there,

M. the householder has committed the act of sacrilege.

N. But if he said to him, "Bring it to me from the window," and he brought it from the chest,

O. or "From the chest," and he brought it from the window,

P. the agent has committed the act of sacrilege.

6:2

A.   [If] he sent by means of [an agent who was] a deaf-mute, an imbecile, or a minor [to purchase goods with money which unbeknownst to the sender, was consecrated],

B.   if they carried out their errand,

C.   the householder has committed the act of sacrilege.

D.   [If] they did not carry out their errand,

E.   the storekeeper has committed the act of sacrilege.

F.   [If] he sent something by means of a person of sound senses,

G.   and realized before he reached the storekeeper [that the coins are consecrated and therefore regretted having sent those coins],

H.   the storekeeper will have committed the act of sacrilege when he pays out [the coins].

I.   What should he [F-G] do?

J.   He should take a *perutah* or a utensil and state, "A *perutah* which is consecrated, wherever it may be, is made unconsecrated by this."

K.   For that which is consecrated is redeemed by money or by something which is worth money.

6:3

A.   [If] he gave him a *perutah* [and] said to him,

B.   "With half of it bring me lamps, and with half of it wicks'"

C.   and [if] he went and brought back lamps for the whole of it or wicks for the whole of it –

D.   or if he said to him, "Bring me lamps for the whole of it," or, "Wicks for the whole of it,"

E.   and he went and brought him lamps for half of it and wicks for half of it,

F.   both of them have not committed an act of sacrilege.

G.   But if he said to him, "Bring me lamps for half of it from such-and-such a place, and wicks for half of it from such-and-such a

H.   and he went and brought for him lamps from the place in which he was supposed to get the wicks, and wicks from the place from which he was supposed to get the lamps,

I.   the agent has committed the act of sacrilege.

6:4

A.   If he gave him two *perutot* [and] said to him, "Bring me an *etrog,* "

B.   and he went and brought him an etrog for a *perutah* and a pomegranate for a *perutah,*

C.   both of them have committed the act of sacrilege.

D.   R. Judah says, "The householder has not committed an act of sacrilege.

E.   "For he says to him, 'I wanted a big *etrog,* and you brought a small and poor one.' "

F.   [If] he gave him a golden denar [= six selas] [and] said to him, "Bring me a shirt,"

G.   and he went and brought him a shirt for three selas and a cloak for three,

H.   both of them have committed an act of sacrilege.

I.   R. Judah says, "The householder has not committed an act of sacrilege,

J.   "For he says to him, 'I wanted a large shirt, and you brought me a small and poor one.'"

The issue here is whether or not the agent has done what he is told. If he has, then the employer is liable, if not, then he is. The issues then concern doing what one is told. M. 6:1 has degrees of doing what one is told. How do we apportion responsibility for sacrilege inadvertently committed upon the consecrated meet? The householder is liable, since his orders have been carried out; the agent is responsible; and here the guests also are responsible for the third piece, that is, sages vis à vis Judah at M. 6:4. Judah wants the exact orders of the employer to be carried out to the letter, or the employer is exempt from the consequences. M. 6:2 introduces the consideration of inadvertence. Once the employer realizes he has sent a consecrated coin, he is no longer responsible for sacrilege, which must be wholly unintentional. The agent is not responsible. The storekeeper inadvertently misappropriates sacred property and is liable when he uses the coin. M. 6:3 asks about the matter of joining or mixing, that is, the agent has misappropriated property to the value of a half *perutah,* and the employer's instructions are carried out to the extent of a half *perutah.* M. 6:4 then sets out the pertinent positions.

6:5

A   He who deposits coins with a money changer –

B.   if they were bound up, he [the money changer] should not make use of them.

C.   Therefore if he paid [them] out, he has committed an act of sacrilege.

D.   If they are loose, he may make use of them.

E.   Therefore if he paid them out, he has not committed an act of sacrilege.

F.   [If the owner of the coins] deposited [them] with a householder,

G.   one way or the other, he [the householder] should not make use of them.

H.   Therefore if he paid them out, he has committed an act of sacrilege.

I.   "A storekeeper is deemed equivalent to a householder," the words of R. Meir.

J.   R. Judah says, "He is equivalent to a money changer."

The money-changer is ordinarily permitted to use coins, and if among them are coins that are consecrated, the money-changer is responsible. But if he is ordinarily not permitted to use the money and does so, he is not responsible.

6:6

A.   A *perutah* which has been consecrated, which fell into a purse [containing other money],

B.   or if one said, "A *perutah* in this purse is consecrated" –

C.   "as soon as one has paid out the first [coin in the purse],

D.   "he has committed an act of sacrilege," the words of R. Aqiba.

E.   And sages say, "[He has not committed an act of sacrilege] until he has paid out all the money in the purse."

F.   And R. Aqiba concedes in the case of one who says, "A *perutah* in this purse is consecrated," that he goes along and pays out the money [without having committed an act of sacrilege] until he will have paid out all the money which is in the purse.

At what point is liability to sacrilege incurred? Aqiba holds that as soon as one coin out of the pouched is used, since it may be the holy one, the user is guilty of sacrilege. Sages want all the coins to be used before we regard sacrilege as having been committed. Here we deal with the issue of probability.

Part Three

A HYPOTHESIS ON
THE MISHNAH'S METHOD AND MESSAGE

32

The Philosophical Issues of Mishnah Tractates Uqsin, Orlah, Besah, Qiddushin, and Meilah

Let us now summarize our findings and so present the hypothesis that we seek. I now answer these questions:

What are the philosophical issues that occur?

What proportion of the several tractates is devoted to issues of general intelligibility?

For each of the five tractates, I catalogue in the same order the philosophical issues I have identified. These are four: the physics of mixtures, encompassing issues of classification and connection; intention and action; potentiality and actuality; rules for the resolution of questions of doubt. (This last item does not seem to me indubitably philosophical, and I several times have expressed some puzzlement on the classification of these rules.) I further list those paragraphs, or pericopes, in which I cannot identify any philosophical principle subject to generalization. Finally, I give an estimate of the philosophical quotient of each tractate, that is to say, a rough guess as to the extent to which a given tractate has centered its discussion on issues of a philosophical character, narrowly defined.

i. Uqsin

1. Mixtures and Taxonomy. The Issue of Classification.

M. Uqs. 1:1: The three relationships of substances to one another: wholly distinct, C, wholly mixed and united, B, and partly joined, partly autonomous, A. This is, of course, a theory of mixtures. Also: M. Uqs. 1:2, 3, 4, 5, 6, 2:1, 2:2, 2:3, 2:4, 2:5, 2:6, 2:7, 2:8, 2:9, 2:10.

M. 3:5: Can something be deemed food for one purpose but not food for some other purpose? Yes, says Aqiba; no, says Yohanan b. Nuri. The same traits that classify in object in one respect classify it in all other respects; and the same decision as to classification for one purpose must apply for all purposes. Also: M. 3:6, 3:7.

2. *The Issue of Intention*

M. 2:1: If the merchant wants the hair, it is deemed connected, and if not, it is deemed null. If the one who did the pickling deemed the leaves merely for the sake of ornament, then the leaves are not regarded as part of the plant. Hence the attitude or intentionality of the owner of the produce is taken into account when we assess whether or not an extrinsic part of the produce is regarded as joined with the main part or is deemed not a component of it at all.

Also: M. 2:5: If the man began to pull the produce apart, we have no reason to suppose that the process of disconnection will inevitably continue; therefore only the food actually taken apart is deemed disconnected. Hence we dismiss the potentiality of what one may do, even though one's intention is to do exactly that; we take account only of what one actually has done.

Also: M. 2:6; 2:10: Since we do not take account of whether the roots have penetrated but only can penetrate, both at A and, conversely, also at B (the pot with the hole), the issue here is whether the potential is deemed actual, and it is.

M. 3:1: There are things which require preparation by the application of liquid, to be made susceptible to uncleanness, but not intention to be deemed edible, intention but not preparation, neither, both. Also: M. 3:2, 3, M. 3:9.

M. 3:4: Once dill has imparted its flavor, it has carried out that for which it is intended and is no longer susceptible to uncleanness as food. The issue of intentionality remains decisive.

3. *Potentiality and Actuality*

The entire issue of intention forms a subset of the larger question of the relationship of the potential to the actual. For attitude or intention remains in the realm of potentiality, until a concrete action brings it to realization. But since, for the tractate at hand (and for the entire Mishnah) these matters come to representation each in its own rubric, we shall keep them separate in these catalogues. Ishmael's position at M. 2:2 introduces not how things are but how they can be. The issue here then is potentiality. If the meat can potentially spread around the bone, we treat it as though it were spread around the bone.

M. 3:2-3: The question of the location of carrion, e.g., in markets, in villages with Jewish populations only, in towns with mixed populations, involves the potentiality of whether or not food can be deemed edible. In a Jewish village, there is no such potentiality, hence the issue of prevailing intent is null. In towns, where gentiles, who eat anything, live, there is that potentiality, and that is taken into account.

M. 3:4: Sprouts of the service tree are potentially edible, when sweetened. But they are not susceptible to uncleanness until they are sweetened. Only when the potentiality has been realized does their status change.

M. 3:8: The issue is whether we deem what must happen as if it already has happened. One position is that while living things are insusceptible, since the fish, once caught, will inevitably perish, it is deemed as if dead now, and susceptibility to uncleanness as food begins as soon as the fish is in the net. The other says that what is inevitably going to happen is not deemed to have happened until it actually will have taken place. M. 3:[10+]11 has already been explained in this same context.

4. The Rules for Dealing with Cases of Doubt

No instances.

5. No Clear Philosophical Issue

Mishnah-Tractate Uqsin: M. 3:10. This is included for redactional reasons.

6. Is Uqsin Philosophical?

One-sidedly so. Mishnah-tractate Uqsin contains 26 pericopes (counting M. 3:10-11 as a single), all of them covering the philosophical issues catalogued above.

ii. Orlah

1. Mixtures and Taxonomy. The Issue of Classification.

The issue of taxonomy is present at M. 1:1, where we distinguish parts of a tree by reference to the function or use to which each part is put. Hence the indicator for taxonomic purposes is the plan of the farmer for the tree or for parts of the tree. M. 1:6 works out the proportion at which two distinct bodies of material, one prohibited, one permitted, are deemed such that the permitted overwhelms the prohibited by its greater volume. It is at a proportion of two hundred to one that we deem the prohibited to be nullified and wholly absorbed into the traits of the permitted. This can take place even when the intention is to accomplish exactly that purpose. M. 1:7 further takes up the question of mixtures. If one curdles milk with the sap of an *orlah*-tree, the milk is forbidden; so the sap imparts its status to the entire mixture. The issue is the classification of the sap. What is like fruit is fruit; what is not like fruit is not. The like follows the rule of the like, so M. 1:7-8. At stake here is whether sap is like fruit, that is, falls into the classification thereof. The same principle of classification of like under the like rule is expressed at M. 1:9.

Chapter Two as a whole is devoted to the issue of how prohibited produce affects mixtures (Essner, p. 123). The basic point throughout is fundamental to mixtures of the first of the three kinds: complete and undifferentiated, so that a single rule applies to the whole. It is, as I said in context, that it is possible to absorb a quantity of a substance of one kind within the body of a quantity of a substance of another classification, so that the mixture is complete, and the traits of the larger quantity of the substance are imparted to the mixture as a whole. This is made explicit at M. 2:1-3. The issue is "joining together," which is to say, accomplishing a complete and unadulterated mixture, so that the traits attaching to the substance that is the greater in volume now apply to the whole. If the prohibited, however, serves to flavor or leaven the food, it has then imparted its character to the whole, and hence also its status. Also: M. 2:4, 5, 6, 7, 8, 9, 10, 11, 12, 13, 14, 15, 16, 17. M. 2:10 adds that spices join together to render forbidden that which they flavor. Here we treat as a single classification diverse spices, each subject to its own prohibition; they form a common mixture because of two traits: all are subject to a prohibition, and all impart something of a flavor to the whole. M. 2:11-12+13 assess the status of the components of leaven. Eliezer maintains that prohibited and permitted leaven are deemed to fall into the same category as that attaching to the portion of the leaven that completed the volume required to raise the bread; sages take the view that only if the prohibited leaven by itself is sufficient do we deem that leaven to impart its status to the whole. So Eliezer takes account of a process of mixing, the leaven mixing together, then mixing with the dough as a whole. He further asks which portion of the mixed leaven has made it possible for the whole portion to do its job, that is to say, he takes account of the result of the mixture, not merely the traits, as to volume, thereof. The same issue is at M. 2:15-17, but expressed in different terms. So the entire chapter works out the rules governing mixtures.

M. 3:1, 2, 3, 4, 5, 6, 7, 8 go over the same principle of neutralization. The details need not detain us, since the same point is made throughout and simply applied over again. The main point of interest is Meir's view that what is distinct cannot be deemed part of a mixture, and sages hold that everything can form a mixture with everything else, except for six specified items. All have something in their nature that makes them distinct (Essner, p. 138). Merely because human beings treat an item as distinct is no reason to hold it cannot form a mixture in the requisite proportion.

2. The Issue of Intention

M. 1:1 takes up the power of intention unaccompanied by deed. But the use of the lumber will be decisive. If one merely makes such a statement, it bears no consequences until the statement is carried out, at which point the taboo will or will not apply. At M. 1:2 the intention of the tree – for public use – removes the tree from the taboo. This is consistent with the foregoing. More to the point, only if the farmer intends to plant the tree and does plant it do the considerations of the taboo come into play. The entire working of the system depends upon the farmer's planting the tree on ground that he owns in the holy land. Outside of that framework the law is null.

3. Potentiality and Actuality

M. 1:3: We take account not of the actual event, but only of the possibility of the event's occurring. Only the possible, and not the actual, survival is taken into account. M. 1:4 likewise assesses the matter by appeal not to the actuality but the potentiality of the tree's survival. M. 1:5 maintains that even though the sunken root can have lived on its own, it is deemed part of the original tree as long as it is attached to it. We here ignore the potentiality and take account only of the actuality.

4. The Rules for Dealing with Cases of Doubt

Where there is a conflict between two or more principles, or where there is doubt as to the facts of the case, regular and orderly rules are spelled out on how to deal with such a matter. These rules are not ad hoc and particular to a case, nor do they appeal to the outcome of the case. They are general rules that can apply everywhere. M. 3:9 is the only such case thus far. Here we have to work out the rule governing matters of doubt. At stake is whether we rule stringently or leniently. Then the rule tells us the answer to that question: in the Holy Land, stringently, nearby, moderately, outside, leniently.

5. No Clear Philosophical Issue

I see no composition of a paragraph or more which does not deal with one of the identified philosophical problems above.

6. Is Orlah Philosophical?

The authorship of Mishnah-tractate Orlah has focused upon the issue of mixtures. Other philosophical principles come into play. The tractate as a whole at no point focuses upon a question that lies beyond principles of general intelligibility, gives no rule that cannot be explained by appeal to a principle that transcends that rule, or otherwise provides merely ad hoc laws lacking relevance to an important philosophical question. The treatment of mixtures is a fine example of what I mean by calling the Mishnah an exercise in practical logic and applied reason, but, more than that, at stake is not merely the mode of correct thought, which can apply as much to theology, exegesis of Scripture, or applying legal principles to legal cases, but the principles that govern a considerable area of *philosophical* interest, in this case, mixtures. It is not enough to identify the presence of rules that transcend cases; we have to show, and in later work I shall show, what is already adumbrated here, which is that the particular principles that are expressed in the cases are distinctively philosophical, and, as I have said elsewhere in these pages, will have been understood as philosophical by other philosophers properly acquainted with the idiom.

iii. Besah

1. Mixtures and Taxonomy. The Issue of Classification.

At M. 1:1 we ask about classifying the egg and the chicken. Is the egg under the rule governing the chicken? Or is it deemed a distinct entity? The House of Shammai classify the egg under the rule governing the dam. The dam is deemed ready, so is the egg. The House of Hillel regard the egg as distinct from the dam. When it is born, it follows its own rule. The egg was not available prior to the festival, so, in it is not permitted on the festival itself. There was no prior act of designation or preparation of the egg for use on the holy day.

The classification of actions is at stake as well. Is the scriptural reference to cooking taxonomic and exemplary or ad hoc and exclusionary? Do we regard the act of cooking as broadly analogous such that all acts connected with cooking are permitted as well? Or do we regard cooking as narrowly analogous, so that only acts that are directly connected with cooking are acceptable on the festival-day? At M. 1:5-6, M. 1:7-9+10, 2:4-5, 2:6-7, the House of Hillel take an inclusionary view, permitting all actions that fall within the basic classification of cooking; the House of Shammai take an exclusionary view, permitted only actions connected with cooking itself. So the interpretation of a metaphor is at stake: broadly classificatory or not taxonomic at all. The House of Shammai do not regard the reference to cooking as taxonomic but specific to itself, and the House of Hillel regard "cooking" as a taxon, covering everything that falls into a single class of actions, connected with food preparation. The debate as to whether a scriptural reference is exclusionary or inclusionary – a particular case or an example of a larger classification of actions – is at M. 1:2 as well.

The other side of the argument concerning exclusion and inclusion within the classification of food-preparation is at M. 3:1-2. Hunting is not involved in food-preparation; therefore preparation of food on the festival excludes an act of hunting. M. 3:3 places another limitation; if there is no usable meat on a beast, on the festival it may not be slaughtered for use, and, moreover, there has also to be time to roast and actually eat a piece of the meat. That is an important exclusionary rule. M. 3:4 (+ 5) is in line with this exclusionary pattern. M. 3:6-8 then distinguish what is part of the process of food-preparation from what is not.

Chapter Four, in particular M. 4:1-5, develops this same issue of excluding some actions and including others within the classification of food-preparation. Some must be done in a manner different from the ordinary way, so as to signify that the act is in connection with preparing food under a special set of rules. Some may not be done at all, e.g., for the former, moving food from here to there, chopping wood, and, for the latter, making utensils for use on the festival in connection with food preparation, building a stove, and the like. See also M. 4:6-7. M. 5:1 adds the detail that within food preparation falls the protection of food from spoilage.

At M. 2:1 we deal with the problem of keeping separate three classifications of time and their rules, an ordinary day, the festival, and the Sabbath. On the second of the three, one may keep; on the third, not. One also may not prepare on the festival food for the Sabbath. This would correspond to that classification in which we do not deem mixed or joined two classes of things that are utterly separate. In this case, what is kept separate are two distinct sanctities, the one of the festival, the other, the Sabbath. Both fall into the single genus, holy time, but each forms a distinct species within that genus, festival sanctity, Sabbath sanctity, respectively. However, an act legitimate on the former may produce results acceptable for the latter. The time is kept separate. Food that is legitimate on the one day remains in the category of permitted food, so permitted on the other day. So this is a very intricate exercise in the making of distinctions and in classification. The appeal to the distinction among sanctities, on the one side, and the single and undifferentiated character of permitted food, on the other, accounts for the two-dimensional definition of the problem, resulting in the simple view that to begin with, one may not prepare food on the festival for the Sabbath, so one cannot begin to do cooking on the festival-day for use on the Sabbath. But if one has begun the cooking-process before that time, he or she may continue to do so. Note also M. 2:6-7, 8.

M. 2:2-3 make the point that water unites completely even through the slightest form of contact. No elaborate process of mixing is required to make of two bodies of water a single body.

M. 2:9, 10 distinguish the parts of a utensil, maintaining that each part is susceptible to uncleanness on its own count. Hence we classify the parts of the utensil differently and so regard them, for that reason, as autonomous entities. Consequently, if one part is rendered insusceptible, e.g., by being broken and so made useless, the other parts remain entirely susceptible, each on its own. There is no mixture whatsoever, and the distinctions among the parts derive from the diverse traits that characterize each part, e.g., something is a receptacle, something is a metal utensil, something is a sieve, and all in the same pepper-mill.

M. 5:2 presents an exercise in the classification of diverse acts in respect to the requirement of Sabbath-rest. These are in three categories: acts for which people are liable on grounds of Sabbath-rest, optional acts, and acts that are religious duties. An optional act may be postponed; a religious duty is not done; and acts of the first category are of course to be penalized. There is no distinction between the Sabbath and festival-days in regard to this classification, and that is an important point in establishing the grid on which this tractate works so mightily. Thus the act of preparation of food in the end is set apart from all other actions; that act alone is permitted on the festival but prohibited on the Sabbath. All other acts that are prohibited on the Sabbath are also prohibited on the festival. Placing this item at the end of the tractate provides a fine conclusion to the taxonomic exercise that occupies so large a portion of the tractate. M. 5:3-5, 6, 7 classify the status of what belongs to a person, e.g., as to location. This is a secondary expansion of the interest in classification of things and persons, now introducing the spatial consideration.

2. *The Issue of Intention*

M. 1:2 (also M. 1:5-6) takes up the definition of the inclusionary or exclusionary character of intentionality. The House of Shammai at M. 1:2 maintain that one's intentionality is general, covering whatever is required for the accomplishment of one's basic purpose. The House of Hillel take an exclusionary view and regard as subject to one's intentionality only the specific action that one has contemplated in advance, not the ancillary actions associated therewith. Note also M. 1:3. Now the House of Hillel dissociate action from intention, and the House of Shammai regard a concrete action as required in the expression of intentionality. M. 1:4 underlines this that the ones that are taken are the ones that were actually designated on the prior day.

M. 2:3C, D, one's purpose in immersing utensils affects matters. If one has immersed utensils intending to make use of them for one purpose and then decides to use them for some other, the utensils require a second immersion.

M. 3:2 raises the issue of designation, that is, explicit expression of intention. If one has not explicitly expressed intention concerning a particular item, that item is deemed unavailable for use on the festival-day, even though one might in general have wanted that category of item. Hence intention must be specific to the item that is supposed to be affected (here: permitted for use) by the act of intention. This same question is in play at M. 4:3, where one has not designated the beams in advance of the festival for use on the festival in cooking food. This intervenes between the potentiality for such use and the actuality of using the wood for that purpose. At M. 4:6, 7, Eliezer regards as adequately designated for use in advance an object that can serve a variety of purposes; any of these purposes is permitted, even when not signified in advance. M. 5:7 makes this same point, that there should be a prior act of designation, now in connection with the transport of food. If the owner has in advance of the festival assigned ownership of food to his guests, then they may carry that food home; but if not, they may not do so.

3. *Potentiality and Actuality*

M. 1:1 takes up the issue of whether we regard what is going to happen as though it already has happened, or whether we interpret a potentiality as tantamount to an actuality. M. 1:3 addresses the issue of whether a concrete action is required along with an inchoate expression of intentionality. The House of Shammai require an action to express in a concrete way whatever intention one has formed. M. 1:9 has the Shammaites take the view that the food must be ready for consumption on the festival-day; the House of Hillel regard it as adequate if the food is potentially edible on that day.

Even though, M. 3:2, we know that the nets for trapping a wild beast, fowl, or fish, set on the eve of the festival-day, enjoy the potentiality of trapping such a thing on the festival-day itself, one may not use such things as are caught, unless one knows for sure that they were caught prior to the festival-day. What is not designated in advance is not available for use. From our perspective, the interesting angle is that what is potential is not deemed as actual.

The consideration of designating in advance one's intention of using on the festival an object for food-preparation contains within itself the consideration of the realization of the potential. Even though wood bears the potential of legitimate use, unless one has taken steps to indicate his intention of actually doing so, we do not take account of that generalized and inchoate potentiality. For a potentiality to be deemed affective, it must be treated as explicit and in a particular way. At M. 4:6-7, Eliezer takes the opposite view. Designation is general, and the object's diverse potential uses, e.g., wood-splinters which can be used for burning or for a toothpick, sweeping which can be used for a fire but may not have been so designated. We accept as valid in connection with cooking on the festival a variety of potential uses without insisting that in advance someone signify precisely which purpose the object is going to serve. The conception of the power of what is merely potential then is different from the one that limits the affective potential to what is virtually actualized.

4. *The Rules for Dealing with Cases of Doubt*

Where we have a case of doubt, M. 1:4A-E, we allow the laws of probability to dictate the outcome. Where probability is that the two that are found are among an original three, then the two are permitted; where three are found and two were designated, they are prohibited, for we do not know for sure that that which of the three that were designated are the two that are found. The significant side is the former of the two cases.

5. *No Clear Philosophical Issue*

M. 1:1D-E: how much leaven is prohibited on Passover?

6. *Is Besah Philosophical?*

This is a philosophically very rich tractate, since a broad repertoire of issues of principle and correct procedure is explored in the distinct cases. The case of the chicken and the egg, M. 1:1, signals the principal interests of the tractate: how do we classify things that are distinct but related? how do we deal with the issue of the potential as against the actual? Between these two questions, we can find a place for most of the specific rulings of the tractate. The classification-process covers both exclusion and inclusion, and that is part of the larger exposition of the taxonomic principle in play. The interplay of intention and designation is a secondary development.

iv. Qiddushin

1. *Mixtures and Taxonomy. The Issue of Classification.*

An exercise of hierarchization by appeal to traits inherent in the various classifications to be set into relationship, the exercise as a whole organizes information and transforms the data into a set of propositions – a deeply philosophical act. For at stake here is more than ordering and regularization of chaotic facts. It is the interest in the meanings of facts, why things are one way, rather than some other, why this, not that. And that attitude of mind, yielding what we now call science, begins in hierarchical classification. The philosophical achievement at M. 1:1ff. is to collect and arrange in a coherent and intelligible manner diverse and otherwise unrelated facts. This is done by drawing into alignment, hence into a hierarchy, the diverse parties, on the one side, and the diverse facts, on the other. M. 1:7-8 presents six items on the liability of two classes of persons, women and men, to diverse kinds of commandments, which are then the predicate for the second construction. M. 1:9+10 finally places into correct order the Land of Israel and other lands. I identify a profoundly philosophical mode of presenting information aimed at establishing an important proposition. For the upshot of the taxonomic exercise is hierarchization, and the setting forth of the relative positions of women, slaves, cattle, and property, on the one side, and men and women, on the other, surely constitutes an argument and a proposition, not merely a neutral repertoire of facts. And I should claim that all hierarchical exercises yield propositions of an imposing order indeed.

M. 2:1A-C deals with hierarchization of man and woman as to betrothals, then the matter of connection, as explained in context. M. 2:1D-I proceed to establish the rule of connection or mixture as it pertains to this case. The conception of joining together or connection is worked out now in terms of spatial or temporal contiguity, e.g., "if all of them together...," and "if she was eating them one by one...."

M. 4:1-8 present yet another exercise in classification, now of castes signified by marital rights. The hierarchization yields a set of overlapping ranks, 1-3, 2-6, 5-10, and that presents us with a different sort of mixing, though the main point is in the classification and hierarchization. Note also M. 4:4-7, which expand on this same matter and add secondary points concerning the consequences of violating the caste taboos as to marriage.

2. The Issue of Intention

M. 2:2-3 introduce the notion that intention or attitude bears upon the fulfillment of the stipulations of an agreement. Simeon takes the view that if a deception is intended for the advantage of the deceived party, then it is a valid one, and that means that he tempers the strict requirements of meeting the conditions of a contract with the consideration of attitude or intention as a countervailing force. That that is what is under debate is shown at M. 2:3, where the opposite viewpoint is introduced. At M. 2:4D, if the instruction is to betrothe the woman, and that is accompanied by information as to her location, then the intent has no bearing on the location of the woman. But, M. 2:4A, where the instruction bears clear evidence that the location of the woman forms a part of the intent, then she is not. So we do introduce the consideration of attitude into the interpretation of contracts, this one between the agent and the source of the agency. At M. 2:6 the intention of the donor plays a role in our interpretation of the result. At M. 2:7's case, we interpret the attitude of the other parties to the transaction in assessing the outcome. M. 2:8 pursues the application of attitude and intention (the issue of inadvertent or advertent action) to the use of Holy Things in a betrothal. Everything depends here upon intentionality.

The language of M. 3:2-3+4 (and see also M. 3:6) introduces conditions which in fact are deemed to state intentions. If someone says, "On condition that I do such and so," that is deemed a condition that the person intends to meet, and hence, the statement is valid and the intention is fully taken into account. This is in contrast with M. 3:1, where an intention to take an act at a specified time is deemed null, not a potentiality worth considering. The betrothal takes effect forthwith, and we take for granted the condition will be met. The issue of intention is modified by the matter of responsibility; if there is deceit that has produced an incorrect attitude, then the action that results is null; but if there is no deceit, then the mere fact that a person intended something that was not realized by itself does not nullify the action.

3. Potentiality and Actuality

I think that M. 3:1's case involves a consideration of the potential and the actual, for reasons specified *ad loc.* What someone says he will do does not establish a potentiality that is taken into account. M. 3:5E-I addresses potentialities that we do not deem worthy of consideration. Even though the death is inevitable, it has not taken place. More to the point, these events not only have not happened but do not lie in the control of the man or the woman. They may come about; but they cannot be brought about solely by the person in question. Here then is a limit on the effect of potentiality. But then 3:5J-M we contrast what may or may not come about with what must come about. Here is a potentiality – the pregnancy – that is certain to be realized.

4. The Rules for Dealing with Cases of Doubt

M. 3:7-9 work out how we deal with betrothals that may or may not have taken place. Essentially, where we cannot resolve matters, we assume that there may have been a betrothal, so that the affected parties must conduct a divorce-procedure. But we do not assume there may have been a betrothal such that we confirm the marriage. Where the one who is in doubt can bring about the situation he says he thinks he has already established, we take him at his word; where not, we dismiss him, so M. 3:8. In all instances we avoid allowing unsubstantiated testimony that is subject to doubt to produce consequences. Where we have conflicted testimony, we believe each party as to himself or herself, but not as to the other. We therefore resolve doubts by taking account of a variety of possibilities but by avoiding a decision that is not made on firm grounds. Whether or not these form principles for resolving cases of doubt beyond the specific subject-matter before us is readily settled. We have a clear policy and a program that will govern a variety of types of cases: believe what you must, doubt the rest and take no action other than on the basis of well-sorted-out facts.

At M. 4:8 we accept in a case of doubt the testimony of someone who can accomplish in the future what he claims has happened in the past, but, otherwise, we reject such testimony. In this case the father cannot in the future do anything to discredit the caste-status of the offspring, so what he says about the past is null. When both parents make the same allegation, Judah maintains we have no case of doubt at all. At M. 4:10-11 the resolution of doubt rests upon establishing the main point, in which case the secondary point is held to be worked out as well. When the mother's status is clear, the children's is not in doubt. When the mother's status is not established, then the children's status is subject to demonstration.

5. No Clear Philosophical Issue

I see no clear philosophical concern at M. 2:7A-C. The issues at M. 2:9-10 work out the status of various consecrated or forbidden objects. I see no point at which any philosophical issue is worked out in the concrete cases at hand. At stake is the extent to which a person owns the objects or materials under discussion, and that is measured by what the rules governing his right to dispose of them. These are legal issues that, so far as I can discern, lack philosophical implications.

M. 3:12-13 seem to me a fine example of a set of rules that serve within the system and that allow the settlement of a variety of specific cases. But these rules bear no implications beyond themselves and do not allow us to work out matters not particular to the subject at hand. Hence when we speak of rules that are of an other-than-philosophical character, here is an excellent example.

M. 4:9's point, that where the agent's act is valid and the initiator's act is also valid, we simply decide the conflicting actions by reference to whose action came first, is a useful and broadly applied rule, but I see no philosophical issue to which it refers. It seems to me no more than a common-sense disposition of a classification of cases of a single sort: first come, first served. If there are profound philosophical issues inherent in that rule, I do not perceive them.

M. 4:12-14 present sayings about appropriate conduct between men and women, suitable choices for trades, and Torah-study. None of the statements here generates a principle that can pertain to an altogether-unrelated case. We have here theological statements, moral principles, immutable truths, and the like, but no philosophy in method or in medium, because nothing in these pericopes is accessible of generalization.

6. Is Qiddushin Philosophical?

The answer to this question is less compelling than for the first three tractates. I find for the matters of taxonomic hierarchization and the matter of intention no doubt that at stake are philosophical issues, philosophically analyzed. The same claim is hardly so strong for the third rubric, potentiality and actuality. The rules for cases of doubt come perilously close to examples of mere common sense: we simply rely on such evidence as we have, and avoid resolving issues where there is no evidence. But by the criterion by which a rule becomes philosophical – availability for application elsewhere or "generalizability," – I think that we may stand on the philosophical side of the boundary, but not far from the line. If we count up the total of pericopes, then, we have in the four chapters 47 in all. Of these, 9 cannot be read as concretizations of philosophical principles, nearly 20 percent of the whole. I see 29 as assuredly philosophical – that is, the items catalogued in Nos. 1, 2, 3 above, or just over 60 percent of the whole. The other 20 percent are less certainly classified. In the balance, the tractate is more general and philosophical than legal, particular, and ad hoc. If we treat as problems of classification matters of doubt as well as the items in list No. 1, then just as Orlah concerns classification and Besah classification and the interplay of potentiality and actuality, so Qiddushin may be deemed a tractate with a primary concern for classification: mixture and the sorting out of mixture. That judgment is assuredly justified by reference to Chapters One, Three and Four. But by contrast to Uqsin, Orlah, and Besah, it is less philosophical and more legal.

v. Meilah

1. Mixtures and Taxonomy. The Issue of Classification.

M. 1:1's main point, that whatever for a single moment has been permissible for priestly use, that is, whatever sacrifice has had its blood properly tossed, even though afterward invalidated for some reason, is not subject to the laws of sacrilege, makes a basic point on classification. It is this. If two traits are antithetical, then if the one is present, the other cannot be present. The laws of sacrilege apply, so that the use by the priesthood or commoners of a beast is prohibited, then God owns the beast. Once God's interest in the beast is fulfilled, then the beast is no longer subject to sacrilege, and, it follows, mortals – priests, commoners – may exercise their rights. Then whatever is done to the beast may be incorrect, but it is not sacrilege. So the two opposites – holy, therefore subject to the laws of sacrilege, profane, therefore not subject to the laws of sacrilege – are shown to be incompatible and mutually exclusive, a fundamental point of classification indeed. The reason the point is important is that it excludes the possibility of a hierarchy of sacrilege and, in the present matter, imposes a severe limitation on the possibilities of hierarchization, invoking, rather, the principle of either this or that but not both in measure. This matter is worked out further at M. 1:2-3, but the discussion concerns only details. The main point established at M. 1:1 is not expanded. M. 1:4 makes this same point that if we invoke trait A, then trait A' cannot be present, and if we invoke trait A', then trait A cannot be present; not only so, but these are explicitly treated as opposites. If we have a lenient ruling in one matter, we have a strict rule in the opposite, and vice versa. I cannot think of a more striking way of expressing the rule of opposites. Then the whole of Chapter Two (M. 2:1-9) restates this same principle, in terms of nine cases. Once the sacrifice is made, one set of prohibitions apply. Once the blood is tossed, a different set of prohibitions come into play. The cessation of the process is specified, e.g., a beast to which the priests lay no claim exits the system when the corpse is fully burned to cinder on the altar. The entire composition seems to me to amplify and extend the basic principle of opposites, though the principle is also muddied by the intrusion of four stages. But these prove immaterial to the basic point of M. 1:1-4. That is why I classify M. 2:1-9 as essentially external to all philosophical thought and discourse. In my view M. 5:3-4 make the same point: something may be subject to sacrilege or not; once it is profaned it cannot then be subjected to another act of sacrilege, since it no longer falls into the category of the sacred.

A second important issue of classification has to do with how we deal with mixtures. In this case, the mixture is an interstitial category, which does not belong wholly on one or in another of two simple classes. In Chapter Three, at M. 3:2-3, 4, 5, 6, 7, we address the issue of cultic property or material that is not subject to the laws of sacrilege but that also may not be used for secular purposes, that is, "not available for secular use but the laws of sacrilege do not apply." The status may be conferred on different counts, e.g., M. 3:5ff., because something cannot be used on the altar but nonetheless has been designated for God, hence sanctified. The issue then is how to dispose of such classes of things. Now this chapter works out what Chapter One has not led us to anticipate, which is, an excluded middle. We thought that something was either one thing or the opposite. But now we have something that is not one thing but also is not the opposite. The sequence – first, something is either one thing or the opposite, then, something may be neither one thing nor the opposite – is absolutely necessary. Reversing the order of the abstract propositions yields no sense. If we are told, something may be neither one thing nor the opposite, we have no principle of consequence; nothing is alleged. It is only with the allegation of Chapter One that the modification of Chapter Three takes on argumentative valence and propositional force. And that seems to me a strong argument that a first-class philosophical mind has determined on the correct order of the exposition, in the details before us, of the important principles of classification that are in hand. Then Simeon's point, M. 3:3, forms a paradox, a problem not covered by the propositions of Chapters One or Three. And that, I think, accounts for the location of the passage here, something that made little sense to me in my original commentary (*A History of the Mishnaic Law of Holy Things* [Leiden: E. J. Brill, 1980] 5:104, 110-111).

Now if we deal with the unmiscibility of substances of diverse, hence opposed, indicative traits, and then if we ask about interstitial cases, can mixtures be far behind? Indeed not! And Chapter Four introduces the case of mixtures, that is, the forming of connections between substances that fall into different and even opposed classifications. Once again, the logical order of the exposition of the philosophical principles of the tractate is compelling and necessary; no other order is possible, if we are to have sense. That the principle of mixtures, not the problem of sacrilege, is primary is stunningly demonstrated by Chapter Four. (I read with genuine astonishment my statement in *Holy Things* 5:124, "The conceptual aridity of the foregoing chapter [referring to Chapter Four] contrasts with the interesting propositions laid before us in the present and following ones [Five and Six, chapters I now see are simply replays of the conceptual principles of the earlier parts of the tractate!]") Only M. 4:1 deals with mixtures of consecrated materials; it asks how these join together or are connected so as to form the requisite volume of material for the law of sacrilege to apply. The remainder of the chapter consists of a sequence of statements, M. 4:2-6, listing things that do or do not join together to form the requisite volume for various purposes, none of them dealing with sacrilege. Hence the principle of mixture and connection, not the case of sacrilege, predominates. The basic principle of mixing is that different categories do not join together, but like categories do – which is to say, the obverse of the principle of M. 1:1! This is stated explicitly in the following language: "All things that are alike in the [duration of] uncleanness of each and in the requisite measure of each join together. [If they are alike] (1) in [duration of] uncleanness but not in requisite measure, (2) in requisite measure but not in [duration of] uncleanness, (3) neither in [duration of] uncleanness nor in requisite measure, they do not join together [to form the volume that is necessary to convey uncleanness]." M. 5:5 goes over the same principle.

2. The Issue of Intention

This is implicit at M. 1:1 in the consideration of the inappropriate intention of the officiating priest, but it is not a principal and generative conception for the composition.

M. 4:1 is clear that if one's attitude toward a substance is that the substance is null, then if one utilizes that substance for a private purpose though it is holy, he has not violated the laws of sacrilege. So the attitude of the person is principal in determining whether or not to invoke the laws of sacrilege. If something is not valued by the person who uses it, then that thing is not subject to sacrilege, even though it is intrinsically holy. Then holiness depends also upon attitude. This is a firm fact in the present pericope. But it is not a principal proposition here.

M. 5:1 maintains that sacrilege depends upon the one who does it, not upon the thing to which it is done. That is to say, the category of sacrilege is invoked by the attitude of the person responsible for dealing with a given bit of *materia sacra*. If that person derives benefit from the thing, even without doing injury to it, he has committed sacrilege. That is Aqiba's conception, and it makes attitude the governing consideration. Sages reject this view, and therefore consider null the issue of attitude, regarding sacrilege as intrinsic to the *materia sacra*. M. 5:4 makes the same point. The same point is made throughout M. 6:1-4, 5. Sacrilege is an inadvertent action to begin with; it cannot be done with intention. Misappropriation of *materia sacra* done intentionally is under a different rubric from sacrilege. Now the issue here is whether or not the agent has done what he is told. If he has, then the employer is liable, if not, then he is. The issues then concern doing what one is told.

3. Potentiality and Actuality

The conception at M. 1:1 is that while the beast may potentially, or even actually, be mishandled, we do not take account of that potentiality, once the blood has been properly tossed, seems to me not a decisive consideration in the formation of this composition. But Aqiba's position at M. 1:2-3 does rest on a judgment as to the relationship of potentiality and actuality. Aqiba's position is that while the potentiality of making an offering of the meat that has been removed from the courtyard is not present, the actuality, that blood has been properly tossed for part of the offering, is taken into account. That is all that registers, with the result that we ignore the potential – here, that we cannot deal with the meat that has been removed from the courtyard at all – but deal only with the actual, which is the blood of the meat that has been left in the courtyard and so not invalidated, and which has been tossed. The parallel to the duplicated sin-offering makes this point still stronger; the beast designated as an exchange for the lost beast is not going to be offered. There is no potential for doing so, since the lost beast has now been found. Nonetheless, we deem the disposition of the blood of the valid beast, the one that was lost and then recovered, to cover the status of the beast that has no potentiality of being offered. What is done is what decides the case, not what can or cannot be done at some indeterminate point in the future. Actualities, not potentialities, are all that are taken into account here. On that basis, I intepret the issue raised by Aqiba – and generative of the case at hand – to concern the relationship of the potential to the actual. Some may think this reading of matters far-fetched, and I would not wish to dismiss that judgment out of hand, but, as I have argued, I think this reading is defensible.

4. The Rules for Dealing with Cases of Doubt

M. 6:6 has a doubt as to which coin, among the lot, is the holy one. Aqiba takes the position that since any of them may be the holy one, as soon as one coin has been used, liability for committing sacrilege has been incurred. Sages want all the coins used. They then insist that only when we know for sure that one has committed sacrilege do we regard the penalty pertaining to sacrilege as having been incurred. We resolve doubt in sages' view by making a decision only as to a case of certainty.

5. No Clear Philosophical Issue

While I see M. 2:1-9 as a clarification and extension of the main points of M. 1:1-4, these points are not repeated and are not generative of the discussion of the passage. What we have in Chapter Two is simply an important piece of information as to when, in connection with a given beast or body of grain or incense, the considerations of sacrilege and other cultic taboos are invoked, and when they cease to apply. While the whole is regular and orderly, it does not seem to me to make a point that can transcend the data at hand or to call upon a philosophical principle that shapes the data before us. Accordingly, in a rigorous sense, we cannot find here a statement of a philosophical principle or even an important illustration of the workings of such a principle.

6. Is Meilah Philosophical?

What I find striking is not the disproportion of philosophical over non-philosophical paragraphs, but the stunningly logical order of the unfolding of problems and their principles. When I took up this tractate, I had in mind a tractate that would exhibit no philosophical character overall; that would allow me to point to evidence of a sort that would contradict my main thesis. This test of falsfication itself fails in the face of the sustained unfolding of simple rules of classification – things that are unlike follow opposed rules, there are interstitial cases, then there are mixtures. No other order is possible, and the order before us is dictated by the logic of the principle to be expounded. Hence the character of the tractate as a whole, not merely of the larger part of its contents, seems to me to point to a deeply philosophical mind and a compelling philosophical problem and purpose. There can be no doubt that this is a profoundly philosophical tractate, not because most of the pericopes deal with philosophical issues, but because, without the considerations of a philosophical order, there can have been no Meilah at all – at least, not the tractate as we know it.

33

Defining the Next Step

So much for the initial probe. What do we now know? One thing is now clear. While I could not have composed a study called "the political Mishnah," though it is a document with a politics, so too "the economical Mishnah," I am entirely justified in characterizing the Mishnah as sufficiently philosophical to allow the title, "the philosophical Mishnah." For this initial probe has now revealed that the basic and definitive traits of the entire writing and its discourse in the five tractates we surveyed are not narrowly legal but abstract and philosophical. Discourse takes place at not one but two (or more) levels, and cases in general are meant for exemplary purposes. That is to say, the issues concern principles that transcend the subject-matter of the law and that in fact affect themes and topics entirely unrelated to the law, physics (mixtures), metaphysics (the potential and the actual), and ethics (intentionality and action), for example. We now know that the five tractates probed treat these important themes that are by their fundamental character philosophical: the nature of mixtures; the relationship of the potential to the actual; the relationship of deed to intentionality; and rules for sorting out issues in doubt. Among our five tractates, these issues are treated not in random proportion; some tractates focus on one, some on another.

Among them, tractate Uqsin centers upon the issues of mixtures and associated questions of classification; intentionality and the matter of the actual and the potential play important parts in the exposition of the subject-matter of connection. Tractate Orlah is a sustained inquiry into issues of mixture, connection, and classification. I see Besah as a cogent account of the interplay between the principles of classification, intentionality and deed (designation), and of the matter of the potential and the actual. None of the three realms excludes a mighty presence for the other two. But the main problems are on the issues of

223

classification and intentionality. Tractate Qiddushin works out its
entire program with reference to hierarchical classification, pure and
simple. Tractate Meilah lays out the principles of mixture and
classification: things that fall into different classifications cannot
share the same rule; if two traits are antithetical, then if the one is
present the other cannot be; but there are interstitial categories; and,
therefore, we have to uncover the principles that dictate the
classification of mixtures. That covers the whole tractate. The upshot
is that our five tractates, covering wildly diverse subjects, join in an
interest in three important philosophical themes, with a secondary
concern for one other (which may or may not turn out to be distinctively
philosophical): classification and mixture, the relationship of the
actual and the potential, and the interplay of deed and intentionality
– those three.

Does this mean that the Mishnah may prove to be a philosophical
treatise on those three subjects in particular? We cannot know the
answer yet. The only way to proceed is to work through the other fifty-
eight tractates of the Mishnah. We have to analyze these tractates on
a grid of two intersecting lines. Two questions require attention.

First, what are the philosophical interests of the document as a
whole? Do the three themes we have identified prove to dominate
throughout, or are there other important topics? Note that this is not
yet the occasion to identify the dogmas or principles of hierarchical
classification and mixture, potentiality and actuality, and
intentionality and action. All we want to know is whether there are
other equally paramount areas of intellectual inquiry that occur within
the various subjects that the Mishnah's authorship takes up.

Second, are Mishnah-tractates essentially philosophical, not
philosophical at all, or in part philosophical, in part not, and is the
Mishnah as a whole philosophical, as the title of this monograph-
series claims: the philosophical Mishnah?

By what criteria shall we answer these questions? A single one, in
three parts, applies. The criteria for whether or not a tractate, or the
Mishnah as a whole, is philosophical may be spelled out in this way:

      1. Are issues "generalizable," that is to say, subject to
generalization and so exemplary, with principles pertinent to a variety
of other cases – a consideration spelled out in Chapter Five? In that
case we can move from cases to principles encompassing a variety of
cases.

      2. And, second, are the principles essentially philosophical
ones (as defined earlier in this book) or are they merely *ad hoc* or legal
ones, lacking any profound philosophical character? Here too the issue
is defined as exemplarity or particularity, with the added

consideration that what must be exemplified is a principle applicable in wholly abstract, not merely concrete and practical, settings.

3. Is the tractate possible, as we now know it, if elements displaying its character as a philosophical discourse are omitted? That is not a question only of the extent to which philosophical principles serve to impart their character on discourse. The issue is not solely or even mainly settled by appeal to the facts of quantity. Rather, it concerns the basic structure and dynamic of a tractate. By that I mean a simple fact, which we have already noted. The potential modes of addressing the subject-matter of Uqsin, Besah, Qiddushin, Orlah, and Meilah are surely without limit. There are many varieties of questions one can bring to those topics. But the tractates as we now have them, covering those topics, cannot have been composed without the prevailing concern for the issues we have identified: classification and mixtures, potentialities, intentionality. In other words, there can be no Uqsin, Besah, Qiddushin, Orlah, or Meilah, without a fundamentally philosophical program of inquiry into the subject-matter of those tractates. Not only so, but, in the case of Meilah at least, the philosophy is worked out in sequence and logical order dictated by the character of the philosophical theorems that are laid out.

The answer to this third question allows us, therefore, to undertake the classification, as to their philosophical structure and substrate, not merely their topical program, of the sixty-three tractates of the Mishnah. There are tractates lacking all philosophical interest. Without address to a single issue of a philosophical character we can have composed some Mishnah-tractates – Yoma, Tamid, and Middot come to mind – even though here and there principles of philosophical interest, e.g., considerations of intention or mixture, may be present. We can have tractates that touch upon philosophical matters, but are essentially focused not on the limited agenda we have identified but on another range of questions altogether. And there are tractates such as the five that we have studied, which can have been composed solely in accord with the limited philosophical agenda we have identified. Indeed, as I just said, my impression is that Mishnah-tractate Meilah forms a systematic and orderly exposition of principles that can occur in this order and in no other order, which is how Euclid sets forth his theorems, requiring us to learn one before allowing us to consider the next and sequential one. If that is the fact, then tractate-Meilah turns out to follow philosophical principles of the exposition of logic as much as a propositional program of an essentially philosophical character – all the while talking of practicalities of an utterly unphilosophical sort, bits of meat, incense, and grain, and inadvertently eating them! So when I ask, can we have a tractate without the philosophical agenda? I frame what is partly a question of extent to which philosophical issues predominate, partly a question of the basic structure and order of the tractate.

A further consideration requires attention. This result – claiming that we have essentially philosophical discourse in the five tractates and possibly in the fifty-eight others – depends upon identifying issues that, as a matter of hypothesis, we regard as philosophical. That is because they meet two criteria. First, they are principles that can apply to a considerable range of specific topics. Second, they are subject to generalization ("generalizable") even beyond the limits of the law, for instance, in matters of metaphysics or physics (as with mixtures and connection), in matters of ethics (as with intentionality), in matters of the fundaments of philosophical inquiry, (as with the interplay of the potential and the actual, which meant so much to Aristotle). The distinction is clear when we realize that there are modes of thought that serve both philosophy and other areas of thought altogether; these modes of thought are methods. There are, then, topics, that is, principles of a broad and encompassing character, and these form the program of thought of philosophy, or of theology, or of the regulation of society we know as law, and the like.

We must then distinguish between the philosophical issues that are right on the surface, e.g., the rules of classification, mixture, taxonomy, the consideration of actuality/potentiality, and the philosophical issues that are present but not articulated, e.g., resolving issues of doubt. The former – the subjects – are programmatic, the latter, methodological. The programmatic ones are the accessible ones, the others reveal modes of thought not necessary particular to philosophy. The former tell us what we have to find in the next stage. The latter have to be noted, and then the specific rules identified, e.g., in resolution of doubt, in modes of classification and so on. The plan of the following studies therefore is clear: to identify the program of philosophy which is active and which imparts its shape to all thought on a variety of diverse themes, the modes of thought that may or may not prove distinctively philosophical.

What has to be done? I see two intersecting tasks and one that lies beyond their accomplishment. The intersecting projects, which yield two accounts of every tractate, are organized within this grid of horizontal and vertical lines:

    1. to survey all *the issues* now identified in all tractates to find out the entire character of the philosophical agenda of the Mishnah as a whole;

2. to survey all *the tractates,* one by one, in terms of the philosophical characteristic of each, as just now explained.

This grid of analysis will yield work organized on the great philosophical themes, a catalogue of discussions on who says what, where, and with regard to which topic, as to mixtures, classification, and taxonomy, potentiality and actuality, intentionality and action, and, possibly, resolution of doubt. This will yield work organized by tractates, just as the present book is. I shall have to characterize the philosophical program, if any, of each tractate and assess whether or not the tractate as we know it will have been possible without the philosophical program that animates it or part of it.

But the stakes are still higher. When the tractates are classified as to their philosophicality, – what philosophy? what extent philosophical? – we have further to draw them into alignment with their status as to their relationship to Scripture, work I have completed in my *Judaism: The Evidence of the Mishnah* and related studies. Is there (as I suspect) a correlation between philosophicality and relationship to Scripture? My guess is that tractates that define their essential or at least their paramount program of thought through philosophical agenda, such as the five we have examined, will stand essentially autonomous of Scripture, even though they make use of facts supplied by Scripture or exegetically derived therefrom.

The basic facts of Orlah, Besah, Qiddushin (in small measure), and Meilah derive from Scripture; nothing in Uqsin does. But knowing the facts of Scripture, e.g., that it is permitted to cook on the festival but not on the Sabbath, as Besah tells us, in no way, by no means, can we have predicted the generative problematic of Besah. Knowing that we cannot use the fruit of a tree in the first three years after planting, we cannot have composed the tractate Orlah we now have. Knowing that sacrilege is a consideration in the cult, that the priests have a right to part of the meat after the blood of the animal has hit the altar wall, we cannot have written tractate Meilah. All the more so for Qiddushin and Uqsin. There are, as a matter of fact, tractates that simply provide a reorganization and reprise of scriptural facts, such as Yoma. I shall be surprised if Yoma systematically works on any identifiable philosophical problems. The upshot is that we have to classify tractates both as to their philosophicality and their interplay with Scripture. If matters work out as I anticipate, then we shall see that the more Scripture predominates, the less philosophical interest shapes discourse, and the more tangential a role is assigned to the philosophical problems we have considered.

The next stage in the work then is clear. I have to catalogue all philosophical paragraphs of the Mishnah in accord with the correct issue or principle, of which, as a matter of hypothesis, we have three certain, and one possible, classes. That work will make possible a complete description of the philosophical program of the Mishnah, not the doctrines or dogmas so much as the range of issues and the shape of inquiry. The position of the Mishnah as such is not important, and there may be none, given the diverse opinions that are preserved. The way in which the Mishnah as a whole – that is to say, the framers or authorship of the document – defines the issue of the potential as against the actual, the physics of mixtures including classification, and the consideration of the interplay of intentionality and actuality, will tell us what came under consideration, and what was not thought and therefore unthinkable. That will make possible comparison and contrast with other programs of thought on these same fundamental questions of metaphysics, physics, and ethics. So one goal is a clear statement of precisely what the Mishnah has to say about the issues of philosophy thus far identified, as well as other recurrent philosophical concerns we may in other tractates find critical.

Further, I shall have to classify whole tractates, e.g., as essentially philosophical in program and in intent, as Meilah, Orlah, Besah, and Uqsin, as essentially non-philosophical in program and in intent, and as possibly philosophical but certainly not essentially so, as (I am inclined to think) we found in the case of Qiddushin. So it will be like the classification of tractates *in re* Scripture – some wholly, some not at all, some in the middle, scriptural in focus and derivation. If the philosophical tractates are essentially autonomous of Scripture, even though using facts supplied by Scripture, and the non-philosophical tractates are essentially restatements of Scriptural facts, as in Yoma, & Middot then we shall finally understand what is really happening in the Mishnah.

Should the correlation of opposites – highly scriptural, not very philosophical, highly philosophical, not very scriptural, – turn out to characterize the bulk of the tractates, we shall see a very interesting fact. The intellects of the Mishnah will appear to have accomplished the union of philosophy and revelation, Scripture and Aristotle – all together, in a seamless statement of wholly coherent and consistent princples, expressed in the nitty-gritty of cases. So everyday life, in the analysis of philosophy, and the realm of the holy and the supernatural, in the account of revelation, will turn out to say the same thing in the same way about everything. If that is how matters emerge, then – to revert to the ultimate hypothesis touched upon in the introduction – we shall see that Aristotle was married to Scripture a thousand years before Maimonides. And the marriage was a permanent and perfect one, so natural and necessary (as the Mishnah represents it) that no one until now even knew about it: two made one in a perfection surpassing understanding.

Index